The Lab, the Temple, and the Market

THE LAB, THE TEMPLE, AND THE MARKET

Reflections
at the Intersection of
Science, Religion, and Development

Edited by Sharon Harper

IDRC ✳ CRDI

KUMARIAN
PRESS

Published in Canada by the International Development Research Centre
PO Box 8500, Ottawa, ON, Canada K1G 3H9
http://www.idrc.ca/books/

Published in Europe and the United States of America by Kumarian Press Inc.
1294 Blue Hills Avenue, Bloomfield, CT 06002, USA
http://www.kpbooks.com/

Canadian Cataloging in Publication Data

Main entry under title:
The lab, the temple and the market : reflections at the intersection of science,
religion and development / edited by Sharon Harper

ISBN 0-88936-920-8
CCG cat. no. E97-7/2000E

1. Economic development — Religious aspects.
2. Technology — Religious aspects.
3. Religion and science.
I. Harper, Sharon, 1965-   .
II. International Development Research Centre (Canada)

HD75.L33 2000   338.9   C00-901336-9

Library of Congress Cataloging-in-Publication Data

The lab, the temple, and the market : reflections at the intersection of science,
religion, and development / edited by Sharon Harper.
    p. cm.
    Includes bibliographical references.
    ISBN 1-56549-116-5 (alk. paper)
    1. Economic development—Religious aspects. 2. Technology—Religious
aspects. 3. Religion and science. I. Harper, Sharon, 1965-

HD75.L33 2000
338.9--dc21   00-055935

Contents

Foreword

Only the most ingenuous or wilfully blind would pretend that after a half century of sustained effort and many, many billions of dollars, international development agencies have at last "got it right." If anything, there is a pervasive sense that, in some very real way, we have failed. True, there have been tremendous achievements: thanks in large part to the programs of these agencies, the dedication of their staff, and the advances of modern science and technology (S&T), more people today have more food, better health, longer lives, more access to education, and faster communications than ever before.

And yet, more people than ever before are living in extreme poverty — physical, social, and moral. Education, health, and employment systems have collapsed in much of sub-Saharan Africa. The Earth is choking in the poison and filth we have generated through ever-increasing industrial growth justified by models of human development that focus on consumption. Population levels outstrip the capacity of many countries to meet basic human needs, let alone the growth in social demand for conspicuous consumption. Both developed and developing countries are facing waves of social disintegration, with crime, corruption, and violence as only the most visible features. The global shift in sociocultural value systems, characterized by Westernized pop culture and the deterioration of collective bonds of community and kinship, has deprived whole societies of their traditional spiritual and cultural reference points and bred disturbing patterns of social and spiritual alienation.

I am not implying that all of these problems can be laid at the door of international development agencies and models. These issues do suggest, however, that somewhere along the line we lost sight of something or that we never saw it in the first place. Most, if not all, development agencies are inspired by a scientific, technological, economic, and positivistic worldview; perhaps, we have been unable to listen to what people outside our agencies and worldview have been saying.

Most people situate themselves, their day-to-day decisions, and their hopes in the context of moral and religious belief systems that have traditionally been seen by development agencies as outside of — if not opposed to — our development models. As an institution with a 30-year history of looking at how S&T can be applied to resolve the development problems of the South, the International Development

Research Centre (IDRC) decided a few years ago to launch a modest inquiry that would help us better understand how our field of action relates to the spiritual and religious dimension of human well-being. This was a new and contentious area for an organization like ours, which has been accustomed to thinking of religion and spirituality as private matters with no place in our professional lives or in a public domain like that of "international development." We were unsure of how to approach the question and of whom to ask.

In the end, we were fortunate to encounter four individuals from different cultural and regional backgrounds, all believers in their own religious traditions and all trained as natural or social scientists, who were willing to work together to explore how science, religion, and development come together in their own personal and professional worldviews. Although we had intended to bring in other actors from various religious traditions and scientific disciplines, we decided to start with these four as a "critical mass" and to trust that others would join in as the inquiry progressed. This book is intended to launch that wider stage of inquiry.

It is unclear to us at IDRC where this experiment in research will lead, either within or beyond IDRC. At the very least, we hope that it will enrich our thinking about development and about how we do our work. We also hope that it will be a useful contribution to the growing international discourse on the relationship between the religious, scientific, and "developmental" worldviews on the improvement of the human condition. And we would, of course, be delighted if there was enough interest to support a continuation of our inquiry into what I believe is one of the great challenges before governments and development agencies: how to harness the scientific, technical, and economic creativity of the modern world to improve the human condition while respecting and reflecting the underlying values about human well-being and our relationship with the world that are offered by religious and cultural traditions.

Pierre Beemans
Vice President
International Development Research Centre

Preface

From the perspective of "research," the conjunction of science, religion, and development (SRD) is an enormous challenge — even to appreciate the scope of the issues. Merely a few of the entry points for research currently being explored in this area are global or universal ethics, ethics and development, religious and faith-based responses to the concern for environmental sustainability, religion and development, religiously based development efforts, issues of globalization and cultural values, indigenous belief systems and knowledge, efforts to create interreligious dialogue and understanding, and religious and faith-based approaches to conflict resolution. The International Development Research Centre (IDRC) SRD project is a modest effort to tease out this knot of questions, concerns, and rich insights. This effort has been specifically designed for a research-for-development organization with an interest in supporting scientific research and research capacity for sustainable development, because, simply put, the SRD project offered the opportunity to investigate what faith and science have to offer each other in the 50-year-old endeavour called development.

One of the strengths of the project is that, given the breadth of the relevant issues, it does not ask people to change their approach to development or to reevaluate the skills they have in their various disciplines but to articulate their disciplinary contribution and the role played by their faith in their approaches. With each person writing from his or her perspective and skill set, we offer an eclectic set of reflections, but we hope that these reflections allow readers to see the relevance of these questions within various scientific and development discourses and to see a richness of methods and results. The project highlights that the governing tenets of organized religion and personal faith are not necessarily divisive or repressive (although, like intellectual and political ideologies, they can be co-opted to that task) and that belief can be deeply motivational and strikingly fruitful in scientific pursuits. Most of the authors emphasize how their faith has brought them a profound understanding of interconnectedness and compassion and thus a wider perspective on their research such that the horizon of their work includes the effects of that research on other people, their community, the ecosystem, minority and marginalized groups, and ultimately the world.

Another strength of the SRD project lies in the people involved. The project brought together a core group of people who, within themselves, unite various disciplines and modes of thought. Without exception, the core group also comprised people with the vision to see another way of doing things, the courage to experiment with conventional ways of thinking, and the self-assurance to challenge their own worldviews when they come into contact with other belief systems. Their forthrightness about their faith is also exceptional, given how little accustomed the academic community is to examining questions of belief and revelation. The reflections found in this text would have been impossible without these people, for they chose to write personally about their faith and their science and it is on the personal level where the intersection of these disciplines can be seen most vividly and concretely. This appreciation extends to all those associated with the SRD project, both within and outside IDRC: Pierre Beemans, Chris Smart, William F. Ryan, S.J., and Kathleen Clancy. Many thanks must be expressed for their guidance, support, wisdom, and just plain hard work. Special thanks must go to Chris Smart for the creative energy behind the perfect title that is drawing so many readers to this publication.

This project frequently faced the question of whether IDRC, a research-for-development organization, should undertake this line of research. Given religious-based conflicts and the ambiguity of some faiths and spirituality, some people are bound to be uncomfortable with this focus and methodology. But those involved in the project found significant encouragement in the recent efforts of the World Bank to open a dialogue with representatives of nine world faiths on the issues of poverty. And the SRD project also uncovered a multitude of voices in a swiftly growing body of literature, in the work of exciting new non-governmental organizations, and in the letters and e-mails (from people in the North and the South) telling us that these questions in development are ripe for research. How might this research be relevant? Could it bring to light — indeed, question — the accepted values that underlie Western economic and scientific assumptions while building an appreciation for the insights and rationalities of other cultures and worldviews? Could it explore the potential for a new symbiosis of science and religion to rethink the question of "human well-being" and address the dilemmas of development? Religion and faith offer other sets of values — some overlapping, some new — and thus new insights and approaches to the pernicious problems of poverty, disease, conflict, and social marginalization.

I feel particularly fortunate to have worked with this project and to have met the people it has brought together. With a background in journalism, law, human rights, and theology, I often wondered where I would find employment that would allow me to explore the issues and skills I had been introduced to at various stages of my education. The

SRD project has brought these areas of knowledge into focus in a meaningful way, allowing me to see how thoughtful and concerned people (secular and religious) and caring and committed organizations (again, secular and religious) devote the best of themselves to the challenges of creating a world that is compassionate, just, peaceful, and sustainable.

Sharon Harper
September 2000

Introduction

Farzam Arbab

The end of the 20th century discloses to the eyes of humanity a vista of stupendous opportunities and grave perils. Some of the more striking phenomena are those associated with globalization, a designation that arouses strong emotions and lends itself to a variety of interpretations. There is no doubt — and this is true irrespective of one's views on the subject — that the forces of globalization have set the nations of the world on a new and irreversible course. Economic activity, political structures, and culture are all undergoing profound change. A global society is being born as barriers that have kept peoples apart crumble and are swept away. The transformation is made possible by accelerated technological advance, an early fruit of which is a mode of communication transcending national boundaries and operating at staggering speed.

However thrilling future prospects may be, present patterns of behaviour do not inspire confidence in the process. It is only natural to wonder whether globalization will, in fact, unify the human race without imposing uniformity or simply propel the universalization of the culture of consumerism. Is it the bearer of prosperity for the masses or the mere expression of the economic interests of a privileged few? Will it lead to the establishment of a just order or the consolidation of existing structures of power?

Such caution is not without justification, for, despite the continual multiplication of the means for improving the human condition, age-old problems persist and new ones present themselves at every turn. Particularly significant in this respect is the inefficacy of the methods of the global development enterprise, now entering its sixth decade. The problem is complex. For one thing, with the exception of certain notable successes, it has not been possible to halt the spread of poverty — not the poverty to which humanity has been accustomed throughout its existence, but one whose impact is rendered intolerable by the disintegration of the bonds of solidarity. For another, the pattern of economic growth being replicated has proven so detrimental to the environment as to call its viability into question. The challenge of bringing prosperity to all the peoples of the world through a process of sustainable development will not be met solely by the application of technology and the expansion of current schemes of organization. It demands a radical departure from the materialistic philosophies that have created today's concurrence of abject poverty and irresponsible wealth.

The thrust of history cannot be understood by the mere analysis of cause and effect. So profound a transformation of society should also be viewed as the exigency of an underlying evolutionary process at a time when the principles of oneness, of interconnectedness, and of justice are imposing themselves on the collective consciousness of humanity. The first global endeavours engendered by such an awakening may be tentative, inadequate, and even motivated by ambition and selfishness. But there is every reason to hope that as experience is gained, energies will increasingly be directed toward the creation of a world civilization embodying both the unity and the diversity of the human race. In this light, reevaluating the field of development, its basic assumptions, and its current strategies is a task that deserves immediate attention.

In the fall of 1997, the International Development Research Centre (IDRC) brought together a small group of us — scientists from diverse religious backgrounds — and challenged us to contribute to this reevaluation by exploring the theme of science, religion, and development. The approach we were to take was straightforward. We were asked to engage in a review of relevant literature and to reflect — from the point of view of our own experiences and belief systems — on issues we considered critical to the theme of this research. We were to meet, as needed, to share and discuss our thoughts. We were to present the results of our personal reflections in working papers, which were in turn to be compiled in one volume and circulated to a wider group for further deliberation. We each found the subject significant enough to add this undertaking to our other obligations for 1 or 2 years.

Before our project, IDRC had carried out an initial analysis of issues related to spirituality and development. Dr William F. Ryan, S.J., had traveled on its behalf to various parts of the world and had interviewed nearly 200 theorists and practitioners working in the field. His conclusions, presented in *Culture, Spirituality, and Economic Development: Opening a Dialogue* (Ryan 1995), were of great assistance to us, as was his active participation in our meetings and discussions. It was clear from his study that the need to give the spiritual dimension of human existence its due place in development thinking was strongly felt in many circles. Dissatisfaction with dominant approaches that search for "the 'perfect package' and the right 'technological fix' for every human development problem" was widespread (Ryan 1995, p. 4). All those interviewed agreed that local cultural and religious values should be integrated into research on sustainable and equitable development. While nearly everyone showed concern about the moral and ethical aspects of development, some went further and sought to "base their committed action" on religion and faith; they were sceptical about the effectiveness of purely rational ethics, especially when rationality was defined by "narrow individualistic premises" (Ryan 1995, p. 42).

Without doubt, the proposition that a purely materialistic approach to development must be abandoned enjoys substantial support. What is not clear is how development theory and practice are to acquire a spiritual perspective. Development efforts rest upon several scientific disciplines and professional fields, each with its own worldview. Is it possible to enter into a rigorous discussion of spirituality — one that is not co-opted by baseless imaginings — when the overall framework within which these disciplines have taken shape holds science and religion in opposition? An inquiry into the relationship between science and religion and their interface with development, then, seems to be a necessary step in any attempt to adjust the present imbalance in development thinking. Our group adopted such a view with confidence, recognizing that the crisis of modern society has already compelled scientists and theologians alike to question the materialistic version of this relationship. The expanding scope of exploration into the subject, combined with the growing awareness of the failures of materialism, assured us of the timeliness of IDRC's decision to promote a discourse on the theme of science, religion, and development.

The papers in this volume are the results of our joint deliberations and individual reflections on the theme. They do not adhere to any specified format, nor do they address the same set of issues. They reflect the decision we made together that whatever approach we adopted, we would do our best to make our own beliefs explicit as we went about analyzing social and intellectual reality. Each paper should be viewed as no more than a first contribution to a conversation that we hope will attract more and more participants.

Dr Promilla Kapur chose to review, in some detail, the teachings of her faith. The paper she is presenting, however, is not a theological treatise on Hinduism. It is an account of the reflections of a social scientist and activist on her own belief system. It begins with a brief discussion of Dr Kapur's personal worldview and spirituality and moves on to an exposition of what she sees as the salient features of the religion of the Hindu people. This is a well-documented section of her paper, supporting her argument that the "syncretic and pluralistic history" of the Hindu religion and "its concept of an ultimate Oneness provide an alternative outlook and an important balance to the divisive effect of modern systems and materialist mind-sets" (Kapur, this volume, pp. 9). This is an important observation, and a much-needed one, given that the religious belief systems of India have been portrayed so frequently as obstacles to development.

Dr Kapur's treatment of development is built around its definition as "the unfoldment of Truth," a process that operates in relation to the

3

individual, society, and the cosmos (Kapur, this volume, pp. 18). Within this context, she has no difficulty arguing that the field of development stands in need of the proper influence of religion. The conception of science to which she adheres leads her naturally to the view that there can be no essential conflict between science and religion. For her, the physical sciences constitute "an inquiry into matter and the nature of the external world" (Kapur, this volume, pp. 27). Religion, she feels, is "an inquiry into consciousness, spirituality, and the nature of the inner world" (Kapur, this volume, pp. 27). As there can be "no separation between the external and internal dimensions" of existence, science and religion cannot but complement each other (Kapur, this volume, pp. 27). She hopes that the two, in harmonious interaction, can be brought to bear on the challenges of development.

4

In describing what she considers to be the Hindu resources for an integrated development, Dr Kapur assumes a markedly Gandhian posture. As such, she draws on the wealth of insights from the struggle for a *Sarvodaya* Order. Her thoughts are clearly in the direction of a search for a development strategy that balances scientific and technological achievement with critically examined values of religion, Western dynamism with Eastern spiritual vision.

Dr Gregory Baum brought to our deliberations at least three concerns: the critical treatment of development by Christian churches, the World Bank's recent promotion of a dialogue with religion, and the subjective dimension of social-science research. In the paper prepared for this publication, he analyzes these concerns. His presentation of the first theme includes instructive examples, largely from the Roman Catholic church, illustrating that ever since the Christian churches "heard the protests of Christian and non-Christian groups in the poorer parts of the world" they have been ill at ease with the idea of development formulated in terms of industrialization (Baum, this volume, pp. 62). In a brief discussion of his personal convictions, he sums up what he sees as a Catholic option, involving two commitments: "to look at society from the perspective of its victims; and to publicly manifest solidarity with their struggle for justice" (Baum, this volume, pp. 69–70). "The option for the poor," he states,

> has released a new inwardness in the Christian churches, marked by a certain spiritual anguish; that is, (1) we are deeply troubled by the suffering of others, especially those who are oppressed (the majority of humankind); (2) we grieve over the Church's past and present complicity with empire, colonialism, and other forms of domination; and (3) we willingly expose ourselves to the painful and unanswerable question of how we can reconcile our faith in a loving and omnipotent God with the evil we see in the world. This new spirituality, which has its own "dark night of the soul," is not devoid of hope and the energy to act.
>
> (Baum, this volume, pp. 70).

Dr Baum's analysis of the effort being made by the World Bank to open a dialogue with religion shows the promise that such a dialogue holds if it is protected from vested interest. By raising the question of subjectivity in research, his third concern, he focuses attention on an issue of particular significance. The exploration on which we have embarked will not advance if constrained by narrow definitions of the scientific method. A question that cannot be avoided is whether the attitude of the social-science researcher toward the existence of a transcendent order influences his or her analysis and conclusion. Dr Baum calls, not for belief in religion, but for empathy and openness. He asks that development research demonstrate "a special sensitivity to the spiritual dimension of people's self-constitution and to the ways the secular presuppositions of contemporary Western culture threaten their identity" (Baum, this volume, pp. 81).

Dr Azizan Baharuddin begins her paper by drawing attention to the consequences of the compartmentalization and reductionism that characterize so much of today's intellectual activity. She then sets out to describe her conception of science, religion, and development, consistently underscoring their interconnectedness. "We have to acquire a holistic, ecological worldview," is her appeal, "and from this reorientation will flow the realignment of our economic and development concepts" (Baharuddin, this volume, pp. 111). In exploring religion, Dr Baharuddin does not shy away from questioning religious precepts and practices she feels are in need of fundamental change. This affords her the freedom to turn to the essence of Islam and present some of its teachings in their full beauty.

The section on metaphysics and its role in human endeavour is a particularly welcome contribution to an emerging discourse on the theme of science, religion, and development. Here, by examining some of the implications of the Qur'anic term *din*, Dr Baharuddin illustrates how Islam "involves the totality of life, if not reality itself" (Baharuddin, this volume, pp. 127). Following Al-Attas' analysis, she explains that submission to God, the foundational precept of Islam, is intimately connected with human indebtedness to God for the gifts of creation and sustenance. In this state of indebtedness, human beings realize that "they possess nothing themselves" and that "everything about them, in them, and from them comes from the Creator" (Baharuddin, this volume, pp. 128). Given that they are in themselves "the very substance of the debt," they have no choice but to repay it "by returning themselves to God" (Baharuddin, this volume, pp. 128). This return means giving themselves in service to God — and thus to humanity — and living in accordance with God's law. It is the profound understanding of a number of metaphysical concepts such as the relationship between indebtedness and submission that, according to Dr Baharuddin, forms the foundation of an Islamic approach to development.

5

My own paper in this collection is based on my work in development, especially in the Latin American sphere. For many years, a group of colleagues and I had the opportunity to make a concerted effort to create an alternative development strategy that sought to apply spiritual principles to the transformation of social and economic processes and structures in rural regions. The theme and approach of the present project served as a framework within which I could make explicit the conception of science and religion that was at the heart of that effort. What I try to describe in my paper is a worldview, informed by the Bahá'í teachings, that considers the generation and application of knowledge the central axis around which development takes place. The main task of development, I argue, is the building of capacity in individuals, communities, and institutions in region after region to participate in the creation of a civilization in which the material and the spiritual join.

The purpose of our endeavour in this IDRC research project was not to reach a consensus or a set of uniform views on the nature of science, religion, or development, and thus the papers reflect a variety of understandings and approaches. However, we shared certain thoughts about fundamental issues, especially in the treatment of religion. None of us wished to deal with religion as a mere instrument, either as a philosophical tool or as a social factor that happens to be useful in furthering material development. We were not interested in aligning religion with consumerism, scientism, or political power. As believers and scientists, we saw both religion and science as concerned with reality. We therefore explored the role of religion in every facet of the development process: purpose, strategy, methodology, and action. Whatever the validity of our specific arguments, we can hope to have conveyed at least one basic message: the various religious traditions of the world have guided humanity throughout its history under a diversity of conditions and, today, can offer humanity a wealth of spiritual insight that it sorely needs. Diversity need not be a cause of conflict and contention as opinions adverse to religion automatically assume. It is not always necessary to think in terms of "religions" and "sects"; it is possible to speak of religion in the same way as one speaks of science and then explore the interactions of the two as they guide human progress.

REFERENCE

Ryan, W.F., S.J. 1995. Culture, spirituality, and economic development: opening a dialogue. International Development Research Centre, Ottawa, ON, Canada. 67 pp.

CHAPTER 1

The Principle of Fundamental Oneness

Promilla Kapur

THE CONTEXT

DOES DEVELOPMENT DIVIDE OR UNITE HUMANITY?

As I look at society today, this is what I see: many worlds and many peoples struggling to find a place for themselves, their traditions, and their ways of life while their realities change around them at an ever-increasing pace. And I see marks of nobility in these struggles: generosity when people have little or nothing themselves, expressions of kindness toward others, and untiring dedication in working for equality, unity of purpose, peace, and harmony with the natural environment. These are good people doing the best they can to manifest the good life that their traditions, myths, religions, and conscience tell them is possible. They work hard to move toward solidarity and cooperation and resist tendencies toward separation, selfishness, and conflict.

But it is impossible to ignore the strength of the forces pulling in the other direction: gender imbalances; gross inequities in the distribution of wealth; the distortion of religion into fundamentalist postures

---

NB: This text would have been impossible without the support, research, and insightful contributions of Tribhuwan Kapur, Associate Professor of the Sociology of Religion at the Indira Gandhi National Open University, New Delhi, India, and author of nine books.

and actions; periodic communal violence; disregard for the principles of moral sexuality; crassly hedonistic consumerism (that is, the production and consumption of goods and items that have little relevance to the real quality of life but provide sensation for the sake of sensation); nonparticipatory development initiatives that rarely profit the beneficiary population; and confusion over culture, religion, and spirituality (for example, how one religion can relate harmoniously and noncompetitively with other religions) — all this occurring within the context of the ever-pervasive and increasingly ominous pollution and destruction of our natural resources. The problems are certainly more than I can list here, but it seems to me that all of them find their roots somewhere in the divided nature of the world.

8

Given the recent emergence of many of these problems, it is hard to identify holistic technological and social solutions to address them. Each "fix" has its own consequences, both good and bad, and it is difficult to see at the moment of its application the ultimate impact of each new "solution." Solutions, without an adequate moral or spiritual grounding, often become problems themselves. For example, although science undoubtedly has made immense and positive contributions to human well-being, it has also been used to build nuclear weapons; computer technology is used to facilitate communications, but it is also used to target "enemy" sites. And behind all these scientific applications gone awry, I again see the marks of a world lacking unity and cohesiveness. It is this insight, I believe, that needs to be brought to an analysis of the prevalent paradigm of development.

In the issues before us, three important areas interplay — modern science, religion and values, and development (broadly defined in economic, social, and psychological terms). I explore their interfaces in this paper from my own perspective as a practicing Hindu woman and social scientist. In these introductory remarks, I elucidate the details of this perspective. In the second section of the paper, "Hinduism: the backdrop," I explain my understanding of Hinduism and Vedanta and some of their cardinal principles, such as *dharma* and "self–Self." In the third section, "Self, society, and development," I explore the approach that Hinduism takes, moving from an inward, personal development to an outward, social development. In the section entitled "Modern science and the Hindu religion," I look at the striking similarities between new discoveries in science and very old wisdom from Hindu scriptures. In the penultimate section, "Devotion, knowledge, and action," I turn to a historical description of religious movements and leaders in India who have spearheaded action for social reform and development, leading us finally into a discussion (in the section "Conclusion: an integrated paradigm") of what resources religion, and Hinduism in particular, can offer to the field of development.

The dilemmas to which I have alluded seem to be so inherent to the modern lifestyle that to reverse them would be no small accomplishment. It would require a great and persistent effort over an appreciable period. The present generation, I think, can do little more than lay the groundwork of an ultimately "united" world. It is exactly in this process that the Hindu religion, for me, offers such valuable resources: its syncretic and pluralistic history and its concept of an ultimate Oneness provide an alternative outlook and an important balance to the divisive effect of modern systems and materialist mind-sets.

A PERSONAL PERSPECTIVE

At the outset, I would like to reflect on how I first encountered the principles of science, religion, and development (SRD), how I use these in my personal life and work, and how I became interested in this project of the International Development Research Centre (IDRC).

I feel that it was my parents, especially my mother, who introduced me to the religious ethos and the Almighty — or Supreme Power — when I was a child. My mother came from an Arya Samaj family background and conveyed, in her own loving way, her understanding that the Supreme Power is One and the Creator of the whole universe. We are all children of that Almighty. She inculcated in me — and my brothers and sisters — the habit of praying to God on getting up in the morning and before going to sleep, to give thanks for God's blessings, to ask for protection from evil, and to impart to us the good sense and positive attitude needed to love, respect, and take care of ourselves and others. Thus, I received these core religious beliefs as part of my socialization in a liberal home, school, and community atmosphere.

I continue these practices even today. I do yogic exercises and pray regularly on waking and again before retiring, to thank the Supreme Power for his blessings and to internalize the divine qualities by linking my personal soul with the Supreme Soul through meditation. I make efforts to put into practice some of the cardinal principles of the Hindu religion (*sanatana dharma*). For example, I have faith in an Ultimate Reality and in the Oneness of that power from which, and in which, all creation lives. I firmly believe that I am a soul (*atman*), as are others, and that the soul is basically and fundamentally divine. I am conscious of the potential divinity inherent in me and in everyone. On these grounds, I try not to distinguish or discriminate between people on the basis of sex, class, religion, region, or nationality, and I work to alleviate discrimination. I make every effort to live out the values of love, understanding, compassion, caring, sharing, nonviolence, and interfaith understanding.

I am a believer in the law of *karma*, a principle that inspires me and gives me the inner strength to carry out my responsibilities and duties to serve humanity to the best of my ability. I work to accumulate good *karma* for a better future in this life and in the lives I believe will come (from my belief in the immortality of the soul and in reincarnation).

My effort (*karma*) is to maximize the good I can do in the world and minimize the evil. I work and pray not only for my family's welfare but also for the well-being of others and society. I endeavour to serve and help others — those who are troubled, poor, weak, and underprivileged — to help themselves. This gives me a great deal of satisfaction when compared with pursuits that centre on economic gain at the cost of values and principles. I try to share my material and nonmaterial achievements — that is, knowledge, education, and training — with others. At the same time, the principle of *karma* gives me strength to bear whatever misfortunes befall me and the courage to face all my problems without blaming anyone else for them.

Throughout my life, my curiosity has led me to learn more, both scientifically and empirically, about religion, exploring such questions as Who is the Creator? and What is the purpose of life? I have read the scriptures of various faiths in translation. I have listened to the religious and spiritual discourses of knowledgeable individuals from diverse belief systems, including the Bahá'í Faith, the Brahma Kumaries, the Ramakrishan Mission, the Sri Aurobindo Society, and the Arya Samaj. I have even tried various kinds of meditation. This has widened my knowledge and appreciation of other religions and the revelations that they each have to offer. I have found that, in essence, the core religious beliefs and values are universal, and this makes me feel very close to people of different faiths.

When I was a student of social science (psychology, counseling, sociology, and religion), I was interested in the debate on whether science and religion contradicted each other. I read literature on science and spirituality, for example, the works of Chander (1988) and Kanal (1991), the writings of Indian scientists such as physics professor D.S. Kothari (1977, 1980, 1997), and texts by spiritualists like Swami Vivekananda (1937, 1968); (see also Swami Bhajanananda 1976–77) and Swami Ranganathananda (1978, 1983, 1987), who argued that there is no clash between science and religion: the two are interrelated and are in harmony with one another.[1] These readings whetted my curiosity to learn more about the interrelationships between these two seemingly unrelated discourses.

Throughout my higher education, I was interested in observing and systematically studying the changes taking place in the socio-psycho-cultural realms and in the political-economic situations of people from diverse societies. I was particularly interested in such changes in relation to the situation of women, especially the women of India. I was keen to study the problems women face and to understand their changing attitudes and feelings. I wanted to investigate how they were being

---

[1] This might be termed the "new approach," the understanding that it is counterproductive to human well-being when people rely on religion or science to the exclusion of the other. When the two are combined, they strengthen one another and bring a holistic expression of human genius and total fulfillment (Ranganathananda 1978).

treated within and outside the family, both now and in ancient India (based on our scriptures). I asked myself what factors had contributed to bringing about these changes. This interest led me to do research on gender issues and women's development for my doctoral and post-doctoral studies. Thus, I was introduced to the concept of development and the social sciences quite a while ago, but I have had less exposure to the physical sciences.

As a social scientist, I have observed developments in science and technology (S&T) and how these affect people's lives — women's lifestyles and well-being in particular. I was also strongly interested in laying out the constitutive elements of women's development in the context of sustainable development. I observed that India, after independence, has seen spectacular progress in S&T, increasing economic growth, industrial development, and self-sufficiency in terms of food and clothing. I found that governments and nongovernmental organizations (NGOs) were taking countless measures to improve the situation of women and bring about overall development. I have been trying to analyze why, despite the vast resources poured into these initiatives, we see increasing problems of communal violence (for example, between Hindu and Muslim groups), a rising incidence of violence generally, widespread corruption, rampant illiteracy, casteism, unemployment, abject poverty, overpopulation, malnutrition, and degradation of the environment. Why do we see so much socioeconomic and gender inequality and injustice? What is the origin of the growing emphasis on the values of materialism and consumerism and the want in quality in public leadership? Why do we see so much crime and violence, especially against women, even in the "developed" countries of the world? In my studies (Kapur 1991a, 1991b, 1992, 1994a, 1994b, 1995), I started exploring whether part of the answer could be found in the crisis of human and spiritual values caused by a decline in attention to these important questions and a lack of education on these subjects.

My efforts in this area have centred on counseling, generating awareness of human and spiritual values, and healing marriage, family, and other interpersonal relationships. As a counselor I try to help people to become cognizant of their strengths and potentialities and thereby help them solve their problems, resolve conflicts, understand themselves and others more fully, and manage their stress. I try to help them help themselves to grow in self-esteem (by helping them find their own positive directions), improve their strong points, and overcome their limitations. Accepting those in trouble as complete individuals, with all their talents and weaknesses, enables me to provide this support.

While working as a counselor, trying to encourage religious and spiritual values, I was continually troubled by certain questions: What is science? What is religion — Hindu as well as other faiths? What have science and religion contributed to development? How have science and religion interacted?

It was at this point that one fine morning, as a pleasant surprise, I learned of IDRC's project in SRD. After some discussion, IDRC invited me to participate in this research, asking me to explore the relevant issues as a believer in the Hindu religion. I was thrilled. Deep in my heart I felt that this opportunity came to me because of God's blessings and will.

I knew that this research would require intensive study and hard work. But I had been keen to do further research in these areas, so I was at once drawn toward the project. I accepted the invitation with great enthusiasm and began the work with the help of my research assistant, Tribhuwan Kapur, who has a doctorate in the sociology of religion. We have found it fascinating and satisfying to work on this research with the knowledgeable, understanding, and friendly IDRC group; the distinguished research team leader, Farzam Arbab; and the other eminent members of the team. I hope that my practical experience with the very intricate motivations and problems of human life (as seen from the eyes of a sociologist and counselor), my experience of India, and my lifelong immersion in a Hindu perspective provide a useful complement to the expertise and knowledge of the other participants in the project.

HINDUISM: THE BACKDROP

THE INDIVIDUAL AND SOCIETY BECOME ONE

It may be appropriate to clarify at the outset what is meant by the terms *Hindu*, *Hindu religion*, and *Hinduism*. According to Ranganathananda (1987) and Badrinath (1993), the words *Hindu* and *Hinduism* were not coined by the people of India to refer to themselves or their religion; these words are not found in any of the ancient or medieval Indian texts. Instead, they suggest that invading Arabs in the 8th century AD or ancient Persians or Iranians used these terms to designate the people living east of the river "Sindhu" (the modern river Indus). Because Persians pronounced *s* as *h*, the word *Sindhu* of Sanskrit became *Hindu*, and the territory became known as Hindustan (Ranganathananda 1987). The Greeks pronounced it as "Indos," from which came the word *India*. Thus, the term *Hinduism* originally meant the religion of the people of Hindustan.

In fact, Hinduism would be hard to define as any one set of beliefs. It has always been a syncretic religion, incorporating several indigenous belief systems in addition to the religions that came to India through war and migration. The Indian thinkers themselves called their religion by the significant term *sanatana dharma*, which can be translated as "Eternal Religion." *Dharma* is the Sanskrit word for "religion," and it is a philosophical concept focused on unity. "The aim of *dharma*," as Badrinath (1993, p. 27) explained, is "to create and sustain individual and social conditions where each individual, in his or her own being and in relationship with others, is able to explore the potential of his or her life and bring it to fruition in such ways that he or she can." He explained the centrality of the concept as follows:

> The one concern from which everything in Indian thought flowed and on which every movement of life ultimately depended, was the idea of *dharma*, order, which was not any positive order but the order that was inherent in all life. Derived from the Sanskrit root word *dhr*, which is "to support," "to sustain," *dharma* means that whereby whatever lives is sustained, upheld, supported.
>
> Badrinath (1993, p. 22)

Badrinath further explained the five elements of the order, or *dharma*, in which our being is firmly grounded: nonviolence; an attitude of equality; peace and tranquility; a lack of aggression and cruelty; and an absence of envy.

13

> While each individual has a relation to himself, he has relationships with others. In the *dharmic* view the two are not separate. It is only when our relationship with ourselves is right, that our relationship with the other can be right: and it is not until we achieve a right relation with the other, that our relation with ourselves can be right.
>
> Badrinath (1993, p. 23)

Swami Vivekananda, a monk in the Ramakrishna order and the most famous disciple of the Bengali mystic, Ramakrishna Paramahans, placed great emphasis on the merging of the scientific attitude with the spiritual dimension. He defined religion as "the manifestation of the divinity already in man" (Ranganathananda 1987, p. 218). By the word *divinity* he meant *Brahman* (Almighty), a concept in which divinity is inseparable from the individual self, or *atman* (soul). As he further stated,

> Religion is realization, not talk nor doctrine, nor theories, however beautiful they might be. It is being and becoming, not hearing or acknowledging; it is the whole soul becoming changed into what it believes. ... All religions are so many stages. Each one of them represents a stage through which the human soul passes to realize God.
>
> Bhajanananda (1976–77, p. 9)

I think Vivekananda used the word *religion* in the special sense of spirituality. For him it meant "the realization of God" and "not just a means of personal salvation but a great creative force in shaping history" (Bhajanananda 1976–77, p. 4). I see echoes of Swami Vivekananda's teaching in the work of Western social scientists like Pitirim Sorokin, a sociologist, who also emphasized that spiritual training is essential to the integration and growth of individuals, society, and culture, which in turn form an indivisible trinity (Sorokin 1958).

Swami Muktinathananda, a scientist, resided in Canada for many years, but ultimately he renounced the world and became a monk with the Ramakrishna Mission. In answer to a question about the nature of the Hindu religion, he responded that it asks the following fundamental questions:

> (i) Who am I? (ii) What is this world? (iii) Who is God? (iv) What is my relation to this world and God? The Hindu concept for a human being is that a person is trichotomous: there is a body, a mind, and the self or *atman*. The aim of every being is to know who exactly he or she is: is it the body, or the mind, or the self. In fact, the Hindu religion begins with this question of knowing myself and my relation to God and my World.
>
> Muktinathananda (personal communication, 1998[2])

14

The notion of the self in Hinduism, classical and modern, differs from that in social science. Whereas social science tends to equate the self with the ego, or the total personality that is presented to society in interaction, in Hinduism the self is equated with the soul (or *atman*) within each living being. Yet, Self also stands for the Supreme Reality (or *Brahman*). The self is seen as a small particle of the Self, and the realization of the oneness of the self with the Self (or the soul with the Supreme Reality) is the goal of human life. Thus, the movement of Creation is a play between self and Self.[3]

Through reincarnation, the self is engaged in virtually endless transmigrations (*samsara*) in order to come to a realization of the oneness of the self with the Self. The doctrine of *samsara* or transmigration holds that *atman* is immortal but deluded with all kinds of desires. According to its *karma* (deeds, totality of action and interaction), the *atman* incarnates in diverse bodies until it is completely purified and finally merges with *Brahman* and attains *moksha* (or spiritual liberation). As the Bhagavad Gita puts it, "Just as a man casts off worn out cloths and puts on others which are new, so the embodied [self] casts off worn out bodies and enters others which are new" (Sastry 1977, p. 49). The *karma* accumulated by a particular *atman* in previous lifetimes determines the situation into which a person is reborn.

Another complementary guide to action found in Hinduism is embedded in the *varnaashram* scheme, a socioreligious framework that

---

[2] Swami Muktinathananda, Ramakrishna Math, Belur, Calcutta, India, personal communication, 1998.

[3] The Bhagavad Gita, the most popular Hindu scripture, states the following: "They say that the senses are superior; superior to the senses is mind; superior to mind is reason; one who is even superior to reason is He [the Self] ... . Then knowing Him who is superior to reason, subduing the self by the Self, slay thou, O mighty armed, the enemy in the form of desire, hard to conquer" (Sastry 1977, p. 117).

divides human life into four distinct stages, each with concomitant privileges and duties:

  ❦ *Bharmacharya* — studenthood and celibacy;

  ❦ *Grihastya* — responsible householdership;

  ❦ *Vanaprastha* — renunciation of all societal attachments; and

  ❦ *Sanyasa* — contemplation of Ultimate Reality (that is, taking on spiritual pursuits on a full-time basis) and retirement from all social links.

This pattern of life, however, is ideal; it is typical that the last stage, which requires separation from the family at a time when a person or couple is most likely to require help, is very hard to achieve. In modern India, the framework of society allows us to aspire only to the first two stages.

Nevertheless, many aged people do turn to a form of renunciation and contemplation by daily reading of the Ramayana, Mahabharata, Bhagavad Gita, and other spiritual texts. They spend money to hold or attend religious gatherings where there are recitations of various prayers and discussions on the teachings of various gurus (or spiritual masters), preachers, and teachers. Hindus continue, by and large, to be ritualistic and to spend conspicuous sums on ceremonies. We can say then that although Hinduism has evolved over the millennia, this evolution has been more in the form than in the content.

VEDANTA: THE ESSENCE OF HINDUISM

Hindu religion is not based on a single personal founder or group of founders; rather, it is based on revelations of the authentic inner experiences of sages and seers deeply involved in the search for Truth. The Veda, Puranas, Upanishads, and Bhagavad Gita form the basic spiritual literature of Hinduism. The Veda is the accumulated treasury of spiritual knowledge discovered by various seers and sages — perfected beings — at various points in history. "The term Veda, according to Sankaracharya, primarily means knowledge, beginningless and endless, capable of leading to liberation, and verifiable by one and all" (Ranganathananda 1987, p. 40). That is why the Veda is the outcome of an inquiry into Truth, very similar in nature and process to modern scientific inquiry.[4]

---

[4] Joshi, a great scholar of the Veda, points out that by studying the Veda one finds that it presents "a dynamic interpretation of the world and assigns to activities in the world a profound meaning and significance. It enjoins upon man to act rather than to renounce his actions. It places before man a method of action which has been discovered after a long and intense search by the vedic seers," who were themselves true scientists and experimenters (Joshi 1991, p. 19).

The Puranas are epics, the ideas and the teachings of the Veda told in story and parable form. The Upanishads collect the concluding and philosophical portions of the vast and varied Vedic literature and contain the quintessence of the Veda. The Gita summarizes the essential teachings of the Upanishads dealing with metaphysical reality, the nature of self, and the need for knowledge of self and presents them in a popular manner. The Gita addresses not only Upanishadic philosophy but also its ethical implications; thus, it both explains the highest reality and provides guidance for everyday life. This is why it has become the scripture of the masses in India.

But the essence of Hinduism is Vedanta, the philosophical and metaphysical part of the Hindu scriptures. Swami Vivekananda could see clearly that Hinduism had a core of sound spiritual principles based on the Upanishads and the Gita and that these principles, when applied in practical life, could solve many of the nation's problems (Bhajanananda 1976–77). I would agree with Vivekananda and suggest that India's contemporary state of decline is not the result of religion but of a failure to apply the principles of Vedanta to solve the social and national problems (Bhajanananda 1976–77). In a lecture entitled "Vedanta Today," Karan Singh, an eminent diplomat, politician, and scholar of Vedanta and interfaith dialogue, explained the central features of *sanatana dharma* as formulated in the five cardinal principles of Vedanta (Singh 1988):

1. *Unity of existence* — Vedantic theory suggests that an all-pervading existence, or single force, permeates the whole universe. Everything that exists — whatever it is and wherever it exists — is illuminated by the same Light that promotes the happiness and welfare of all beings.

2. *Divinity inherent in all existence (includes the potential divinity of human souls)* — In Vedanta, human beings are children of immortality, with the capacity for spiritual realization. In explaining the concept of religion, Vivekananda stated this well-known article of Vedantic faith:

    > Each soul is potentially divine. The goal is to manifest this divinity within, by controlling nature, external and internal. Do this either by work, or worship, or psychic control, or philosophy — by one or more or all of these — and be free. This is the whole religion. Doctrine or dogmas, or rituals, or books, or temples, or forms, are but secondary details.
    >
    > Ranganathananda (1987, p. 45)

    Vedanta is the realization of the divinity within oneself and in each one of us. The crowning idea of Vedanta is the unity of the divine within us and the divine beyond us. Vedanta describes *Brahman*, the Ultimate Reality, as *Sat-cit-Ananda* (existence, knowledge, and bliss). If bliss is a constituent of the Ultimate Reality of the universe, it is also a constituent of the individual (Ranganathananda 1987, p. 23).

To manifest one's inherent potential for divinity, one follows the three paths to self-realization offered in Vedanta through which the individual soul finds a link with the Supreme Soul: *bhakti yoga*, or the path of devotion to the Supreme Reality or Soul; *jnana yoga*, the path of knowledge; and *karma yoga*, the path of action and work. As Gangrade (1995) pointed out, no one of these paths can alone suffice or permanently stand isolated from the other two. A person must follow *jnana*, *karma*, and *bhakti* together to completely develop his or her character and personality.

3. *The entire human race like one extended family* (vasudhaiva kutumbhkam — The bond of spirituality binds people belonging to various parts of the human race, despite all their differences. Ideally, **all** the members of an extended family care and share, demonstrate mutual love and respect, and take responsibility for and cooperate in maintaining and furthering the welfare of the family; these ideals can be extended to provide models of behaviour for each individual toward the rest of the human race.

4. *Essential unity of all religions* — The perception of the spiritual unity of all existence in Hinduism and the emphasis on spiritual realization as the goal of religion foster interreligious harmony (Ranganathananda 1987). In Hinduism, various paths lead to the Divine: one can worship a female or male deity, trees, plants, herbs, the sun, the moon, stars, fire, the incorporeal God, the Supreme Soul–Reality, or an idol. This pluralism is apparent in Swami Vivekananda's idea of the harmony of the religions of the world and in that of a universal religion providing for the coexistence of all religions, each accepting the best elements in the others. I feel that people today very much need the pluralism of Vedanta and the interfaith understanding it espouses.

5. *The welfare, progress, development, and happiness of all* — Vedanta promotes not only the fulfillment and liberation of the self but also the welfare and development of all beings. This is indicated by a popular Vedic prayer that all may be happy and healthy and participate in and be the recipient of welfare, progress, and prosperity and that none may be unhealthy, unhappy, or ignorant. This prayer is recited in Sanskrit during various religious ceremonies; similar prayers are found in the Bahá'í Faith and in other religions.[5]

17

---

[5] Swami Jitatmananda (1992) has brought out the five concepts, or cardinal principles, of the Upanishads (Vedanta) very effectively in the book *Modern Physics and Vedanta*, which offers an alternative to the current, primarily materialistic, paradigm.

Vedanta is both a philosophy and a religion, but it has no set dogma or method:

> While asserting the truth as one, and its mystic vision as the only means, [Vedanta] accords recognition to multiple approaches to this vision ... . Each generation has felt free to interpret the basic truth in the language and cultural mores of his own generation ... though strictly adhering and following the original texts. ... Thus Vedanta is the science of Reality rather than a dogma, religious or philosophical.
>
> Giri (1985, pp. 34–35)

Today, people are engaged in a tremendous search for new approaches and broader understandings to guide their actions. And for me, it is this search that makes Vedanta so relevant. Vivekananda pointed out that the Vedantic principles are applicable not only in India but throughout the world (Bhajanananda 1976–77) and that Vedanta has an important part to play in the life of modern humans. It provides them with, among other values, a philosophy of social service so lacking in modern society (Bhajanananda 1976–77). Vivekananda believed, as I do, that religion properly understood can be applied to help solve both the mundane and the existential problems of humanity.

SELF, SOCIETY, AND DEVELOPMENT

> Science is discovering the Truth. Religion is the manifestation of Truth. Spirituality is Truth itself. Morality is holding on to Truth. Ethics is application of Truth in social life.
>
> Muktinathananda (personal communication, 1998 [6])

The concept of development according to *sanatana dharma* is the "unfoldment of Truth." It embraces the development of the self (body, mind, and spirit), others, and the entire universe (that is, the well-being of all living beings, including the environment[7]). Real development

---

[6] Swami Muktinathananda, Ramakrishna Math, Belur, Calcutta, India, personal communication, 1998.

[7] Hinduism lays stress on the psychophysical environment as a cocoon for the growth of goodness and harmony. The Veda devotes a great deal of attention to agriculture, livestock, rains, and harvests (Balasubramanian 1999). An entire branch of medicine — *Ayurveda* — has its base in various herbal remedies: *Vrkshayurveda*, classical Indian plant science, is highly advanced (Balasubramanian 1999). Hindus greatly venerate several plants, including *tulsi* (basil) and neem, and use them medicinally. The ashrams of the Vedic *rishis* (seers), which taught young disciples the Veda and the way of *dharma*, were forest retreats. The vivid descriptions of forest and fauna in the Ramayana and Mahabharata indicate quite clearly that there was then no environmental crisis of the sort witnessed in the 20th century. These accounts and indicators suggest that living according to the principles of *dharma* includes, and results in, an understanding and appreciation for the natural world and a "right" relationship with the natural environment, as well as with others in society.

18

from a Hindu perspective is the development of one and all in terms of both the inner and the outer environment. As Swami Muktinathananda said,

> According to Hinduism, real development in any area consists in removal of all imperfections and bringing about perfection. Thus, the essential elements of real development are helping in the removal of everything that is unreal, false or imperfect, providing education to remove ignorance, and helping one and all to understand the necessity and implications of development.
>
> Muktinathananda (personal communication, 1998[8])

SELF AND DEVELOPMENT

> That man attains peace, who, abandoning all desires, moves about without attachment, without selfishness, without vanity.
>
> Sastry (1977, p. 80)

> He who hates no single being, who is friendly and compassionate to all, who is free from attachment and egoism, to whom pain and pleasure are equal, who is enduring, ever-content and balanced in mind, self controlled, and possessed of firm conviction, whose thought and reason are directed to Me, he who is (thus) devoted to Me is dear to Me.
>
> Sastry (1977, p. 311)

> He by whom the world is not afflicted and who is not afflicted by the world, who is free from joy, envy, fear and sorrow, he is dear to Me.
>
> Sastry (1977, p. 312)

> Those who ever contemplate the Imperishable, the Indefinable, the Eternal, having restrained all the senses, always equanimous, intent on the welfare of all beings, — they reach Myself.
>
> Sastry (1977, p. 304)[9]

Whereas we know that the concept of the self is related to an immortal spark of inner consciousness, the word *I* or *me* (*aham*) refers to the accretions that cloud the pure perception of the immortal soul within every being. The purpose then of *sanatana dharma* is to evolve a way of dealing with society that removes the accretions of doubt, vanity, anger, and misery and brings the *atman* within every member of society ever closer to the realization of total fusion (*moksha*) with the *Brahman*. This fusion

---

[8] Swami Muktinathananda, Ramakrishna Math, Belur, Calcutta, India, personal communication, 1998.

[9] Sastry (1977) contains an English translation of Sri Sankaracharya's original Sanskrit commentary on the Bhagavad Gita.

is the goal of pursuing good *karma* in everyday life, and in India it provides a raison d'être for human existence.

The scriptural injunctions of the *purusarthas* (the doctrine of the four goals of life) convey the four ways to fulfill one's inner being:

🦋 *Dharma* — moral code of conduct, rightful action;

🦋 *Artha* — economic pursuits for self-sufficiency;

🦋 *Kama* — satisfaction of desires (physical or other); and

🦋 *Moksha* — total liberation, release from delusion.

Of these, the most significant is *moksha*. Our discussion of this path of the *purusarthas*, however, must be couched in the basic premise of Hinduism that the soul within a human is immortal: "Him weapons cut not, Him fire burns not, and Him water wets not; Him wind dries not. He cannot be cut, burnt, nor wetted, nor dried up. He is everlasting, all pervading, stable, firm, eternal" (Sastry 1977, pp. 49–50). Thus, the quest for *moksha* is a quest for a sort of immortality.

Dharma is neither a doctrine nor a dogma. In practical terms, *dharma* is the overarching principle guiding a dutiful and responsible life. It relies on reason no less than on intuition (the inner feeling and apprehension of any situation). As one of the fundamental ideals of human life it aims at life's fullest manifestation and upholds and sustains the individual and universal life principles, including spiritual and social values. *Dharma* is the urge to grow.

Rama in the Ramayana is often cited as a mythological example of a man–god who followed the path of *dharma*, even though it led him to abdicate his right to the throne of his father, Dasratha, and go into exile for 14 years in the forest as a result of the selfish wish of one of Dasratha's wives, Kaikeyi. This story demonstrates that the path of *dharma* is not always pleasurable but also involves duty, even that which is unpleasant. Following the path of *dharma* leads to the accumulation of good *karma*, which itself leads to a better rebirth in a family that pursues the path of the *sanatana dharma*. This is the beginning of the process toward the goal of *moksha* or liberation from *samsara*. The Bhagavad Gita (ch. III 19) emphasizes this: "Therefore, without attachment, constantly perform the action which should be done; for, performing action without attachment, man reaches the Supreme" (Sastry 1977, p. 104).

The fulfillment of *kama*, which is the principle of lawful desire (including sexual desire within marriage) is also part of the *purusarthas*. For Hindus, the fulfillment of desire within the limits of their understanding is also part of the *sanatana dharma*. Thus, it is clear that people in society should be moral and not obsessed by the sensual to the extent that it damages their psychological and physical health, or the fabric of society, through extramarital sexuality.

The *purusarthas* also enjoin the principle of *artha*, or economic independence. This is considered to be one of the pillars of a moral life, as economic dependence creates a flaw in all aspects of life, including that of morality. Thus, in making *kama* and *artha* some of the cardinal points of human fulfillment, along with spiritual and social goals, the *purusarthas* encourage a sane and balanced approach to living in society; in the case of *artha*, one balances the support of oneself and one's family (materialistic achievements and comfort) with the pursuit of other equally important aims in human life. In Hindu and Indian society, however, the drive for economic independence as a means to a life of plenty is evident everywhere — in all aspects of the media and in conversation with college students, as well as with corporate executives. Rural people who derive much of their income from agriculture or crafts are far closer to the life of the *purusarthas* and might therefore be considered more exemplary of the Hindu moral system.

21

The *purusarthas* provided a path of life that applied to both men and women. In Hindu society, societal, physical, and mental hygiene depended on living up to the *purusarthas'* high standards, and these basic notions enjoyed wide currency in India. Yet, although the ideals remain the same, modern Indians are unlikely to adhere fully to the *purusartha* system as a guide to personal growth or social interaction.

SOCIETY AND DEVELOPMENT

One might ask whether the diversity of India and Hinduism has led to division and conflicts and whether such controversies have been in themselves detrimental to overall development, including economic progress. Has the emphasis on spiritual development, evident right from the era of the Veda, come at the cost of economic development, perhaps even itself fostering self-centredness and apathy?

How widely are the Hindu beliefs and schemes of life accepted by the general population in India? This question is extremely important for gauging the effect of religion on economic development. The reality of Hinduism on the ground, both in urban centres and in villages, is that there is a vast proliferation of sects — the two main cults being the Viashnavite and the Saivite — which have their own local variations and imagery, chants, *bhajans* (hymns), and *mantras* (spiritually uplifting words, phrases, and concepts, usually derived from traditional scripture and musically intoned to purify the mind, elevate one's understanding of the self, and realize the divine Oneness). Yet, the sects all have in common their belief in God, known as Bhagwan, Ishwara, or Parmatma, and they all claim allegiance to *sanatana dharma*.

Religious messages are widely disseminated. Although a sizable proportion of Hindus may be illiterate in the sense of modern education, they certainly are well informed regarding the precepts of the Bhagavad Gita and the moral and ethical questions raised by the epics — the Ramayana and the Mahabharata — enacted in whole and in part each year throughout India. In modern India, radio, television, and cinema reinforce this educational process; programs frequently include discourses on religion or religious stories. These modes of communication serve to popularize and reinforce the values of *sanatana dharma*: the honour and dignity of women, tolerance, forgiveness, patience, humility, and obedience to the will of one's parents.

Hindu social life is life within the community. One's immediate family and the wider network of kin and friends, as well as the whole community, participate in all life-cycle rituals (weddings, funerals, etc.), festivals, and special ceremonies. These ceremonial and ritualistic occasions regenerate the religious life and bring harmony to those who take part in them. During these ceremonies, priests recite various holy books and scriptures and give discourses on many scriptures, including the epics and the Gita. Local customs make a unique contribution to these events in each region but never go against the tenor of the Veda.[10]

From India's inception, its history has been one of invasions and conquests, commencing with the Aryans and culminating with the British colonization. Many diverse ideologies have gone into making Hinduism what it is today. An outstanding consequence of Hinduism's eclectic origins is that it has sufficient tolerance and patience to forge new syntheses without totally losing its direction and basic spiritual content. In the medieval era, for example, when the Moguls dominated India, Hinduism survived by incorporating some of the better aspects of other faiths. This is true also of India's response to the Christian rulers and missionaries under British colonization.

Hinduism's acceptance and assimilation of such varieties and polarities of faiths emerged from an underlying truth, eloquently expressed by the Vedic seers in the phrase "Truth is one, Sages call it by various names" (*Ekam Sat vipra bahudha vadanti*). This is one of the greatest pronouncements in the Rig Veda and provides the foundational philosophy of the Hindu faith. Swami Vivekananda considered this statement the Magna Carta of religion (Ranganathananda 1987).

Enlightened Hindus have a deep faith in syncretism, that is, in the practice of incorporating the best principles and elements of all religions. Thus, Hinduism displays an understanding of an underlying and overarching unity, a hard-earned tolerance for all aspects of truth, and a willingness to incorporate the truths of other faiths. As such,

---

[10] Even in contemporary India, 47.5% of the population is still more or less illiterate. The main sources of people's knowledge of Hinduism are in the oral tradition, passed down from parents to children; sermons delivered by itinerant preachers; discourses given by priests on a daily basis at the temple or at the numerous religious festivals, rituals, and ceremonies; the daily prayers to male or female deities in temples or at the home altar (which most Hindu households have, no matter how affluent or poor); and interchanges during pilgrimages to holy shrines at the four cardinal points of India. On these pilgrimages, people exchange and absorb religious ideas from other pilgrims, especially the legends and myths connected with the shrines.

philosophically, it is not prone to intra- or interreligious conflict. This is not to deny that conflicts have ensued but to suggest that they are not in accord with the fundamental tenets of Hinduism. Given the heterogeneity of Indian society, one might ask whether these conflicts would have been much worse without this philosophical and spiritual underpinning.

Related to Hinduism's syncretic tendencies is the Indian understanding of the term *secularism*. India's society is pluralistic, with a variety of cultures, ethnicities, races, languages, and religions. Although Hinduism is the majority religion in India and a large proportion of the Indian population is Hindu, the milieu of Hinduism contains several other religions, like Islam, Christianity, Sikhism, Zoroastrianism, the Bahá'í Faith, and Jainism. One of the major issues that occupied Gandhi and Nehru was determining what position on this multiplicity of religions would best suit an independent India. This position would have to define "clearly the relation between religion and politics and between religion and the nation-state" (Joshi 1995, p. 3). Secularism was the approach chosen, but a secularism with a politically convenient and distinctly Indian interpretation. "Secularism is defined as 'equal respect for all faiths' and a call for cultivation of religious tolerance and harmony" (Kanal 1988, p. 1). Mahatma Gandhi summed up the secular approach of India as follows:

23

> Hindustan belongs to all those who are born and bred here and who have no other country to look to. Therefore it belongs to Parsis, Beni Israelis, to Indian Christians, Muslims and other non Hindus as much as to Hindus ... . Religion is a personal matter, which should have no place in politics.
> Gandhi (1992 [1947], pp. 277–278)

Nehru, the first Prime Minister of independent India (and Gandhi's chosen disciple), had a similar appreciation of the question of secularism and felt that it was not merely a question of tolerating other religions — it was a question of social and political justice, of creating an equitable society (Joshi 1995). Thus, the preamble to the new Constitution of India declared the country "a sovereign secular, democratic republic." The state was not to interfere with people's freedom to practice or believe in any faith.

If this idea had been truly accepted, it would have laid the foundations for an integrated development, because it would have created the conditions for subcontinental harmony. But of all the various types of socialization and conditioning, the religiocentric bias yields least to any kind of pressure to change. It is very difficult to let go of the central tenet of each religion that makes believers claim, "our religion is the best!" I would say that this is mainly a result of paranoia and the absence of knowledge and understanding of one's own religion and, more so, of other religions. If India is to realize its goal of interfaith harmony, then

Hindus must use the syncretism of Hinduism to take the lead in this process.

India's experiment in "secularism" is now about 50 years old and bears many scars; it has not managed to avoid carnage and violence, including the great strife during the partition of India into India and Pakistan. On numerous occasions, communal violence has occurred between Hindus and Muslims. These events indicate that the ethos of secularism has not percolated into the psyche of the common person in India. The experiment, however, goes on, and perhaps with deep knowledge, understanding, appreciation, and respect for one's own religion, as well as for the religions of others, India's secularism will fully succeed. Outside India, interfaith understanding and interfaith movements are also growing in every corner of the world; these beliefs, I feel, will form the basis of global unity and integrated development.

In examining the question of Hinduism's role in economic development, I take as an example an argument put forward in the early part of the 20th century by the sociologist Max Weber. For Weber (1958), the caste system and the Hindu religious beliefs of *karma*, *samsara*, and *kismet* (Urdu for fate) meant that Hindu society was otherworldly in orientation and not geared to respond to new economic challenges. Weber, however, did not seriously consider other factors — colonialism and repeated invasions — that led to the conditions he observed in India. Moreover, Hinduism is a lived and in many respects still oral tradition: it is very difficult to understand from texts. Thus, although Weber's viewpoint is scholarly, it is not holistic. A number of social scientists have, in fact, rejected his perspective. On the basis of research among entrepreneurs, Singer et al. (1966) found that the "stagnant economy" of India could not be related to otherworldly religious values; they observed that the family orientation of these entrepreneurs, as opposed to Western-style individualism, was an asset in capitalist development (see also Brzezinski 1997). Singer et al. also found that Indians used adaptive strategies — such as compartmentalization, ritual neutralization of the work sphere, and vicarious ritualization — to successfully combine the economic and religious spheres (Singer 1972). Moreover, the economist Arvind Sharma (1980) suggested that the basis for a strong work ethic can be gleaned from Hindu scriptural tradition (Brzezinski 1997).

The reason why India has seen little economic development might be found in the nonparticipatory policies and practices that have always governed its primarily agricultural economy. Farmers, especially those with small holdings, have been exploited by the landowners, bureaucrats, and rulers; for the landless, the situation is still worse. As a result, in most parts of India the benefits of agricultural production have accrued only to those who exploited both the people and the resources and refused to share these benefits with those who worked for them or with the general population. The most recent spate of economic development in India began with the unification of the various pre-existing nation-states into a single sovereign Republic of India on 15 August 1947; at that time, India's leaders confronted a host of historical problems but failed, for various reasons, to fully enlist the progressive and reformist ethos of that period, including its participatory, indigenous methodologies. I will return to this issue when I discuss Gandhi's *sarvodaya* (or welfare of all) model of village-based economic development and Nehru's preference for the heavy-industrialization model.

ISSUES FOR HINDUISM AND DEVELOPMENT

Westerners raise some pertinent questions when they encounter Hindu-based social action and development strategies: Does belief in reincarnation, *karma*, and *samsara* have a deleterious effect on people's awareness of, or their action on, social problems, such as poverty and the denial of women's rights? Further, to what extent is "fatalism" a major influence in people's daily life, and is it based on Hindu religious belief? Does the caste system create and reinforce inequity?

The concepts of reincarnation, *karma*, and *samsara* are closely inter-related and convey the belief in the "cycle of birth and rebirth," the immortality of the soul, and the idea that "as you sow, so shall you reap." It would be incorrect to assess the Hindu attitude as fatalistic, for this would imply the existence of a large Hindu community without any intellection or direction. Fatalism is the attitude of people who believe and act as if their efforts, whether great or small, will make no difference to the ultimate outcome of plans or actions. This attitude would result in utter indifference to efforts to bring about development. Yet, *karma* (in Hindi) and *bhagayavad* (in Sanskrit) do not carry the negative connotations of fatalistic passivity and laziness; rather, they carry the positive connotation of reconciliation after the event. This is the approach, in practice, of a vast section of Hindu society; these people use it to accept gracefully and with great courage, calmness, and strength the outcome of adverse economic and social situations. *Karma* suggests that such circumstances must stem from people's own deeds, yet *karma* also imparts confidence that people have the strength and capacity to shape their own future in this life and in subsequent ones. I feel that this understanding of *karma* has, on balance, a positive rather than negative effect on poverty alleviation, women's rights, and developmental activities in general because it allows people to sustain their hope during inevitable setbacks and to believe that their endeavours will yield fruit.

Besides, the existing socioeconomic system adequately inculcates norms of competition, individuality, and ceaseless striving to better the situation in one's family, business, or career. This has removed all but a token recognition of the passive side of fate and fatalism. Even though Hindus refer to "fate" whenever they encounter a life event they cannot control or even understand, they exert strenuous efforts to follow their desires and achieve their goals. This dual approach is consistent with passages in the Gita that clearly refute Weber's argument. The Gita preaches constant action in all that one does **and** deep meditation as part of action. One is instructed not only to strive in all spheres of life but also to do this in a cool and detached manner, keeping all the consequences of action in view. Hinduism is therefore not a religion that teaches passivity; rather, it is both outward and inward looking, with a logical connection between these dimensions.

The caste system also causes great comment and consternation. Each caste is related to a *varna*, of which there are four: *brahmin*, *kshatriya*, *vaisya*, and *shudra*. Each of these has a role to play in society:

- *Brahmins* are in charge of ritual and religious matters;

- *Kshatriyas* are warriors and allied to the defence of society;

- *Vaisyas* are the merchants and given to commercial pursuits; and

- *Shudras* serve all people belonging to the other *varnas*.

Another group of people, who live outside the caste system, were once known as the "untouchables" and then as *dalits*[11]; contact with an untouchable was considered polluting by caste Hindus.

Many Hindus believe that the *varna* into which one is born is due to fate or *karma,* because *varna* is immutable. Although the practical effect of this system has often been inequality — with rural, illiterate, and often destitute people bearing the brunt of exploitation by higher castes — it can be argued that this was not the intention of the *varna* system as set out in ancient Hinduism. The functional, rather than hierarchical, nature of the *varna* system is manifest in Balinese Hinduism:

> In the history of Hinduism, the doctrine of varnas appears *before* the doctrine of karma. This raises the suspicion that the doctrine of karma may have provided a post facto rationalization for a birth-oriented division of society that was already in place when the doctrine of karma became widespread. ... It is possible though that Balinese Hinduism represents the original concept of varnas ... .
> "In Bali *varna* is simply occupation. A businessman is a vaisya, a teacher a brahmin, an employee a sudra and so on. No inferior or superior stature is attached, and if one switches profession — say from teacher to shopkeeper — one changes caste from brahmin to vaisya."
>
> Sharma (1993, p. 25, emphasis in the original)

---

[11] In 1937 Dr Ambedkar coined this term for untouchables, but it later came to refer to people of all oppressed classes.

The exploitation of lower castes and untouchables was condemned by the Bhakti mystics and by numerous modern Hindu activists, such as Gandhi. In more concrete terms, certain provisions in the Indian Constitution also combat the discrimination caused by this system, and the Indian people are changing their attitudes and behaviour toward these classes. The history of the caste system in India leads me to think that all human systems carry the potential for abuse when material and status considerations are foremost in our minds and we ignore spiritual and human values.

MODERN SCIENCE AND THE HINDU RELIGION

Scientific knowledge is built upon facts. The medical side is fairly well developed, though the causes and cures of certain ailments are yet to be discovered. But what science does know, it is more or less sure about, because the various factors concerned have been tested: theories have been tried and proven. In religion it is different. People are given certain facts or truths and told to believe them. After a little while when their belief is not fulfilled, doubt creeps in; and then they go from religion to religion in trying to find proof. You hear about God in churches and temples; you can read about Him in books; but you can experience God only through Self-realisation attained by practicing definite scientific techniques. In India, religion is based upon such scientific methods. By experimentation, India has proved the truths in religion. In the future, religion everywhere will be a matter of experimentation; it will not be based solely on belief.

Yogananda (1944, p. 35)

Science without religion is lame, religion without science is blind.

Einstein (1950)

Turning to the nexus between science and religion, I should state that I believe that as objects of study, external phenomena and the inner dimensions of human existence are equally significant. Thus, inasmuch as science is a search for truth, religion is also a search for Truth. The physical sciences are an inquiry into matter and the nature of the external world. Religion, in contrast, is an inquiry into consciousness, spirituality, and the nature of the inner world. In the final analysis, however, one may find no separation between the external and internal dimensions, but a continuum between these states. Science inquires through experiment, and religion inquires through inner experience. In this sense, religion is scientific.

One of the most noticeable trends in science and religion in India is that spiritual savants are recognizing the great significance of science; they have begun to acknowledge that contemporary humans are living in an age dominated by science. They do not see religion as opposed to science but as having much to learn from the methods and temper of science. Thus, Ranganathananda recorded the following statement of Yogananda:

> Pure science needs to cover a wider ground than the external phys-ical world constituting only the external physical environment of human life. Science has to study the inner world of man as well, besides the outer world of nature. But in the modern context, unfor-tunately the sciences of physical nature have far outstripped the sciences of man ... . If the physical sciences have lifted man from many fears and uncertainties of his primitive past, it has landed him also in new fears and uncertainties arising from ignorance of his own inner nature. The modern man has to realise that such a study of the *"within"* of nature, as revealed in nature's evolutionary product, that is man, is also a science like the other study by the physical sciences, of the *"without"* of nature.
>
> Ranganathananda (1983, p. 3, emphasis in the original)

I find this statement important because people often assume that mod-ern science alone has verifiable methods, experimentation, and testing. But, as Yogananda suggested in the epigram that began this section, spiritual aspirants can internally verify and replicate specific stages in spiritual progress as set out in Hinduism and Buddhism. We can then say we have a "science" of religion, which, apart from the sociological side of it — as represented in ceremony and ritual observances — is quite capable of providing a topography of the "within" of humans.

In answer to the question of whether the Hindu religion is scien-tific, Swami Muktinathananda (personal communication, 1998[12]) gave the following response: "If we define the scientific in this way that to be practical is to be scientific, then Hinduism is perfectly scientific."

In his lecture on religion and science, Vivekananda said, "Religion deals with the truth of the metaphysical world just as chemistry and other natural sciences deal with the truth of the physical world" (Ranganathananda 1987, p. 175). Vivekananda also taught that "reli-gion is the science which learns the transcendental in nature through the transcendental in man" (Jitatmananda 1992, p. 68). In Swami Vivekananda's view, the physicist and the mystic reach the truth of unity by following different approaches. As he noted, "physics today is relating itself increasingly to philosophy and drawing closer to Vedanta philosophy" (Jitatmananda 1992, p. 70). "What the Vedic sages discov-ered through mystic intuition, modern scientists are confirming with the help of sophisticated instruments" (Jitatmananda 1992, p. 86). American physicist, Fritjof Capra, also supported this view:

> Thus the mystic and the physicist arrive at the same conclusions; one starting from the inner realm, the other from the outer world.

[12] Swami Muktinathananda, Ramakrishna Math, Belur, Calcutta, India, personal communication, 1998.

The harmony of their views confirms the ancient Indian wisdom that *brahman*, the ultimate reality without, is identical to *Atman*, the reality within.

(Capra 1983, p. 338)

Another trend in Hindu religion is the discovery of various parallels in religion and science where the two seem increasingly to be speaking the same language, that is, language that points toward the unity of all existing phenomena:

Modern particle physics shows the folly of trying to search for a single object, a sub-atomic particle or electron as a separate independent reality. Such a thing does not exist. The very experience of the independent existence of one thing is unreal. Vedanta terms it *mithya*. The right vision is to perceive the whole in the so-called isolated entity. This is what the Vedantist means by the statement "*brahman* alone is real."

Jitatmananda (1992, p. 27)

As mentioned before, the Ultimate Reality for the ancient Indian seers was *Brahman* (or the Self), from which all *atmans* (or selves) emanate. The realization of the preexisting oneness with *Brahman* was the goal of all life, but to describe *Brahman*, or the Supreme Reality, was considered beyond the capacities of human language or even human conception. For example, Yajnavalkya, a Vedic seer, attempted the following description of Supreme Reality for his wife, Maitreyi, many centuries ago:

For where there is duality as it were, there one sees the other, one smells the other, one tastes the other, one speaks to the other, one hears the other, one thinks of the other, one touches the other, one knows the other. But where everything has become just one's own self, by what and whom should one know? By what should one know Him by whom all this is known? He is indestructible for He cannot be destroyed. He is unattached for He does not attach himself. He is unfettered, He does not suffer, He is not injured. Indeed by what would one know the knower?

Radhakrishnan (1974, p. 286)

A well-known mystic from medieval India, Kabir, also preached the merging of selfhood with the *nirguna* (beyond any attributes), which is clearly a linguistic reformulation of the "not this, not this" (*neti, neti*) of the Upanishads' description of *Brahman*.[13]

---

[13] See Pande (1989, p. 122): "Kabir's object of devotion is qualityless (nirguna). This reality cannot be identified by any creator. Kabir, in fact, identifies the creator with the created world. In this notion of transcendent immanent unity he is reminiscent of Upanishadic or Kasmira Saiva monism as also of Madhyamika absolutism."

Thus, two features frequently characterize the Hindu perception of the nature of reality:

❦ Ultimate Reality exists, but it cannot be adequately described, or at least it cannot be described with a great deal of precision; and

❦ The Ultimate Reality can be experienced in the consciousness of the self by the latter's merging with the consciousness of the ultimate Self.

Further, certain other subfeatures emerge from this characterization:

❦ The experience of an Ultimate Reality is not the monopoly of any single religious tradition. Buddhism, for instance, speaks of the "void" into which everything returns and from which everything emerges.

❦ It is not possible to quantify the "voidic experience," and in fact this linguistic awkwardness indicates the difficulty.

Modern physics suffers from similar difficulties when it attempts to describe or predict the behaviour of quantum particles, which physicists have described as forms of energy "dancing" without any cause or purpose, a field of energy existing for and in itself.

Hindu scientists, religionists, social scientists, and medical practitioners have noted other base-level similarities between the findings of modern science and the experiential discoveries of Hindu mystics; they have also tried to conceive of new paradigms in which the scientific and religious understandings converge. For example, Mukhopadhyay (a pathologist) developed the *Akhanda* ("unbreakable" or "whole") paradigm that treats the entire universe as a living organism. He pointed out that the "evolution or involution of species is intimately related to evolution or involution of its environment" (Mukhopadhyay 1995). He felt that the question of morality is intimately related to the evolution of consciousness, and this is clear from the wisdom of the sage and savant Sri Aurobindo, whom Mukhopadhyay acknowledged as a seminal influence on his work. In the following quotation, Mukhopadhyay expressed, in modern language, the ancient insight of the Vedas that *Brahman* created the "multiverse," to use Mukhopadhyay's language, as a form of play, where the self would lose consciousness of Self, and the entire purpose of Creation would be the drama of mind, body, and spirit, in which the self would once again merge with the Self:

The "self" within the brain understands its imprisonment within five overlapping concentric spheres. Who am I? What am I supposed to do? Where from I have come? Where shall I be doomed, if proper precautions are not taken before hand? It is "self", seeking the "Self", through "self", for "Self". If "self" is successful in this mission, then inside is out and outside is in. There is inversion of the neuraxis.

Mukhopadhyay (1995, p. 171)

Mukhopadhyay's seminal work was thus a transformation of the ancient religious insights of India into the modern scientific language of pathology and biology.

Certain scientific discoveries — such as the theory of evolution, the law of conservation of matter, and the theory of relativity — bear striking similarities to Vedantic concepts of the universe. Sri Ramakrishna used the concept of the nonduality of consciousness (*Advaita*) to build his theory of the harmony of religions (Bhajanananda 1976–77), and Vivekananda saw nonduality as the basis for the underlying similarities of art, science, and religion.[14] Likewise, Einstein, in his special theory of relativity, used the constancy of the velocity of light to formulate the principle of invariance (Bhajanananda 1976–77, p. 23). The close agreement between Vedantic principles and those of the modern scientific discoveries, despite the difference in their expression, is noteworthy (Bhajanananda 1976–77). As Jitatmananda pointed out,

31

> The entire world of modern physics is moving toward a knowledge of final unity in the universe. The Vedanta, the philosophical and the metaphysical portions of the Vedas, affirmed this unity as the very basis of all existence and the ultimate goal of all knowledge.
>
> Jitatmananda (1992, pp. 6–7)

Another commonality of science and religion is the idea that the mind, or subjective consciousness, plays a great role in creating the world and lays down the laws of perception. When mystics go "inward," their consciousness alters and they can perceive worlds not possible if consciousness were not capable of altering dimensions and adapting itself to new perceptions. Social-science researchers have recognized this link between subject and object, in terms of the continuum of consciousness, and suggest that each person "creates" a particular perception of the world, both mental and sociophysical. Similarly, as Jitatmananda remarked,

> Unless we know the Knower we cannot also know that the known is only the projection of the Knower. This Knower is our Pure Consciousness, which is the only seer, the one all-pervading Existence, the one all-inclusive knowledge. This Pure Consciousness projects the entire universe just as a spider projects its web. The external and a separate universe is, therefore, only a superimposition, due to our desires and will, on the Pure Consciousness which knows everything as One.
>
> Jitatmananda (1991, p. 50)

---

[14] According to Vivekananda, "Art, science and religion are but three different ways of expressing the single truth. But in order to understand this we must have the theory of Advaita" (that is, nonduality of consciousness) (Bhajanananda 1976–77, p. 26).

The importance of the observer has, by now, also been recognized in the physical sciences.

Backed by these eminent thinkers and with these comments on the similarities between scientific and religious inquiry, I subscribe to, and try to manifest in my work, the following statement by Ranganathananda:

> There is no conflict between science and religion, between the physical sciences and the science of spirituality. Both have the identical aim of discovering truth and helping man to grow physically, mentally and spiritually, and achieve fulfillment. But each by itself is insufficient and helpless.

DEVOTION, KNOWLEDGE, AND ACTION

THE ORIGINS OF THE HINDU SOCIAL ETHIC

Between the 12th and 16th centuries AD, Hinduism experienced an extraordinary efflorescence. This medieval spiritual renaissance indicates that Hinduism not only survived but prospered under the foreign rule of the Moguls. Some of the better known mystics of this age were Jnanadeva (d. 1296), Namadeva (d. 1346), Kabir (15th century), Nanak (1469–1539), Mira (16th century), Tulsidas (1532–1623), and Eknath (1533–99). Together, they are referred to as the Bhakti gurus. They were spiritual masters–preceptors, who imparted knowledge to their disciples, dispelling ignorance from their minds.

The concept of a living spiritual master has been of extreme importance in Hinduism, and even today many cults and sects with living gurus flourish in India and in other parts of the world where Hinduism has spread. The guru mediates between the disciple and *Brahman*, bringing the disciple closer to *Brahman* through counsel, discourse, exercise, and example. In due course, perhaps after several lifetimes, the disciple is freed from the bonds of delusion and the ongoing cycle of transmigration; then the disciple can merge with *Brahman*.

There were a number of commonalities among the Bhakti mystics and saints, several of whom, like Kabir, came from the lowest caste. The medieval Indian spiritual preceptors, like the Vedic seers, enjoined hard work in the form of service to the spiritual preceptor, community, and society. Devotion to *Brahman* by means of devotion to the guru was another common aspect of their teachings. Most advocated that caste "untouchability" was an age-old evil and that the exploitation of the lower castes and outcastes was a reprehensible practice that must be reversed. They therefore made no distinctions of caste or gender in their ashrams and attempted to influence society by their example. They initiated men and women of all castes into their faith and promised them that they, too, could aspire to and fulfill the desire of spiritual liberation.

Mira stands out as a mystical luminary who was regarded as a saint, even as a woman living in medieval times.

Kabir, for example,

> refused to acknowledge caste distinctions or to recognise the authority of the six schools of philosophy. He did not set any store by the four divisions of life (*ashramas*) prescribed for *Bhramanas*. He held that religion (*dharma*) without devotion (*bhakti*) was no religion at all (*adharma*), and that asceticism, fasting, and alms giving had no value if not accompanied by adoration (*bhajana* — the singing of devotional songs).
>
> Pande (1989, p. 102)

Kabir taught the worship of a Reality that cannot be described. He felt deeply that the guru was the only route to salvation.

There was a great deal of cross-pollination among the religions of the region during this time: Islam[15] and Sufism (mystical Islam) had a strong influence on the Bhakti gurus. In the case of Nanak, the synthesis between Hinduism and Sufism was seminal in the creation of Sikhism.[16] A description of the medieval renaissance would be incomplete without a reference to the insights of Nanak. He was a spiritual teacher who came from a Hindu family, founded Sikhism, and set in motion a lineage of 10 spiritual masters. Nanak believed that the Creator is a single principle from which all things evolve. Although he believed that the Creator is beyond any specific description, he felt that God is capable of forming a pervasive personal relationship with humans. Nanak described God as a "pure light" that pervades everything; in this sense, everything exists in God and the world is his play (*lila*) (Pande 1989). Humans, according to Nanak, emanate from the light of God and are born as a result of the desires of the mind. Humans, by following the will (*hukum*) of God, can evolve in stages and realize spiritual salvation. In this process, nothing is achievable in the spiritual realm without the presence and guidance of the guru. In terms of action, humans must be balanced and objective and live in the world with love and dedication. Nanak said, "Truth is higher than everything, but the living of Truth is higher than everything else." Clear Upanishadic strains appear in Nanak's insights, and he, too, worked against idolatry, ritualism, the caste system, and exploitative relationships.

The medieval Indian saints had a very pronounced impact on the evolution of Hindu ideas. Almost every reformer or mystic after Kabir and Nanak denounced casteism and tried to purge Hinduism of the pernicious practices that had crept into it, including discrimination against

33

---

[15] See Pande (1989, p. 121): "A pervasive influence of Islam on the medieval Bhakti movement has been asserted and even Sankaracharya is said to have been influenced by Islamic monotheism."

[16] In Sikhism, the "Holy Book" (Guru Granth Sahib) is treated as a living guru and given every consideration that a living master would be given. For its recitations and interpretation there are Sikh priests called "granthies."

women. Some of the 18th- and 19th-century reformers were outright in their condemnation of such discrimination; they praised the role of women as mothers — as representative of the Divine Principle. Others, like Dayanand, campaigned to abolish ghastly ritualistic customs, such as *sati* (the self-immolation of widows on the funeral pyres of their husbands) and the then-prevalent custom of child marriage, in which even prepubescent children were married. He was also firmly opposed to social restrictions against the remarriage of widows, which went so far as to prevent a widow from remarrying even if she was only a child when her husband died. This first recrudescence of devotion, knowledge, and action, in medieval times, paved the way for the second Hindu renaissance, the effects of which are still evident. The various sects and cults of the 20th century owe allegiance to, and freely quote, the teachings of Kabir, Nanak, Namdeva, Jnanadeva, Mira, and others.

34

THE SECOND HINDU RENAISSANCE

By the 18th and 19th centuries, despite the teachings of the mystics of the Bhakti Renaissance, many social problems remained unresolved. In fact, these conditions and practices — *sati*, obstruction of widow remarriages, caste exploitation, untouchability, and poverty — remained intact under both Mogul and colonial rule. Nevertheless, certain exemplary movements in the fields of SRD emerged and significantly improved the economic and social conditions of marginalized people. I will now turn to a brief examination of these movements, with a view to outlining their ethical guiding principles and how their principles inform their developmental activities.

Arya Samaj movements

Founded near the turn of the century (1875) by Swami Dayanand Saraswati, under the slogan "back to the Vedas," the Arya Samaj was characterized by the development of an elaborate monotheistic system of beliefs. Swami Dayanand had an acute sense of social awareness and was active in the field of women's rights, women's education, and gender equality. The Arya Samaj started movements for India's freedom, the education of girls and women, the care of orphan children and the poor, and the revival of religious studies and debate. Through these movements, Dayanand attempted to eradicate superstition, obsessive ritualism, and blind faith; caste, class, and sex discrimination; and the social evils of dowry and untouchability. He started a movement to revive the dignity of hard work and individual virtues. He propagated regular prayers and "Havens" (recitations of Vedic verses while herbs, incense, or cereals are burned to purify the inner and outer environment). He encouraged the concept of the oneness of the incorporeal God and gave impetus to economic development through education, vocational training, creation of jobs and small-scale industry, and publications. The Arya Samaj has generated an enormous amount of literature on social, religious, scientific, and literary topics (Gupta 1998).

Dayanand acted to change society through the classical system of education (*gurukul*) in which knowledge about *dharma*, as well as human and spiritual values, was imparted and the ideal of equality practiced. In Satyarth Prakash, a book that provides the fundamental principles of Arya Samaj, Dayanand proposed education for young boys and girls in a three-language formula — Sanskrit, Hindi, and a foreign language. He propounded continence for students and opposed child marriage. The Arya Samaj has founded many Dayanand Anglo Vedic (DAV) schools, especially in the Punjab; the DAV schools provide modern education with a traditional and Vedic tinge. The Arya Samaj runs a large number of Vyayam Shalas–Akharas (gymnasiums and sports centres) for physical health. It was involved to some extent in the anticolonial movement, supporting the production and consumption of indigenous goods (*swadeshi*) and the use of Hindi as a national language, and it remains active in contemporary India, especially in the northern belt (Jordens 1978).[17]

Ramakrishna Mission

The Ramakrishna Mission was founded at the end of the 19th century and named after the Bengali mystic, Sri Ramakrishna Paramahans. Its founder, Swami Vivekananda, was one of Ramakrishna's chief disciples. The Mission teaches the principles of Vedanta and also provides concrete service to communities with its schools, colleges, hospitals, and orphanages.

Sri Ramakrishna emphasized, among other principles, "the equal validity of all religions, the potential divinity of man, and service to man as a way of worshipping God."[18] Ramakrishna was basically a devotee of Kali, the Divine Mother. As a mystic, Ramakrishna emphasized the spiritual side of life and the limitation of human wants. One of his most urgent dictums was that humans should avoid the trap of sensuality and obsession with material things. He also emphasized people's need for the spiritual and cultural traditions of the past to help them move meaningfully into the future.

Today, the Mission addresses the question of spirituality and science and is now preaching that science has begun to validate the Vedantic viewpoint of the oneness of the universe — nothing can exist outside the Spirit. The Mission's ideal is freedom of the self and service to humankind. Its aim is to practice and preach the *sanatana dharma* as embodied in the lives and teachings of Sri Ramakrishna and Swami Vivekananda, who undertook their spiritual quest through social action

35

---

[17] For more information, consult the Arya Samaj website (www.whereisgod.com), which, at the time of writing, was still under construction.

[18] See the Ramakrishna Mission website (www.sriramakrishna.org).

and the gospel of love. The motto of the Mission is "renunciation, service, and harmony of religions"; its method is work and worship — religious preaching and training of monastic aspirants. The preachers are all monks in the Mission and have specific regulations governing their clothing and food. The two components of the Ramakrishna Mission are the *math* (or monastic order) for contemplative activities, such as meditation and preaching the Vedanta, and the Mission per se, which has ashrams and institutions all over the country. The activities of these bodies include the following (Gambhirananda 1957):

❦ Religious teaching and discourses;

❦ Operation of schools at all educational levels, including general technical education, language training, and character building from an ethical–spiritual perspective;

❦ Creation of libraries;

❦ Social work among marginalized peoples;

❦ Medical service (creation of hospitals, clinics, dispensaries, and sanitoriums and distribution of medicines to those unable to afford them);

❦ Projects for poverty alleviation and income generation;

❦ Relief projects; and

❦ Agricultural and scientific research.

These organizations work closely with local communities on problems the communities have themselves deemed relevant. They infuse their actions with the teachings of Swami Vivekananda and Sri Ramakrishna.

Sri Aurobindo Society

The life, message, and teachings of Sri Aurobindo inspired the creation of the Sri Aurobindo Society:

> Sri Aurobindo's teaching starts with the ancient perception of the seers of the Vedanta that there is a supreme reality that is absolute, eternal, and indeterminable. This is *Brahman*, the one Truth, Sole and Entire … . All this is a manifestation of *Brahman*, by *Brahman*, and in *Brahman*.
>
> Pandit (1959, pp. 3–4)

The integral truth of Sri Aurobindo's teachings is corroborated by the hymns of Veda, the Upanishads, and the Gita. The basic aim of the Sri Aurobindo Society is to work toward "individual perfection, social transformation, and human unity based on a spiritual foundation."[19]

---

[19] See the Sri Aurobindo Society's website (www.sriaurobindosociety.org.in).

The Society has established a number of research centres to investigate ways to integrate spirituality into various aspects of human life, such as the social sciences, health, management, commerce and business, and applied scientific research.[20] One of the developmental activities of the Society and the Sri Aurobindo ashram is to promote "integral education" to balance and integrate the four aspects of the individual: the physical, the vital (dynamic energy, passions, will), the mental (thinking and reasoning), and the psychic and spiritual (the seat of the highest truths of existence). The Sri Aurobindo Society promulgates this education through various means (children's books, educational games and toys, teacher-training programs, and distance and digital education) and institutions (an institute of vocational training and mass communication; study and youth camps; and health centres, with yoga and "nature-cure" wings). Through its Women's Council, the Sri Aurobindo Society also focuses on women's development premised on the full development of the spirituality of the individual woman and an inherent equality based in the divine source of all humanity. Through lectures, seminars, and publications, the Sri Aurobindo Society promotes prenatal and parental education, equal opportunity for women to work and be of service to humanity, and economic independence for women.

World Spiritual University

Seeing illiteracy, ignorance, superstition, and blind faith and realizing the grave erosion of India's moral values and national character, Prajapita Brahma (later known as Brahma Baba) started the World Spiritual University (Prajapita Brahma Kumaris Ishwariya Vishwa Vidyalaya) to cultivate the seeds of knowledge, wisdom, and virtuous behaviour.

The World Spiritual University is an international organization with 450 000 members or students. It has more than 3 000 educational centres teaching Rajyoga meditation and moral and spiritual values in more than 60 countries. It is administered primarily by women. It is dedicated to education for all-round development, and it focuses on spiritual growth through contemplation, development of higher values, and service to community. Education in moral and spiritual values is emphasized to bring about transformation in attitudes and behaviour, build human character, and develop an integrated personality. Enrollment in the university is free and open to individuals who wish to

---

[20] The Sri Aurobindo Institute for Applied Scientific Research focuses on innovations in alternative energy sources and appropriate technology to solve worker-identified problems while consciously emphasizing deeper psychological and spiritual values. In its literature, the institute suggests that, "while it is important to reach and work at the frontiers of science, it is equally important to develop a technology which will be appropriate for rural and semi-urban India and other developing countries. The need is for a technology which will have the least side effects and touch immediately a large number of people directly in their lives. It will help them do their work more efficiently, faster, with less health hazards and at a lower cost" (SAS n.d.).

engage in an active change process through personal growth and meditation.[21]

Prajapita Brahma's vision for the world was grounded in truth, justice, and equality, an equality based on a foundation of harmony and balance between the sexes. At the time of the university's inception, Prajapita Brahma, a respected 60-year-old diamond merchant, surrendered all his property and assets to a trust administered by eight young women. Women and young girls have been chosen as administrators and spiritual teachers. The university is based on principles of equality of the sexes and teaches that "any form of discrimination and prejudice is destructive to a world which depends on the strategic balance of a full and equal partnership between women and men" (BKWSO 1995b).

The university has general consultative status with the Economic and Social Council of the United Nations, has consultative status with the United Nations Children's Fund, and is associated with the United Nations Peace University. The World Spiritual University works primarily in the areas of environmental improvement (for example, a project to demonstrate solar–wind–battery hybrid systems technology in India[22]), health awareness and medicine, world unity and peace, and the eradication of poverty. It has participated in a number of United Nations conferences, published position papers taking value-based approaches to various development problems,[23] and received seven United Nations Peace Messenger Awards.

Swadhyaya

Another spiritual movement engaged in development activities is the *Swadhyaya* movement (a Sanskrit word meaning "self-study"), which works primarily in Gujarat and Maharashtra. Using the Bhagavad Gita and the traditional Indian worldview as its philosophical basis, Pandurang Shastri Athavale, its founder, asked people to recognize the self as a manifestation of divine being and thus to acknowledge the divinity of all individuals. The followers of this movement — the "swadhyayees" — consider service to God their main purpose and

---

[21] See the Brahma Kumaris World Spiritual University website (www.bkwsu.com).

[22] The project is summarized on a web page of the International Centre for the Application of Solar Energy (www.case.gov.au/complete3.htm) (CASE n.d.).

[23] For example, the World Spiritual University explored a spiritual response to poverty in its statement for the 1996 International Year for the Eradication of Poverty, which emphasized that the interconnected root causes of poverty go beyond material considerations and advised careful consideration of poverty in relationships, spiritual bankruptcy, spiritual causes of poverty, the greed factor, and conditioning and poverty consciousness. It recommended that solutions to poverty emphasize self-worth, simplicity, creativity, and self-reliance. It saw its role in poverty eradication as planting the seeds for long-term changes in attitudes, behaviours, and lifestyles through positive-thinking programs, developing and sharing values, inculcating abilities and responsibilities, promoting self-reliance–empowerment of the self and community, and encouraging intellectual development and inner knowledge (www.bkwsu.com/bkun/wit/wit6.html) (BKWSO 1995a).

translate this purpose into initiatives to improve the socioeconomic conditions in swadhyayee villages. Swadhyayees, for example, tend communal farms and regard the wealth thus generated as belonging to God, to be distributed to those in need or to villagers to support their efforts to become more productive. Any individual, however, only works a few days a year on any one plot and does this as a form of devotion. The principle has also been expanded to fruit-tree planting and fishing. *Swadhyaya* is credited with teaching equal treatment of individuals, regardless of sex, caste, class, or faith. It has no formal hierarchy or paid workers. It does not attempt to convert people away from their professed religion; instead, Athavale recommended that the wisdom of *swadhyaya* be shared through example and by heart-to-heart or mind-to-mind discussion (Ekins 1992; Ramashray Roy 1993).

Gandhi and the *Sarvodaya* Order

The developmental nexus is most pronounced in Mahatma Gandhi's ideas espousing "welfare of all" (*sarvodaya*). This concept–movement represents a stream of thought developing from the beginning of the 20th century until Gandhi's assassination in 1948. It propounds a model of sustainable development as an alternative to the capital-intensive, industrial paradigm of the West and to the nonparticipatory communist model, which also set store in expeditious economic growth. Gandhi preached the participation of people in decision-making and the decentralization of power to the many villages of India. Gandhi, in his struggle for a *Sarvodaya* Order, linked his economic agenda with a non-violent (*ahimsa*) struggle for Indian political independence (*swaraj*). He made *swadeshi* (indigenous production and consumption) part of his overall developmental philosophy.

Gandhi was a self-confessed Hindu, who regularly read the Bhagavad Gita; as such, he represents a continuity in the Hindu tradition. He injected the spirit of religion into politics and everything he did. In Gandhi, the voice of ancient Hinduism found an interpreter who envisioned the development of India from the bottom up, rather than from the top down as in conventional development paradigms (Khoshoo 1997b). In fact, his entire approach to development differed from prevailing methodologies that pay no attention to the depletion of the resource base, ecological imbalances, or the needs of future generations. Gandhi said, "The earth provides enough for every man's needs, but not for every man's greed" (Khoshoo 1997a, p. 6).

Perhaps it was his adherence to the precepts of Hinduism that led Gandhi to comprehend and articulate the inextricable link between social transformation and self-transformation:

> This method of self-transformation [Gandhi] called "satyagraha" and it was characterized by an earnest desire and effort to make truth, non-violence and justice pervade every aspect of one's personality as well as inter-personal transactions. He founded

ashrams, communities where these principles could be deliberately practised.

Palshikar (1998, p. 15)

Gandhi was also aware of social marginalization and its effects; he fought, for example, against untouchability and for the liberation of women, saying

> I shall work for an India in which the poorest shall feel that it is their country, in whose making they have an effective voice, an India in which there is no high class or low class of people, and an India in which all communities will live in harmony. Women will enjoy the same rights as men. This is the India of my dreams.

Chowdhry (1994, p. 19)

For Gandhi, the *charkah* (spinning wheel) was symbolic of a proper perspective on economic development — it should provide a minimum income and employment to the people at large (Mashruwala 1971). In that early era of Indian development, theories were not obsessed with stimulating materialistic wants. The population of India was just one-third of what it is now, allowing for sustainable levels of economic consumption. Gandhi could envision a good and simple life for the people of his country.

The *Sarvodaya* Order proposes that economics be based on renewable resources and that power be decentralized to independent, but interlinked, villages, where employment would be generated through agriculture and simple crafts. Kamla Chowdhry, in her *Mahatma Gandhi: Lessons for Sustainable Development* (1994, p. 19), observed that "Gandhi's priorities for development were village development and village industries. Development to Gandhi was abolition of poverty, misery and fear." Gandhi visualized a village society in India in which all the basic amenities would be available and people would be economically self-sufficient but mutually dependent. He saw cities as "clearinghouses" for village products. Gandhi also believed in making use of all human waste to produce gas or manure to replenish the Earth for agriculture.

Gandhi was highly critical of Western-style industrialization, writing

> God forbid that India should ever take to industrialism after the manner of the west. The economic imperialism of a single tiny Island Kingdom is today keeping the world in chains ... . Industrialism is, I am afraid, going to be a curse of mankind. Industrialism depends entirely on your capacity to exploit.

Khoshoo (1995, p. 33)

Yet, Gandhi was not against machinery per se, only against machinery designed for the exploitation of people.

Gandhi wanted to decentralize the state structure and create "fully participatory village 'republics' founded on a non-violent revolution, in which landlords would voluntarily transfer their property to the people" (Annan, cited in Starcevic 1998). Gandhi also wrote that "independence must begin at the bottom ... . It follows, therefore, that every village has to be self sustained and capable of managing its affairs. The Government of the village will be conducted by the Panchayat (Village Council)" (Khoshoo 1995, p. 40).

One could say that the special features of the *sarvodaya* approach are the following:

- National governance accountable to local governance;

- Self-sustaining local economies;

- Decentralized production system;

- Industry in trusteeship of, and accountable to, the community; and

- Secularism as a confluence of all religions.

The desire of Gandhi's heart was "to wipe every tear from every eye" by encouraging India to follow its own path of development, taking into account its own realities, its own people, and its own culture. Although Nehru agreed with Gandhi that certain objectives, like sufficient food, clothing, housing, and education, were the minimum requirements for the country and all its citizens, he wanted to attain these objectives "speedily." "Speedily to Nehru meant modernization, industrialization, building of big dams, establishing institutional infrastructure for science and technology. In other words catching up with the West, for, according to Nehru there was no way out but to have them" (Chowdhry 1994, p. 19). After Gandhi's death, therefore, India embarked on a development strategy very different from the one he had envisaged.

Nehru's approach to development has been the credo for more than five decades in India. His development strategy undoubtedly brought about very impressive progress in many directions, but it also led to many failures. Chowdhry (1994, p. 23) pointed out that these strategies neglected issues such as "rural poverty, primary education and illiteracy, unemployment, increasing inequalities and women's drudgery." She went on to explain that widening disparities in income and consumption were causing social and political unrest, widespread corruption, and the decay of the social fabric. We cannot say with certainty that Gandhi's approach would have played itself out more positively and successfully, but we can see certain results of the Gandhian approach, such as the effects on the 8 600 villages adopted by the well-respected Sri Lankan Sarvodaya Shramadana movement. Moreover, his thinking has influenced some of the most important social-justice and environmental movements in India. Some examples of these movements are described below.

41

The contemporary environmental movement in India

The contemporary environmental movement in India started with the Chipko Andolan in April 1973. From the Chipko Andolan to the Narmada Bachao Andolan, environmental activists have relied heavily on Gandhian techniques of nonviolent protest and *sarvodaya* philosophy, as well as drawing abundantly on Gandhi's polemic against heavy industrialization. Some of the movement's better known figures — for example, Chandi Prasad Bhatt, Sunderlal Bahuguna, Baba Amte, and Medha Patkar — have repeatedly emphasized their debt to Gandhi (Guha 1993). Other influences on the Indian environmental movement include Marxism (in Kerala), socialism, liberation theology, and the self-help traditions.

42

The organizations participating in the environmental movement in India demonstrate an interesting amalgamation of modern scientific technique and traditional motivation. Take, for example, the Sankat Mochan Foundation. The head of this Varanasi-based institution is Professor Veer Bhadra Mishra, a priest of the Sankat Mochan Temple and a professor of hydraulic engineering at Benares University. He is convinced that science and religion have to mesh if India is to clean and save the river Ganges. He says, "Life is like a stream. One bank is the 'Vedas' and the other bank is the contemporary world, including its science and technology. If both banks are not firm the water will scatter. If both banks are firm the river will run its course" (Chowdhry 1998).

Other participants in this movement also seem to display a firm awareness of the interconnection of spiritual, environmental, social-justice, and economic concerns and their solutions. Ramchandra Guha is a professor, sociologist, and historian; his work has focused on historical and present-day interactions between humans and the natural environment. In a lecture on Gandhi and the environmental movement (Guha 1993), he commented on Gandhi's approaches and those of two well-known followers — Kumarappa and Mira Behn — who had applied Gandhi's ideas to environmental questions. Guha (1993, p. 9) noted that "at the level of the individual, Gandhi's code of voluntary simplicity offers a sustainable alternative to modern life styles." Guha also commented that Behn's primary concern, like that of Gandhi and Kumarappa,[24] "was with rehabilitating the village economy of India." And Kumarappa himself stated that "forest management should be guided not by considerations of revenue but by the needs of the people" (Guha 1993, pp. 11–13).

---

[24] See *The Economy of Permanence: A Quest for a Social Order Based on Non-violence* (Kumarappa 1984 [1948]).

The women's movement

In India, the women's movement started in the late 19th and early 20th centuries. Unlike the women's liberation movement in the West, which adopted a militant stance and often took an adversarial posture toward the opposite sex, in India the women's movement was the creation of social reformers like Raja Ram Mohan Roy, Ishwarchandra Vidya Sagar, Keshav Chandra Sen, Dayanand Sarasvati, and Maharishi Karve — almost all of them men. It started as a fight against social injustice suffered by women, the dominant-male–inferior-female mind-set, and social customs such as *sati,* the ill-treatment of widows, the custom of demanding a dowry, and female infanticide. Lord William Bentick, Anne Besant, and Margaret Cousins were some of the foreigners who actively supported the first phase of the women's movement in India. The relevant issues were also taken up by pioneer women's organizations, like the All India Women's Conference. This phase was marked by an overall, middle-class urban leadership.

In the preindependence period, the drive for women's rights was very much a part of the nationalist movement. Mahatma Gandhi brought masses of women from behind the four walls of their homes to take part in the struggle for freedom. He encouraged them to be partners in the endeavour to gain India's independence. He supported women's equality and recognized their potential to advance the country's development.

After independence, the Indian Constitution guaranteed women's equality, and India established autonomous bodies like the Social Welfare Board. It was felt that welfare-oriented programs for women would ensure gender equality. The emphasis in government policies was on women's welfare: women were to be the passive beneficiaries of this support. And for almost two decades, the women's movement was inactive. These decades were marked by apathy toward women's issues and a general attitude of acquiescence (Desai 1988).

During the 1960s, women did not become involved in the political arena for women's issues specifically, yet they participated in large numbers in the general struggle to improve the conditions of the rural poor and indigenous peoples, as well as participating in other mass movements, like the Chipko Andolin. This participation definitely provided a backdrop for later struggles focused on women's issues. The declaration of International Women's Year and of the Decade of Women, the creation of the National Committee on the Status of Women in India, and the submission of its report in 1974 provided leverage to the women's movement in India. These factors also contributed to the emergence of some autonomous organizations (for example, the Self-employed Women's Association, in 1972; the Rural Development Society, in 1976; and the Centre for Women's

43

Development Studies, in 1980) and the revitalization of some main-stream organizations.

With the National Committee on the Status of Women in the 1970s and the propagation of the government's sixth five-year plan (1980–85), the focus of the movement shifted from social welfare to the developmental activities of women. Many women's organizations concentrated on issues in education, economic independence, and health, emphasizing women's participation in all these developmental activities. The first three World Conferences on Women addressed the themes of equality, development, and peace, respectively. At the Fourth World Conference on Women, in Beijing in 1995, the emphasis was on women's rights as human rights and on the introduction of the concept of a "partnership" of men and women in development. The Fourth World Conference on Women chalked out a Plan of Action for achieving the goals of women's equality, development, and peace and for ensuring that all participating nations would be committed to this plan. The focus of the women's movement then shifted to women's empowerment and women's equal participation in all decision-making and developmental activities. Yet, despite national- and international-level efforts to achieve the goals of women's equality and development, these goals are far from being achieved.

Women's development and empowerment are imperative for nationally and globally integrated development. I feel that to make this a reality, we must collectively work for the transformation of the psyche and consciousness of men, women, and society, which would involve awakening the spiritual powers for the conversion of the heart and mind. As suggested in the book *A Global Ethic* (Kung and Kuschel 1993), all men and women need to make a commitment to a culture of equal human rights and obligations, a culture based on human, spiritual, and religious ethical principles and a common ethic of mutual understanding, peace, and Earth-friendly ways of life.

HINDU RESOURCES FOR AN INTEGRATED DEVELOPMENT

> Religion can help development by encouraging the spirit of service and sacrifice; by showing ways to attain the Truth ... and by improving the quality of life for all. The Hindu religion gives the exalted ideals of *Atman* — self — to everyone and that through the awakening and realisation of the self, one could achieve success and development in every field.
>
> Muktinathananda (personal communication, 1998[25])

Hinduism brings a holistic approach to development, because it does not concentrate simply on the question of economic well-being but also incorporates ideals of spiritual and sociopsychological satisfaction. In

[25] Swami Muktinathananda, Ramakrishna Math, Belur, Calcutta, India, personal communication, 1998.

the book *Bhagavad Gita and Contemporary Crisis*, the great Vedic scholar Kireet Joshi (1996) pointed out how our modern culture looks on a person first and foremost as an economic agent. Even attitudes are conditioned by the demands and needs of the economic imperative. Modern culture has developed the science of material life but neglected the science of self-control and self-discipline and, as a result, cannot present remedies for the crises of violence affecting individuals, societies, and nations from time to time. We are gradually becoming dehumanized because we do not have the leisure to grow inwardly (Joshi 1996).

As Joshi (1996, p. 8) further emphasized, "We need the knowledge of what is within us, beyond our economic being, beyond our physical, vital, mental and intellectual faculties. We need to know if there is a source of peace and tranquility ... free from turbulence of hurried struggle [and competition]." The Gita, in a practical manner, unites knowledge, action, and the third crowning element in the soul's completeness, divine love and devotion;[26] the *jnana*, *karma*, and *bhakti* *yogas* provide interrelated paths to this self-realization. Wisdom such as this can solve the contemporary crisis of personal, and socioeconomic, and spiritual development (Joshi 1996).

Thus, life for a Hindu is basically meant to be a spiritual journey. When development becomes merely a means to fight off hunger and disease, without encompassing the spiritual dimension, then to that extent it fails to provide the essential fuel of enthusiasm and hope. The contemporary discourse of development is geared toward the physical, without incorporating any idea of what lies beyond the attainment of plenty. The notion of sustainability has gained credence, to my mind, because it addresses this imbalance.

This spiritual dimension is most evident in the fourth of life's aims in Hinduism — *moksha*. Ultimately, all life action and development activities must lead to spiritual liberation, even as they create better economic conditions and release us from physical pain and disease. Development efforts must create, or at least not suppress, conditions that provide intellectual and spiritual satisfaction; "development" should not be thankless toil — in the sense of working under compulsion — for one's own material gains. Yet, despite Hinduism's spiritual orientation, it is not entirely otherworldly. Hinduism acknowledges the need for people to appropriately enjoy the mind, spirit, body, and senses, in its idea of *kama*; and economic accomplishment, in its idea of *artha* — both *kama* and *artha* are included in life's goals. As Danesh

45

---

[26] Joshi (1991, p. 20) pointed out that "in practical terms the veda prescribes that every action of man should be sacrifice offered by him to higher and higher forces and beings, to the *devas* and ultimately to the Supreme Being itself. ... It is, in fact, in the Gita that we find a comprehensive and abundant exposition of the principle of sacrifice [not ritualistic sacrifice] and of the method of performing actions as a sacrifice to the Divine." It is this approach that is needed for self-development and holistic socioeconomic and ecological development.

(1993) stated in his examination of the psychology of spirituality, the living person requires this integration, because the true nature of a human being is in the total unity of the two distinctive expressions of reality — the material and the spiritual. To achieve individual self-transformation or self-development — and this must precede the transformation or development of others and broader society — it is essential that the individual work simultaneously at both levels of reality (Danesh 1993).

Looking at the situation in India today, I see that uninhibited materialism has certainly increased among the affluent classes since economic globalization made its recent appearance. In addition to promoting a consumeristic paradigm of economic development, globalization has been lopsided: it caters to those who are already privileged, making them richer. Moreover, it marginalizes the poor, the weak, and the underprivileged, categories that often include a disproportionate number of women. Although globalization "reduces" the geographic distance through efficient communication technologies and trade networks, it concurrently increases socioeconomic distance and disparity. In India, it is felt that globalization adversely affects people's human rights and lures them away from their culture.

According to Hassija (1991, 1998), unless people retain the ability to look inward, globalization will unleash bitter competition, stark materialism, commercialism, and the disintegration of the human and spiritual values of world unity, compassion, and cooperation. These effects of globalization would not only destabilize financial markets but also create disharmony in social and human relations. As such, globalization in business and trade without globalization of spiritual values will create imbalance and tension in the world order. Hassija (1998, p. 2) suggested that "a happy blend of economics and spirituality — both based on values — is necessary."

Hindu beliefs and religion certainly caution against uninhibited consumerism and materialism. I feel that a greater emphasis on limiting human wants and on the ideology of simple living and high thinking could counterbalance today's consumerist ideology. The approach and concept of the *Sarvodaya* Order, for example — which provides an outline of the voluntary limitation of human wants — can certainly help temper unmitigated consumerism, materialism, and hedonism. I feel that Gandhi could become an important symbol in the fight against the present-day consumer ideology and the violence it nurtures.

Gandhi's principles also provide us with another important resource for integrated development: *ahimsa* (nonviolence), an ancient Hindu principle that mandates noninjury of others in thought, word, and deed. One of the central principles of Mahatma Gandhi in his movement against the colonial British powers was nonviolence, which he adopted as a personal credo and preached to the Indian people. A truly nonviolent person will not retaliate with violence, even in self-defence.

The concept of nonviolence is found throughout Indian religious traditions, and it is especially emphasized in Buddhism and Jainism.

Hinduism also brings to the paradigm of development the idea that all life in the cosmos is interrelated and interwoven — a firm spiritual basis for ecological balance and protection of the environment. In the Isho Upanishad, for example, we read the following:

> The whole universe with its creatures belongs to the Lord (Nature).
> No creature is superior to any other, and the human being should
> not have absolute power over Nature. Let no species encroach upon
> the rights and privileges of other species. However one can enjoy
> the bounties of Nature by giving up greed.
>
> Khoshoo (1995, p. 13)

Kumar (1997) remarked that at the centre of the Vedic vision is the human–nature relationship, as articulated in sacred incantations and rituals that repeatedly remind us of the need to sustain the ecological balance of nature. The "Bhumisukta" of the Atharvaveda (12.1.35 is one of the most important sources of information on the relationship of humans to their environment and their duty to preserve it. In this hymn, the seer Atharvan presents a beautiful picture of Mother Earth as the basis of our sustenance and a symbol for the entire environment:

> Whatever I dig from thee, O Mother Earth
> May it have quick growth again!
> Purifier, We may not injure thy vitals or thy heart.
>
> Quoted in Kumar (1997, p. 6)

The holism practiced in Hinduism has other ramifications for the environment. The current paradigm defines sustainable development as development that meets the current generation's needs without compromising the ability of future generations to meet their own needs (WCED 1987). The problem is that one nation's sustainability very often comes at the cost of another's resources. We have no "world sustainable-growth model" that takes into account even the poorest nation. With Gandhi's *sarvodaya* approach, the notion of sustainability would involve all the nations of the world, not just the countries of the North in isolation from those of the South. In an increasingly individualistic world, this all-encompassing concept of sustainable development could be very difficult to comprehend, accept, and act on.

But the chief influence of Hindu belief in promoting integrated development, I believe, would be a deep-rooted belief in God and in the notion that we are all children of the same father, in the Oneness of the universe, in the potential divinity and immortality of the soul, and in spiritual values. The approach of the Hindus is to insist that development have a conscience. This is encoded in the idea of *dharma*, wherein all action, including development interventions, must be weighed carefully in terms of an altruistic concern for village, region, nation, and all other countries on the globe; all actions must be weighed holistically.

47

According to Hindu belief, developmental efforts must incorporate the spiritual welfare of the entire beneficiary population and, indeed, anyone who would be affected by it. Development should not come at the cost of exploiting the resources in other countries at cheap rates, displacing marginalized populations, and living extravagantly at the ultimate expense of others, for Hinduism conceives of the world as a global family. The idea of a global family is essentially a religious one, found in Hinduism and other traditions. The percolation of this idea into the psyche of development practitioners might change the insidiously exploitative bent of 20th-century development.[27]

WHERE TODAY'S HINDUISM AND DEVELOPMENT MEET: THE PROMISE REAPPRAISED

48

I now turn to the question of how today's Hinduism can be incorporated into the idea of sustainable development. Agreeing with Einstein's observation about how peace can be brought to the world, Chowdhry (1994, p. 33) wrote that "the problem of peace, as well as that of sustainable development and environmental concerns, will only be solved by employing Gandhi's method on a large scale." Echoes of Gandhi's voice seem to be emerging even from institutions such as the World Bank. After visiting some 25 countries, the World Bank's president, James Wolfensohn, said these visits had brought home to him that the "World Bank's central mission is to weld economic assistance with spiritual, ethical and moral development" (Chowdhry 1996, p. 10). Some recent World Bank initiatives (known as the World Faiths and Development Dialogue), in which the Bank met with leaders of nine world faiths to broaden opportunities for a base of common understanding and action in tackling global poverty, may raise suspicions among Bank critics, but they suggest that the Bank is at least trying to make good on Wolfensohn's insight.

Development experts, like Kamla Chowdhry, Ashok Khosla, and S.K. Sharma, and religious leaders, like Swami Muktinathananda,[28]

---

[27] It must be admitted, however, that many religions and many religious leaders talk about love, compassion, and altruism; they say there should be equity, cooperation, and the absence of force and violence. Yet, for centuries and centuries this message, which is both simple and profound, does not seem to have percolated very deeply into the human psyche. Instead of *Ram Rajya* (Rule of Virtue and Truth) and the Kingdom of Heaven, we have seen endless wars backed by religious jingoism. It would be safe to say that love and compassion, though widely preached, are concepts not widely understood or practiced in their truest sense.

[28] Swami Muktinathananda observed that science can help development in the following ways: (1) by providing adequate knowledge to remove ignorance and superstition; (2) by adding to the happiness of human beings through the removal of disease, poverty, and want; (3) by providing technological means to enhance lifestyles; and (4) by reducing destructive items and by not adding to the already existing ones (Swami Muktinathananda, Ramakrishna Math, Belur, Calcutta, India, personal communication, 1998).

agree that sustainable development needs technology and science to solve its problems. Yet, they also feel that this relationship should be subject, in Chowdhry's words, to the condition that it also be accompanied by public awareness, political action, and a way to ignite the moral and ethical values of the Indian heritage and psyche. Chowdhry further suggested that we should start with a new paradigm of development, which she described as "a people-led development, an alternative development, a development which is 'pro-poor, pro-nature and pro-women', not borrowed development" (Chowdhry 1994, p. 37). She also summed up the elements involved in sustainable development:

> Eradication of hunger and poverty is not merely an intellectual exercise of science, technology or economics, but also involves an inner change. To alter the system, it is necessary to alter the paradigm of development, and to take cognisance of the spiritual, of the inner voice, of the ethics and values that promote sustainable development.
>
> Chowdhry (1996, p. 11)

49

Khosla, founder of the NGO called Development Alternatives, and Sharma, founder of the NGO called People First, observed that technology can change lifestyles but does not usually change the quality of human existence.[29] The goal, they emphasized, should be to realize a sustainable society in which people work toward attaining a high level of human and spiritual development. In their opinion, this society could be achieved by combining Gandhian ideology (based on the Indian ethos and tradition of grass-roots democracy) and contemporary Western democratic experience.

The experience of 50 years of independence in India has shown us that borrowed models of development do not work. The mindless imitation of Western models by developing nations has led to all kinds of environmental disasters (Siddhartha 1998) and social malaise. When formulating and implementing an indigenous paradigm of development based on the Gandhian model, we have to understand and take into account the social, cultural, ethical, and spiritual background and values of the people concerned. Khoshoo (1997a) stated that this model of development aims at building local self-reliance and self-respect in villagers, alleviating poverty, and striving for social justice. He wrote that the need for a "creative synthesis" of the Gandhian and Nehruvian (or Western) models is imperative because the Gandhian model leads to decentralized economic planning — an economy of permanence — whereas the Nehruvian model of industrial economy runs the danger of making the rich richer and the poor poorer (Khoshoo 1997a). We need to appropriately blend tradition and modernity, religion and science in

---

[29] More information about Development Alternatives can be found at www.ecouncil.ac.cr /devalt/damain.htm; and about People First, at www.ecouncil.ac.cr/devalt/peoplef.htm.

such a way that human-made capital does not become destructive of the natural capital needed for development (Khoshoo 1997a).

These realizations are also manifesting themselves outside India as international development agencies like the United Nations Development Programme (UNDP) discard or revamp many of their old concepts of development. Chowdhry (1994) felt that their focus on participatory approaches in the last decade means that these organizations are moving more toward a Gandhian-like focus on people. She pointed to UNDP 's use of phrases like "men, women and children must be the centre of attention," development strategies are "to be woven around people and not people around development," and "the durable solution to today's problems of poverty, unemployment, social disintegration and environmental deterioration cannot be achieved through just more development of the past kind" (Chowdhry 1994, p. 23).

Chowdhry's point is well-taken. The UNDP's *Human Development Report 1993* offers some indications of this change in approach. The report calls for

> new models of sustainable human development [to] invest in human potential and to create an enabling environment for the full use of human capabilities. ... The purpose of development is to widen the range of people's choices. Income is one of those choices — but it is not the sum-total of human life. Human development is development *of* the people *for* the people *by* the people.
>
> UNDP (1993, p. 3, emphasis in the original)

At the end of the overview, the report notes,

> The implications of placing people at the centre of political and economic change are profound. They challenge traditional concepts of security, old models of development, ideological debates on the role of the market and outmoded forms of international cooperation. They call for nothing less than a revolution in our thinking.
>
> UNDP (1993, p. 8)

These words give me hope that international agencies are open to new ideas, that is, to hearing what experience has been telling them, but I am left to wonder how this emphasis on "people centredness" will manifest itself without a more explicit focus on spiritual principles. Are the challenges of tapping into creativity, distributing benefits justly, and providing equal access to opportunities (UNDP 1993) not, in the final analysis, asking what motivates people to act and (perhaps more important) to act compassionately? And does that question not require us to ask what is at the centre of ourselves?

CONCLUSION: AN INTEGRATED PARADIGM

> The Hindu religion stands for the good of humanity — social, cultural, moral and spiritual. Development and science are related to Hinduism in this sense: the ideal of benefiting humanity in all ways possible.
>
> Thus it is the paradigm of development in which there is a synthesis of the two complementary disciplines — science and religion — being used for the well being of self and society, that will produce fully integrated and developed human beings, and would bring about holistic development — physical, economic, social, environmental, moral, and spiritual.
>
> Muktinathananda (personal communication, 1998[30])

Tremendous confusion surrounds the question of whether science and religion have a meeting point and, if so, what its precise nature is.[31] The general perception in the Hindu world, today, apart from some of the intelligentsia, is that there is no connection, or at best a tenuous one. The relationship between science and development is well accepted, but the nexus between religion, economic development, and the role of science seems to many very vague.

The way forward for the Hindu world as it faces the next century is, I believe, to integrate science and religion, broadly speaking, in all spheres of life; development is a process that seeks to sustain and improve human life and well-being and, as such, needs to understand, incorporate, and implement the strengths of both discourses. Religion provides, for example, access to the inner being — human hopes, goals, and motivations — the place from whence all action stems. It provides insight into thousands of years of experience and experiment with how to live a fulfilling and balanced human life. Equally important, science

---

[30] Swami Muktinathananda, Ramakrishna Math, Belur, Calcutta, India, personal communication, 1998.

[31] Among the religionists and the scientists in India, one encounters various perspectives on the convergence of science and religion. An informal survey based on structured conversations with a cross-section of employees at various levels at a New Delhi university indicates that many Hindus approach the question from the perspective that both science and religion are made by God (expressed as Bhagwan, Ishwara, Sri Krishna, or Ram). Nothing God made can be bad, but humankind has made use of both science and religion in negative ways. I found that many informants thought of science in terms of the help it can provide in enhancing daily life, whereas the role of religion was to inculcate faith in God and encourage people to do good deeds to improve present and future lives and to accept one's conditions in the present life. Some pointed out that science would ultimately "prove" the findings of religion, and people had a strong bias in favour of religion as the primary source of any lasting spiritual benefits. For many Hindus, science is "Godless" and "atheistic," whereas religion has the concept of a transcendent Ultimate Reality. Certain knowledgeable persons among the sample insisted that the world could advance only if science recognized the validity of religion, rather than treating it as an aberration or an elaborate superstition.

provides both insight into the workings of the outer world and the means to effect change in that world.

One way to bring about such integration at the personal, community, national, and international levels is to provide for a much broader dissemination and much better understanding of the spiritual component of the scriptures and holy texts so as to help make them relevant to today's issues. We should gradually reduce obsessive rituals, ceremonies, and festivals. We should work to do away with the misuse of science and religion for selfish gains, along with the obsession with economic and political power for personal aggrandizement and ill-gotten fame. With the help of modern S&T and the media, the cardinal principles of Vedanta can, through proper understanding, practice, and dissemination, change the attitudes and behaviour of the masses of people and revive the human and spiritual values of mutual love, respect, and sharing and caring.

Above, I discussed the problems of the unequal division of wealth and distribution of resources. In India, however, one cannot ignore population growth as one of the biggest problems standing in the way of socioeconomic development. Every year, the population of India grows at almost the same rate as the economy, thus negating whatever positive effect new economic growth might have on poverty, unemployment, or related problems. Indian demographers and economists have been working on population control with considerable success in some states, such as Kerala, but with little success in others. The *varnaashram* system (described earlier) divides human life into four stages and prescribes celibacy before marriage, moderate sexual indulgence within marriage, and complete marital fidelity. I feel that reviving the *varnaashram* scheme might provide guidance and part of a solution to the population problem, as well as to the problem of HIV–AIDS. In addition, education for girls and women, as well as for boys and men, with the consequent employment potential that it creates, would be one of the key factors in controlling population growth.

Along with education and awareness, what is acutely needed is change, through formal and informal mass media, in the attitudes of all members of society toward girls and women. In this way, Indian society can work (as so many societies need to work) to become female positive and egalitarian, that is, to empower women and girls and to improve their status.

I strongly feel that we cannot pursue and achieve development without the integrated development of women, who after all constitute half the world's population. We must, for this reason, increase, implement, and realize the measures already being undertaken all over the world for women's development and empowerment. For these efforts, we can take inspiration and guidance from the spiritual texts of other faiths, such as those of the Bahá'í Faith, in which one can find the following: "The world of humanity has two wings — one is woman and the other man. Not until both wings are equally developed can the Bird fly. Should one wing remain weak, flight is impossible" (BPT 1994, p. 11). Here again, I feel that regenerating ancient Vedic values of gender equality and equity would be of great help in improving the situation of women.[32] Metaphors for an approach to equality could be derived from the depiction of the gods and their consorts together in Indian religious culture. The consorts are worshipped along with the gods, and, during rituals, prayers, and devotional songs, the names of the consorts are often used first (for example, Radha–Krishna, Sita–Ram, Parvati–Shankar, and Lakshmi–Narayan). The symbol of *Ardhnareshwar* — the god Shiva as half male and half female — also indicates that men and women should have the same status in society.

The most important task for the Hindu community (and for the other great faiths) is to evolve a national syllabus for education that includes spiritual factors. In presenting Vivekananda's ideas about education and religion, Bhajanananda wrote that the purpose of education is to make humans. With that purpose, religion and spirituality sit at the innermost core of education and should be a core subject. Vivekananda strongly felt that the purpose of education is not merely to provide information but also to impart knowledge and wisdom, "by which character is formed, strength of mind is increased, the intellect is expanding, and by which one can stand on one's own feet" and face the problems of life (Bhajanananda 1976–77, p.39). Of course, education should also take up internationally important issues in science, religion, spirituality, and development and add lessons on the nexus among them. Education has the twin responsibility of equipping people with the latest technical skills to enable them to become economically independent and providing them with the relevant spiritual and moral strengths to enable them to improve the world in which they live (for example, by making them aware of the thoughts and insights of spiritual masters, scientists, and philosophers).

Education should build capacity and character, self-confidence, and the ability to manifest for self- and social transformation the potential divinity that is in each of us. Educators can accomplish these goals by conveying to students the principles and elements of religion (along with its inherent human and spiritual values) through stories, parables, and the life stories of religious masters and divine messengers. Accompanying this should be instruction in the scientific techniques of concentration and yogic meditation. These ideas have been in circulation for some time now, variously articulated by scholars such as Kireet

53

---

[32] Certain contemporary Hindu sects also provide inspiration for female equality and equity. Take, for instance, the Brahma Kumaris World Spiritual University, which is run by and caters mainly to women and provides knowledge about the Creator and creation. It asks questions such as, Who am I? Who is God? What is the world? It preaches spirituality, promotes universal values of life, and teaches Rajyoga meditation for the betterment of self, others, and the universe. It also preaches celibacy and purity of mind, body, and soul.

Joshi and institutions like Aurobindo Ashram. But until these ideas gain currency in the formal and informal education systems, they will have little therapeutic effect on the psyche of humankind or do little to bring about the needed development. I feel it is important to go back and remember that source of guidance — God — and have religious faith, because that is what ultimately empowers people.

After all, in the final analysis, development involves changing people's psyche and behaviour, for it is people who are behind all the planning and execution of development paradigms and it is people who are intended to benefit from them. And I believe that people cannot be fundamentally changed unless they receive divine guidance or wisdom, whether through holy scriptures or through the writings of divine messengers, such as Bahá'u'lláh, Buddha, Jesus, Krishna, Mohammad, or Guru Nanak. Global unity begins with a global mind; the best way to think globally is to at least have a working knowledge of religions, Eastern and Western. Only religion and spirituality — as approaches that strive after the ultimate realization of truth — will provide the guidance and inspiration human beings require to rise above the instincts of retaliation and unmitigated self-interest and to solve their problems with dignity and nonviolence, recognizing contributions from all cultures, particularly indigenous ones. Obviously, this is easier said than done, as vested interests support the current system and many people wish to live for themselves, even at the cost of future generations. Thus, science and religion have to create a more balanced development in which people seriously consider the consequences of their lifestyles for future generations.

I would like to conclude this piece with the words of Swami Jitatmananda (1997, p. 11): "Truth Unites. Newton's laws of motion or Einstein's Relativity is common to all humanity. Universal truths of all religions, compatible with reason, will unite humanity." Jitatmananda (1997, p. 10) draws his model for a new society, based on practical Vedanta, from Vivekananda's words to European scholar Jules Bios: "[It will be] a successful "Superior Fusion" of Brahmin's spiritual culture with Kshtriya's administrative efficiency, Vaisaya's wealth-generating capacity, and Shudra's dignified dedication to all labour, as service to mankind." Jitatmananda also clarified the changes that could be made at an individual level:

> Acceptance of the spiritual and holistic values by today's high-tech econo-socio experts like scientists, technicians, industrialists, managers or state leaders will help us to create complete human beings equally enriched with the higher excellence of Western science, technology, the Western dynamism, and organisation, along with Eastern spiritual vision of the infinite capacity and excellence hidden within each individual. The ultimate success, and wealth, as the Bhagavad Gita asserts, are available through a holistic living for all.
>
> Jitatmananda (1997, pp. 10–11)

I strongly feel that the existing development paradigm, with its overemphasis on economic development and scientific–technological achievement, should be balanced with the critically examined concepts and values of religion. Thus, the empowerment of marginalized peoples and the creation of a just society, which should be the goals of any integrated development paradigm, could be brought about through education and individual and societal synthesis of science and religion, the cardinal elements of which are universal in nature.

ANNEX 1:
SELECTED ETHICAL PRINCIPLES OF
HINDUISM-INSPIRED MOVEMENTS FOR DEVELOPMENT

The ethical guiding principles of the movements discussed in the text can be synthesized into some basic premises that help to elucidate the principles of ethical action in Hinduism:

1. God is incorporeal, eternal, omnipotent, all intelligent, all compassionate, all truth, love, beauty, and bliss, the creator of the universe.

2. The ancient scriptures of India — the Vedas, the Upanishads, and the Bhagavad Gita — are sources of the true knowledge, the highest truth, and a guide to living. They should be studied, lived, and taught to all.

3. The power of love and necessity of world unity are paramount, because we are all children of the same Supreme Power.

4. The principles of a good life include work, worship, and selfless service to humanity — including physical, mental, social, moral, and spiritual improvement — especially for the benefit of women and the weaker segments of society.

5. Humans should cultivate a constant remembrance of God.

6. Humans should inculcate in themselves divine qualities by acquiring wisdom through spiritual–religious study, education, and prayer.

7. Humans should work to improve and care for both their inner and their outer environments.

8. Humans should work to bring about communal and interfaith harmony.

9. Humans should practice nondiscrimination, refusing to discriminate on the basis of caste, class, sex, race, creed, or religion.

10. Humans should accept the concept of the world as one family and live and practice in accordance with this principle.

11. Humans should work for the welfare and well-being of all. Humans should live at peace with themselves and their fellow beings.

12. Humans should work to bring aid and solace to less-privileged people in an altruistic spirit.

13. Humans should act according to the idea that an inherent divinity exists in all life and within each one of us. We are all equally worthy human beings. There is a fundamental unity in diversity.

14. Humans should not cause suffering to anyone.

15. Humans should devote themselves to truth and nonviolence in thoughts, words, and action.

16. Humans should proceed with their actions without expecting specific fruits or benefits from them.

17. Humans should carry out their duties toward themselves and others; it is through duty that a human reaches perfection.

18. Humans should be guided by the principle that our present life is the result of our good or bad actions in the past and that our present conduct moulds our future lives.

19. Humans should know their human rights and responsibilities and respect those of others, treating others as they would like to be treated themselves.

20. Humans should be guided in their conduct by the principles of love, respect, righteousness, justice, equity, equality, and service toward one and all.

21. Humans should limit their wants and needs and thereby live a simple life without exaggerated materialistic desires.

22. Humans should work constantly and seek wealth but share it with those in need; riches are but the means to do good and should not become the goal of life.

23. Humans should pursue the aims of becoming good human beings and help others in their efforts to do the same.

REFERENCES

Badrinath, C. 1993. Dharma, India, and the world order: twenty-one essays. St Andrew Press, Hungary. 352 pp.

Balasubramanian, A.V. 1999. Testing classical Indian knowledge. COMPAS Newsletter, 1 (Feb), 26–27.

Bhajanananda, Swami. 1976–77. Swami Vivekananda's discoveries about India. Reprint from Prabuddha Bharata. Journal of the Ramakrishna Mission, Belur, Calcutta, India. 46 pp.

BKWSO (Brahma Kumaris World Spiritual Organization). 1995a. Eradication of poverty. BKWSO, Rajasthan, India. Internet: www.bkwsu.com/bkun/wit/wit6.html

——— 1995b. Wisdom in action. BKWSO, Rajasthan, India. Internet: www.bkwsu.com/bkun/wia/index.html

BPT (Bahá'í Publishing Trust). 1994. Selections from the writings of 'Abdu'l-Baha. In Women. Research Department of the Universal House of Justice, BPT, New Delhi, India. 90 pp.

Brzezinski, J. 1997. The work ethic and world religions: a study of bibliographic resources. International Development Research Centre, Ottawa, ON, Canada. 72 pp.

Capra, F. 1983. The Tao of physics. Fontana Paperbacks, London, UK. 384 pp.

CASE (International Centre for Application of Solar Energy). n.d. Completed projects: project summary sheet 3. CASE, Perth, Australia. Internet: www.case.gov.au/complete3.htm

Chander, J. Rajayogi Brahmakumar. 1988. Science and spirituality. Brahma Kumaris, Mount Abu, India. 215 pp.

Chowdhry, K. 1994. Mahatma Gandhi: lessons for sustainable development. Vikram Sarabhai Foundation, New Delhi, India. 43 pp.

——— 1996. Gandhi: the voice in the wilderness — no more. National Foundation for India, New Delhi, India. Lecture in Sustainable Development and Environment Series, No. 1, Jun 1996, New Delhi. 11 pp.

——— 1998. Development and spirituality. The Hindustan Times, New Delhi, 26 Jul, p. 13.

Danesh, H.B. 1993. The psychology of spirituality — from divided self to integrated self. Juxta Publishing Limited, Hong Kong. 270 pp.

Desai, N. 1988. A decade of women's movement in India. Research Centre for Women's Studies, Shrimati Nathibai Damodar Thakersay Women's University; Himalaya Publishing House, Bombay, India.

Einstein, A. 1950. Out of my later years. Greenwood Press, Westport, CT, USA. 282 pp.

Ekins, P. 1992. A new world order: grassroots movements for global change. Routledge, New York, NY, USA. 248 pp.

Gambhirananda, Swami. 1957. History of the Ramakrishna Math and Mission. Advaita Ashram, Calcutta, India. 380 pp.

Gandhi, M.K. 1992 [1947]. India of my dreams (4th reprint; compiled by R.K. Prabhu). Navjivan, Admedabad, India. 344 pp.

Gangrade, K.D. 1995. Religion and ideal society — a Gandhian perspective. Paper presented at the International Congress on Realising the Ideal: The Responsibility of the World Religions, Aug 1995, Soeul, Korea. Inter-Religious Federation for World Peace, New York, NY, USA. 24 pp.

Giri, M. Swami. 1985. Vedanta philosophy for the 21st century. Bharatiya Sanskriti Samaj, Delhi, India. 44 pp.

Guha, R. 1993. Mahatma Gandhi and the environmental movement. The Parisar Annual Lecture, Parisar, Pune, India. 23 pp.

Gupta, R.P. 1998. Developmental activities and ethical guidelines of Arya Samaj. Maharishi Dayanand Memorial Centre, New Delhi, India. 5 pp.

Hassija, J.C. Brahmakumar. 1991. Science, spirituality, ethics and environment. Brahma Kumaries World Spiritual University, Mount Abu, India. 31 pp.

——— 1998. Globalisation: ethical or unethical economics. Purity — Newsletter of Prajapita Brahma Kumaries Ishwariya Vishwa Vidyalaya, 17(8), 2.

Jitatmananda, Swami. 1991. Holistic science and Vedanta. Bhartiya Vidya Bhavan, Bombay, India. 156 pp.

——— 1992. Modern physics and Vedanta. Bhartiya Vidya Bhavan, Bombay, India. 87 pp.

——— 1997. Holistic and spiritual values needed for the emergence of Asia in the 21st century. Paper presented at the Seminar on Religion, Politics and Society in South and South-East Asia, Dec 1997, New Delhi, India. India International Centre, New Delhi, India. 11 pp.

Jordens, J.T.F. 1978. Dayananda Saraswati: his life and ideas. Oxford University Press, Bombay, India. 368 pp.

Joshi, K. 1991. The Veda and Indian culture. Rashtriya Veda Vidya Pratishthan, New Delhi, India. 115 pp.

——— 1996. Bhagavad Gita and contemporary crisis. Nag Publishers, New Delhi, India. 317 pp.

Joshi, P.C. 1995. Secularism and development: the Indian experiment. Vikas Publishing House Pvt Ltd, New Delhi, India. 247 pp.

Kanal, S.P. 1988. Value education for a secular society. Dev Samaj Prakashan, Chandigarh, India. 16 pp.

——— 1991. Religion and science. Dev Samaj Prakashan, Chandigarh, India. 26 pp.

Kapur, P. 1991a. Religion and culture. Paper presented at the Second International Conference of Non-Resident Indians, Jan 1991, Parliament Annexe, New Delhi, India. Non-Resident Indians Welfare Society of India, New Delhi, India. 9 pp.

——— 1991b. Family violence on women as a great obstacle in human resource development. Paper presented at the One-day National Seminar on Women and Human Resource Development, Aug 1991, New Delhi, India. Parliamentarian Forum for Human Development, New Delhi, India. 14 pp.

——— 1992. Rajyoga — its role in bringing about universal peace — a must for development. Paper presented at Third International Scientific Public Conference, Novosibirsk, Russia. Gorno-Altaisk Republican Department of Culture; Commission on Culture and Art of the Novosibirsk City Society of People's Deputies; Novosibirsk Roerich Society, Novosibirsk and Indian Cultural Centre, Moscow, Russia. 11 pp.

——— 1994a. Role of the family in the development of individual and society. Presidential Address in a seminar of the Prachi Educational Society, Apr 1994, New Delhi, India. Prachi Educational Society, New Delhi, India.

——— 1994b. Violation of human rights in gender bias as a great hindrance in overall development. Paper presented at the Global Conference on

Human Rights and Terrorism, Jul 1994, Indian Institute for Non-Aligned Studies, New Delhi, India. 10 pp.

———— 1995. World peace through ideal family. Paper presented at the International Congress on Realising the Ideal: The Responsibility of the World Religions, Aug 1995, Soeul, Korea. Inter-Religious Federation for World Peace, New York, NY, USA. 39 pp.

Khoshoo, T.N. 1995. Mahatma Gandhi: an apostle of applied human ecology. Tata Energy Research Institute, New Delhi, India. 71 pp.

———— 1997a. Gandhian environmentalism: an unfinished task. Indian Association of Social Sciences Institute Quarterly, 16(1), 1–16.

———— 1997b. Open letter to leaders of South Asian Countries in Rio, five years later. Ecodecision: Environment and Policy Journal, 24 (Spring), 68–69.

Kothari, D.S. 1977. Some thoughts on science and religion. Shri Raj Krishan Jain Charitable Trust, New Delhi, India. 56 pp.

———— 1980. Atom and self. Meghnad Saha Memorial Lecture 1978. Proceedings of the Indian National Science Academy (Part A, Physical Science), 46(1), 1–28.

———— 1997. Science and self-knowledge. Ninth J.N. Tata Lecture (in memory of Jamsetjee Nusserwanjee Tata), Mar 1997, India Institute of Science, Bangalore, India. Dorab Tata Trust, Bangalore, India. 27 pp.

Kumar, S.P. 1997. Ecology and conservation in BhumiSukta of the Atharvaveda. Paper presented at a meeting held by Dr Kireet Joshi, President of Dharam Hinduja International Centre of Indic Research, Dec 1997, New Delhi, India. Dharam Hinduja International Centre of Indic Research, New Delhi, India. 12 pp.

Kumarappa, J.C. 1984 [1948]. The economy of permanence: a quest for a social order based on non-violence. Sarva Seva Sangh, Varanasi, India. 208 pp.

Kung, H.; Kuschel, K.-J., ed. 1993. A global ethic: the declaration of the Parliament of the World Religions. Continuum Publishing, New York, NY, USA. 124 pp.

Mashruwala, K.G. 1971. Towards Sarvodaya Order. Navajivan Publishing House, Ahmedabad, India. 150 pp.

Mukhopadhyay, A.K. 1995. Conquering the brain. Conscious Publications, New Delhi, India. 281 pp.

Palshikar, V. 1998. Gandhi — a model of alternative thinking. *In* Report of the workshop: Cultural Values and Sustainable Alternatives, December 1997, Bangalore. Alliance for a Responsible and United World; Pipal Tree, Bangalore, India. p. 15.

Pande, S. 1989. Medieval Bhakti movement. Kusumanjali Prakashan, Meerut, India. 168 pp.

Pandit, M.P. 1959. The teachings of Sri Aurobindo. Dipti Publications, Sri Aurobindo Ashram, Pondicherry, India. 68 pp.

Radhakrishnan, S, ed. 1974. The principal Upanishads. Oxford University Press, Delhi, India. 956 pp.

Ranganathananda, Swami. 1978. Science and religion. Advaita Ashram Mayavati, Pithoragarh, Himalayus, India. 235 pp.

———— 1983. Science and spirituality. Ramakrishna Math, Hyderbad, India. 38 pp.

———— 1987. Eternal values for a changing society: philosophy and spirituality (vol. I). Bhartiya Vidya Bhavan, Bombay, India. 572 pp.

59

Roy, R. 1993. Swadhyaya: values and message. *In* Wignaraja, P., ed., New social movements in the South. Zed Books, London, UK. pp. 183–194.

SAS (Sri Aurobindo Society). n.d. SAIASR: Sri Aurobindo Institute for Applied Scientific Research. SAS, Pondicherry, India. Internet: www.sriaurobindosociety.org.in/activity/scitech.htm

Sastry, A.M., trans. 1977. The Bhagavad Gita: with the commentary of Sri Sankaracharya. Samata Books, Madras, India. 522 pp.

Sharma, A. 1980. Hindu scriptural value system and the economic development of India. Heritage, New Delhi, India. 113 pp.

———— 1993. Hinduism. *In* Sharma, A., ed., Our religions. HarperCollins, New York, NY, USA. pp. 3–67.

Siddhartha. 1998. Introduction. *In* Report of the workshop: Cultural Values and Sustainable Alternatives, December 1997, Bangalore. Alliance for a Responsible and United World; Pipal Tree, Bangalore, India. p. 2.

Singer, M. 1972. When a great tradition modernizes: an anthropological approach to Indian civilization. University of Chicago Press, Chicago, IL, USA. 430 pp.

Singer, M.; Srinivas, M.N.; Cohn, B.S. 1966. The modernization of religious beliefs. *In* Weiner, M., ed., Modernization: the dynamics of growth. Basic Books, New York, NY, USA.

Singh, K. 1998. Vedanta today. Lecture presented at Habitat Centre, New Delhi, India, 20 Apr 1998.

Sorokin, P.A. 1958. Reconstruction of humanity. Bharatiya Vidya Bhavan, Bombay, India. 223 pp.

Starcevic, F. 1998. Human rights and development. Opening remarks on the occasion of the 50th Anniversary of the Declaration of Human Rights, Aug 1998, New Delhi, India. United Nations Information Centre; Forum of Indian NGOs for Cooperation with the UN, New Delhi, India. 3 pp.

UNDP (United Nations Development Programme). 1993. Human development report 1993. Oxford University Press, New York, NY, USA. 230 pp.

Vivekananda, Swami. 1937. Essentials of Hinduism. Advaita Ashrama Mayavati, Pithoragarh, Himalayas, India. 72 pp.

———— 1968. Hinduism (7th ed.). Sri Ramakrishna Math, Mylapore, Madras, India. 88 pp.

WCED (World Commission on Environment and Development). 1987. Our common future. Oxford University Press, New York, NY, USA. Brundtland Commission Report. 383 pp.

Weber, M. 1958. The religion of India: the sociology of Hinduism and Buddhism. The Free Press, Glencoe, IL, USA. 392 pp.

Yogananda, Sri Sri Paramahansa. 1994. The divine romance. Yogoda Satasnga Society of India, New Delhi, India. 468 pp.

CHAPTER 2

Solidarity with the Poor

Gregory Baum

A ROMAN CATHOLIC IDEA OF DEVELOPMENT

The idea of development that emerged in the 1950s envisaged the rescue of poor people from their misery through the industrialization of their societies. The hope was that the economic system that produced the wealth of Western nations could be exported to the developing countries and eventually make them wealthy too. W.W. Rostow (1960) elaborated this idea in detail in his celebrated work, *The Stages of Economic Growth: A Non-Communist Manifesto.* This book offered a vision and a plan for overcoming poverty in the world, as an alternative superior to the Marxist enterprise. Rostow, director of Policy and Planning in the US State Department during the Kennedy administration, is said to have inspired President J.F. Kennedy's Alliance for Progress. The intention of this program was to promote the modernization of Latin America by supporting industrial development and fostering an entrepreneurial culture of self-reliance and competitiveness.

To render a full account of how the Christian churches have viewed the idea of development would demand an entire book. Both the Roman Catholic Church and the Geneva-based World Council of Churches have produced significant, critical literature on the topic of development. What I wish to do in this paper is much more modest. In this section, I draw on a number of papal documents to provide a summary of a Roman Catholic idea of development; in the second section, I show that in recent years the World Bank has come to regard religion as a possible factor in the promotion of economic development; and in the final section, I argue that the social and economic sciences are never entirely value free and that the researcher's political vision and attitude toward religion are likely to influence her or his conclusions.

CRITICS OF THE IDEA OF DEVELOPMENT

At first, the Christian churches were ill at ease with the new idea of development. They had heard the protests of Christian and non-Christian groups in the poorer parts of the world, denouncing the aggressive modernization of their regions. I will mention but two of their objections. One is from Latin American liberation theology. The theologians of this school, in dialogue with political economists, recognized that the industrialization of the South by Northern capital created patterns of dependency that prevented the countries of the South from creating their own future in accordance with their own culture. If industrialization was supported by Northern capital, they argued, it would be guided by the North; it would produce goods for export to sell at high prices on the world market, not goods needed by the local population; it would use sophisticated technologies, not those appropriate to the skills of the people; it would exploit the simple workers, paying them in accordance with the law of supply and demand. More than that, these Christians opposed the globalization of Western culture, with its competitive spirit, ideals of personal autonomy, unrelenting work ethic, and impatience with celebration and contemplation. Liberation theologians replaced the notion of "development" (*desarrollismo*) with the concept of "liberation" (Gutierrez 1973). They advocated the creation of a regional, low-scale economy, based to a large extent on local resources, relying mainly on local skills, and serving, for the most part, the needs of the local population. Is there still room in today's world, they asked, for alternatives to Western industrial culture?

Liberation theology made use of dependency theory to interpret the situation of the continents at the periphery of the global capitalist system. To many observers this appeared to be an infiltration of Catholic theology by Marxist ideas. Not so to Canadian observers. By the 1930s, the Canadian liberal economist Harold Innis had already analyzed the evolution of Canadian society in terms of the exploitative dynamics between the "metropolis" and the "hinterland" (Drache 1995).

The arguments of liberation theology against Western-style development are mainly economic and cultural. Yet, some communities have also had specifically religious reasons to protest the globalization of capitalist culture. In Canada, we are keenly aware of this as First Nations defend themselves against private developers and government-sponsored development projects by affirming the sacredness of their understanding of the land and their relationship to it. They claim that, in the first place, natural resources are not commodities, means of creating wealth, or even objects of barter to enrich First Nation communities; natural resources, they insist, sustain a specific lifestyle, support a local community, and form part of a living entity. For these people, land is not real estate to be bought and sold: it is something sacred. They venerate it as something that has given them life and continues to support and protect them. The land claims of First Nations are not based on a Western liberal idea of property: they demand the power to protect their land from the invasion of developers and preserve it to ensure the continuance of their lifestyle. Yet, they are quite willing to share this land with people from the dominant population, as long as these people have the same reverence for the natural environment.

First Nation peoples, whether they are Christians or practice their traditional cosmic religion, regard with great suspicion the secular approach to life taken for granted in business, government, economics, and other social sciences. As all these endeavours systematically exclude the spiritual dimension of life, native peoples often regard them as a form of brainwashing designed to undermine their cultural identity.

63

This theme is developed at length by the Ecumenical Association of Third World Theologians, which was founded in Tanzania in 1976 and has been meeting since then at regular intervals. Here, Christian theologians from Africa and Asia offer critical reflections on the secularism of the industrialized world (Fabella 1997). They argue that political science, economics, and other social sciences and development projects based on the dominant model presuppose an anthropology — a vision of humankind — that severs the human being from the realm of the Spirit and contradicts the understanding of human life in African and Asian cultures. Some of these theologians are even critical of Latin American liberation theology: they feel that in relying primarily on an economic critique of the oppressive conditions of their continent, liberation theology has become excessively influenced by the secularism of the oppressors. The position of these theologians is that the Western economic empire makes people in Africa and Asia suffer "anthropological oppression," that is, the people find themselves caught in institutions and overwhelmed by a set of symbols that rob them of their cultural identity and produce religious anguish. If this analysis is correct, it may not be surprising that in many parts of the world people turn to religious fundamentalism to protect themselves from the invasion of the Western empire and mind-set.

It is not surprising that after listening to these and other voices of protest, the Christian churches, especially the World Council of Churches, made "development" an important issue, calling for a response of faith. The major churches, Protestant and Roman Catholic, have denounced the purely economic understanding of development and the aggressive globalization of the free-market economy. In the present world, marked by soul-destroying and often death-dealing inequality, the Christian churches have expressed in public statements their solidarity with the poor and their commitment to analyzing their own societies and the world system from the perspective of the marginalized and excluded. This expression of solidarity has produced a new understanding of the church's mission to serve God's reign in the world, to bear, in other words, the burden with the victims of society and promote love, justice, and peace.

The literature on the churches and development is extensive.[1] As I indicated above, I confine myself in this paper to a résumé of the Roman Catholic idea of development proposed in two papal encyclicals — Pope Paul VI's (1967) "Populorum Progressio" and Pope John Paul II's (1987) "Sollicitudo Rei Socialis" (see excerpts of both in Annex 1).

PAUL VI'S "POPULORUM PROGRESSIO"

64

In the "Populorum Progressio," Paul VI showed himself keenly aware of the protest against development mounted by Christian and non-Christian groups in the poorer parts of the world. As we shall see, he pays attention to their economic and religious arguments. As John Paul II (1987, p. 12) later noted, the "Populorum Progressio" emphasized "the ethical and cultural character of the problems connected with development" and the legitimacy of the Church's intervention in the field.

Paul VI supported the idea that the wealthy nations of the North must help the poorer nations of the South overcome the conditions that produce misery and suffering. International solidarity is an obligation of love and justice. Love of God and neighbour, which is the heart of biblical faith, implies a commitment to universal solidarity, beginning with the poor and oppressed. But even strict justice, required of Christians and non-Christians alike, demands that rich people and nations do their utmost to help poor people and nations gain access to the wealth of the Earth. Because God intended the goods of the Earth for the whole of humanity, the current scandalous maldistribution of wealth is an offence against justice and a grave sin. Paul VI praised the efforts of international organizations, particularly the United Nations, to try to restructure the economic order, support development projects in the poor countries, and demand the reduction of their public debt.

Paul VI supported the modern idea of development, but in an alternative mode. He appreciated, in particular, the humanistic development theory of Father Louis Lebret (1959). The Pope took with utmost seriousness the economic and religious arguments against the dominant form of development. He gave an extended critique of liberal capitalism and its impacts on the poorer continents. He recognized that the plight of many Southern nations is, at least in part, the result of the precarious economic conditions created by the colonial powers, such as

---

[1] For a useful summary of this literature, see the *Dictionary of Mission* (Orbis Books 1997).

the concentration of agricultural production on a single crop, which left these nations vulnerable when they became independent (Paul VI 1967, s. 7). He also recognized the fear that "under the cloak of financial aid or technical assistance, there lurk certain manifestations of what has come to be called neo-colonialism, in the form of political pressures and economic suzerainty aimed at maintaining or acquiring complete dominance" (Paul VI 1967, s. 52). In more general terms, the Pope lamented the emergence of neoliberalism, that is, the globalization, in theory and in practice, of the self-regulating market system.

> It is unfortunate that ... a system has been constructed which considers profit as the key motive for economic progress, competition as the supreme law of economics, and private ownership of the means of production as an absolute right that has no limits and carries no corresponding social obligations. This unchecked liberalism leads to dictatorship rightly denounced by Pius XI as producing "the international imperialism of money."[2] One cannot condemn such abuses too strongly by solemnly recalling once again that the economy is at the service of man.
>
> Paul VI (1967, s. 26)

65

Paul VI argued that "if certain landed estates impede the general prosperity because they are extensive, unused or poorly used, or because they bring hardship to peoples or are detrimental to the interests of the country, the common good sometimes demands their expropriation" (Paul VI 1967, s. 24). The Pope also considered it "unacceptable that citizens with abundant incomes from the resources and activity of their country should transfer a considerable part of this income abroad purely for their own advantage, without care for the manifest wrong they inflict on their country by doing this" (Paul VI 1967, s. 24). In certain situations, the Pope continued, injustice cries to heaven:

> When whole populations destitute of necessities live in a state of dependence barring them from all initiative and responsibility, and all opportunity to advance culturally and share in social and political life, recourse to violence, as a means to right these wrongs to human dignity, is a grave temptation. ... We know, however, that a revolutionary uprising — save where there is manifest, long-standing tyranny which would do great damage to fundamental personal rights and dangerous harm to the common good of the country — produces new injustices, throws more elements out of balance and brings on new disasters.
>
> Paul VI (1967, ss. 30 and 31)

---

[2] The reference is to paragraph 109 of Pope Pius XI's "Quadragesimo anno" (O'Brien and Shannon 1992).

The Pope also asked us to question even the sacred cow of technology, in a passage particularly prescient of today's issues in development:

> It is not sufficient to promote technology to render the world a more humane place in which to live. The mistakes of their predecessors should warn those on the road to development of the dangers to be avoided in this field. Tomorrow's technocracy can beget evils no less redoubtable that those due to the liberalism of yesterday. Economics and technology have no meaning except from man whom they should serve.
>
> Paul VI (1967, s. 34)

The Pope favoured the reform of these circumstances and dynamics, calling for "bold transformations, innovations that go deep" (Paul VI 1967, s. 32) and encouraging individual involvement in the necessary reforms, each according to his or her resources and capacity for action.

Yet, after reflecting on the nature of the human vocation and the current condition of the world, he came to the conclusion that the industrialization of society had become a necessity. According to the Christian understanding of the human being, the Pope argued, the quest for self-fulfillment is not optional. People must work, and work hard, to humanize the conditions of their lives. One sentence of the encyclical has a particularly "Western" ring:

> By persistent work and use of his intelligence man gradually wrests nature's secrets from her and finds better application of her riches. As his self-mastery increases, he develops a taste for research and discovery, an ability to take a calculated risk, boldness in enterprises, generosity in what he does and a sense of responsibility.
>
> Paul VI (1967, s. 25)

In this passage, the Pope endorsed modernization. In an earlier passage, he supported industrialization. The evils of neoliberal capitalism, according to Paul VI, must not be attributed to industrialization as such. Industrialization can take place in a mixed economy in which market forces — regulated by government, contained by the labour movement, and tamed by a culture of solidarity — are made to serve the common good of society.

Paul VI also took seriously the religious arguments against development. He repudiated the generally accepted and purely materialistic idea of development current at the time and suggested, instead, what he called "integral" development, that is to say, a development that improves people's material conditions in the context of the fuller realization of humanity in social, political, cultural, and religious terms. Economic development must go hand in hand with the intensification of social solidarity, political freedom and responsibility, access to education, cultural continuity, and the search for greater religious depth:

> If further development calls for work of more and more technicians, even more necessary is the deep thought and reflection of wise men

[and women] in search of a new humanism which will enable modern [persons] to find [themselves] anew by embracing the higher
values of love and friendship, of prayer and contemplation.

Paul vi (1967, s. 20)

A purely secular culture has no access to this new humanism.
According to Paul vi, it is only by calling on the hidden divine powers,
graciously and undeservedly made available to us, that humans can
make progress on the road of love, justice, and peace in today's complex
global society. Christian faith, hope, and love are not meant as an entry
into personal piety; rather, they constitute a world-transforming power
that dwells in people's hearts and summons forth a transpersonal piety
of solidarity[3] and concern for others.

The "Populorum Progressio," it seems to me, is a document that
supports development, but from a particular perspective. First, it
affirms the need for worldwide industrialization; second, it endorses the
idea that the North must assist the development of the South, albeit in
an alternative fashion; and third, it understands the presence of God in
human life as a means to rescue us from personal and social sin and to
empower us for the sanctification of human history.

The passage of time has shown us that many questions remain.
First, can the resources of the Earth afford industrialization on a global
scale? Are all subsistence economies destined to disappear? Second,
should the somewhat paternalistic idea that the rich North must help
the poor South be replaced by a more cooperative model that recognizes
the distinct contributions of both partners to mutually beneficial interaction? The 1971 World Synod of Bishops moved beyond Paul vi's
analysis when it insisted that Southern nations receiving help from the
North should remain the principal architects of their development and
the guardians of their culture (SBSGA 1971). And third, is the humanistic theology of Paul vi, which I fully and joyfully endorse, shared by all
people who believe in God? Members of other religions may have different ideas. Many Christians may interpret God as other than the
redeemer and transformer of human history — that is, acting in the here
and now — but look on God as the saviour rescuing them from history
and offering them a refuge in the sacred temple (in the afterlife).

[3] Pope John Paul ii explained the term *solidarity* in "Sollicitudo Rei Socialis": "political leaders, and citizens of rich countries considered as individuals, especially if they are
Christians, have the moral obligation, according to the degree of each one's responsibility,
to *take into consideration*, in personal decisions and decisions of government, this relationship of universality, this interdependence which exists between their conduct and the
poverty and underdevelopment of so many millions of people" (John Paul ii 1987, s. 9,
emphasis in the original).

John Paul ii's "Sollicitudo Rei Socialis"

To commemorate the 20th anniversary of the "Populorum Progressio,"
Pope John Paul ii (1987) composed the encyclical "Sollicitudo Rei
Socialis." He reexamined the question of development in the light of
more recent events and, through theological reflections on present-day
culture, demonstrated the need for a more nuanced concept of development. John Paul ii agreed with the positions adopted by his predecessor
in the "Populorum Progressio," namely, the need for industrialization,
the deleterious material and cultural consequences of neoliberalism, and
the need for international solidarity to promote the integral development of developing countries. John Paul ii grieved with his predecessor
over the misery, oppression, and marginalization imposed on masses of
people in the South. He lamented that despite major political and economic efforts made in the North and the South, several indicators of
basic needs revealed that the global situation was getting worse and that
the social and economic inequalities between rich and poor countries
and between rich and poor people in each country were increasing.

In this paper, I mention only one issue introduced by John Paul ii's
encyclical, namely, the cultural causes that, in conjunction with economic and political ones, are responsible for the increasing misery in the
world. John Paul ii mentioned in particular the economistic understanding of human beings; and the belief, sustained and guided by science, in humanity's orientation toward limitless progress. The Pope
reminded his readers that both liberals and Marxists share these two
convictions, even if they interpret them differently. He pointed an
accusing finger at contemporary Western culture and suggested that to
account for the "underdevelopment" of the South, we have to examine
the "superdevelopment" of the North; in other words, to understand the
troubling situation of the poor, we must examine the trouble-creating
situation of the rich:

> A *disconcerting conclusion* about the most recent period should serve
> to enlighten us: side-by-side with the miseries of underdevelop-
> ment, themselves unacceptable, we find ourselves up against a form
> of *superdevelopment*, equally inadmissible, because like the former it
> is contrary to what is good and to true happiness. This superdevel-
> opment, which consists in an excessive availability of every kind of
> material goods for the benefit of certain social groups, easily makes
> people slaves of "possession" and of immediate gratification, with
> no other horizon than the multiplication or continual replacement
> of the things already owned with others still better. This is the so-
> called civilization of "consumption" or "consumerism" ... .
> John Paul ii (1987, s. 28, emphasis in the original)

John Paul ii analyzed "consumerism" from an ethical and theological perspective. He argued that the urgent task of helping developing
countries overcome the conditions of hunger and misery demands a

moral conversion of wealthy countries and people everywhere. British sociologist John Hargreaves, in his book *Sport, Power and Culture*, offered a detailed analysis of consumerist, capitalist culture:

> It is the way discourses and practices are articulated around features of a consumer culture, and the way this whole complex is orchestrated by certain key themes, that gives [contemporary capitalism] its coherence and power. The orchestrating themes of this culture are directed at selling a specifically modern, secular version of the good life. The dominant discourse/practice is of youth, beauty, romance, sexual attraction, energy, fitness, health, movement, excitement, adventure, freedom, exotica, luxury, enjoyment, entertainment, fun. Above all, it is a culture that esteems "self-expression." A truly astonishing variety of goods and services — from washing powder, cars and foreign holidays, to cosmetics, fashion-wear, eating and aerobics — circulate on this basis: and concomitantly, major segments of social life are organized around this consumer culture.
>
> Hargreaves (1975, p. 131)

According to John Paul II, the North needs to transform its culture, reject the consumerist mentality, and reenter the spiritual life.

The new idea that John Paul II added to Paul VI's idea of development was that the goal of a world of justice and peace that meets the basic needs of all people is wholly unrealistic unless rich nations are willing to undergo a spiritual conversion. This is a bold assertion. Most of the development literature, including reports by the United Nations and the World Bank,[4] deal with the situation of the poor. If the Pope was correct, then what we need is research on the rich: their power, ideals, culture, and worldview and the impact of their institutions on the world at large.[5]

A PERSONAL SPIRITUALITY

Before turning to the other questions I want to address, I will make a few remarks on where I stand as a Catholic theologian and what inspires me in my work of exploring the meaning and power of the Gospel in today's world. One important influence on my life has been the concept of an "option for the poor," first articulated in Latin American liberation theology and then endorsed in papal and episcopal documents. This option involves two commitments: to look at society from the

---

[4] Most recently, the "World Development Report 2000/01: Poverty and Development" (to be published by the World Bank in September 2000).

[5] Susan George, Associate Director of the Transnational Institute in Amsterdam and a well-known critic of economic globalization, said, "Let the poor study themselves. They already know what is wrong with their lives and if you truly want to help them, the best you can do is give them an idea of how the oppressors are working now and can be expected to work in the future" (George 1976, p. 289).

perspective of its victims; and to publicly manifest solidarity with their struggle for justice. Whereas the implications of this option are secular, its inner spirit is religious and grounded in the Bible. Its roots are particularly evident in the Exodus story (the rescue of the people of Israel from pharaonic oppression), the divine demand of social justice announced by the Hebrew prophets, and the provocative preaching of Jesus Christ that led to his condemnation as a troublemaker and to his death on the Roman cross.

The option for the poor has released a new inwardness in the Christian churches, marked by a certain spiritual anguish; that is, (1) we are deeply troubled by the suffering of others, especially those who are oppressed (the majority of humankind); (2) we grieve over the Church's past and present complicity with empire, colonialism, and other forms of domination; and (3) we willingly expose ourselves to the painful and unanswerable question of how we can reconcile our faith in a loving and omnipotent God with the evil we see in the world. This new spirituality, which has its own "dark night of the soul," is not devoid of hope and the energy to act. In situations of grave injustice, Christian love transforms itself into a yearning for justice and an impulse to act to lift the heavy burdens from the shoulders of the oppressed.

What amazes many Christians, like me, is that in our association with secular men and women committed to justice we often discover that they also have a "spirituality." By this I mean an inwardness of compassion, urgency, and hope that inspires them and guides their lives, even though they never talk about it. Perhaps they never talk about this motivation because traditional spiritual language appears otherworldly to them and they do not possess an alternative discourse to describe such feelings. I often feel closer to such inwardly blessed secular people than I do to those members of my own church who are insensitive to the divine summons for justice. I do not speak of God to these secular associates of mine. It does not occur to me to desire their "conversion"; on the contrary, I marvel at their spiritual experience of standing aloof from the dominant culture, feeling compassion for the unjustly treated, and being empowered to act on their behalf. I detect there a moment of transcendence. As a Catholic in the theological tradition of St Augustine (354–430 AD), I am greatly impressed — as he was — by the sinful dimension of society's dominant structures and, at the same time, the gratuity or "grace" of people's capacity to love, do justice, and make peace. Just as I respect their "secular spirituality" and have no intention to "convert" my friends, I hope that they also respect — in their social-scientific research and their support for public policies — the "otherness" in the mind-set of religious people.

THE WORLD BANK'S NEW INTEREST IN RELIGION

STRUCTURAL-ADJUSTMENT POLICIES IMPOSED BY THE WORLD BANK

After World War II, the Bretton Woods Agreement created the World Bank and the International Monetary Fund (IMF) to monitor the world economy, loan money to poor countries in urgent need, and prevent financial collapse on a universal scale. At the time, the British participants were unhappy that (on the insistence of the Americans) the Bretton Woods institutions would be guided by a liberal economic philosophy that conceived the free market as the engine moving history forward toward universal well-being. When, in the early 1980s, Prime Minister Thatcher of the United Kingdom and President Reagan of the United States implemented neoliberal economic policies in their countries, the Bretton Woods institutions were confirmed in their neoliberalism and pursued it with even greater vigour.

71

The neoliberal policies had devastating effects on many of the developing countries of the South. To promote free trade and the free reign of market forces, the World Bank and the IMF imposed the so-called structural-adjustment policies (SAPs) on these countries. These countries were to get no further loans unless they

&- Opened their borders to free trade and the entry of foreign corporations;

&- Deregulated their national economies;

&- Privatized publicly owned enterprises;

&- Reduced government spending by cutting social programs and laying off government employees; and

&- Shifted production from the local market to the export market.

The SAPs increased hunger and misery in many countries. Instead of growing their own food and producing the goods they needed, people were obliged to produce for export and thus increase their dependency on the centre of world power. In the eyes of the World Bank and the IMF, this bitter medicine was needed to contain what they judged to be irresponsible governments, discipline what they thought to be lazy populations, and convince people that in the long run the self-regulating market system would be the wealth-creating engine of world development.

Neoliberalism has become the new orthodoxy. In response to critics, the World Bank and the IMF claim that they have no alternative. Yet, others have offered alternatives. A well-known example is the 1989 report of the Economic Commission for Africa entitled *African Alternative Framework to Structural Adjustment Programmes for Socio-Economic Recovery and Transformation* (ECA 1989). Pressure from the World Bank seems to have been a strong contributing factor in the stagnation of this report (Mihevc n.d.).

The industrialized countries of the North, I note, have increasingly applied the SAPs to their own economies, and this has brought about a major shift in the distribution of power and wealth. There are signs that we are entering a new phase of human history. Central controlling power has moved to international financial institutions and transnational corporations (TNCs), which are accountable to neither the public nor any supervisory agency. National governments have lost the capacity to promote the well-being of their people and protect them from the TNCs that enter their countries, destabilize their local economies, and invest local profits in other countries (Martin and Schumann 1997). As a policy and ideology, neoliberalism has widened the gap between rich and poor in the industrialized countries; it has produced a growing sector of chronically unemployed people and promoted a culture of competitive individualism devoid of both social solidarity and self-restraint. Only minority movements of spirited people resist this culture. One such movement among the churches is the world-wide ecumenical Jubilee 2000 Initiative,[6] which addresses itself to the Northern nations, the World Bank, and the IMF. Based on the Jubilee texts of Leviticus (25:13–24), in which God commands the Israelites to redistribute wealth, release slaves, and cancel debts at regular intervals, this initiative demands the cancelation of the heavy debt load that currently burdens developing countries. Accompanying this ecumenical initiative is a major educational effort to raise the awareness of church-going Christians.

MOUNTING CRITICISM OF THE WORLD BANK

We saw in the first part of this paper that the major Christian churches on all continents have condemned neoliberal philosophy and demanded political and economic policies based on international solidarity and a desire for social justice. A growing number of nongovernmental organizations (NGOs) active in the South have also formulated criticisms of the World Bank and the SAPs. This wave of complaints climaxed in 1994, the 50th anniversary of the Bank's foundation, when, under the slogan "50 Years Is Enough," the NGOs succeeded in organizing a major campaign critical of the Bank. This campaign informed the public of the destructive, undemocratic, and unaccountable policies adopted by the

---

[6] The Canadian Ecumenical Jubilee Initiative published a 30-page brochure, entitled "A New Beginning: A Call for Jubilee," about this initiative. It is available from the Canadian Ecumenical Jubilee Initiative, PO Box 772, Station F, Toronto, ON, Canada M4Y 2N6. More information on the Jubilee 2000 Debt Campaign can also be found on the Canadian Ecumenical Jubilee Initiative homepage (www.web.net/~jubilee/debt.htm).

Bank and called for fundamental reforms of this institution. The campaign received massive support. In fact, the leaders of the G7 countries put reform of the World Bank on the agenda of their 1995 meeting in Halifax.

In 1994, under its new president, James Wolfensohn, the World Bank decided to listen to these complaints, enter into dialogue with the NGOs, and modify some of its policies. The Bank canceled its involvement in a controversial project in India — the Narmada Dam. It admitted that in many countries foreign debt was a serious problem and prepared measures to alleviate it; it strengthened its commitment to reduce poverty in the world; and, most significantly, it began to hold meetings with the NGOs. The World Bank admitted NGOs to the 1995 assembly of the Bank and IMF and created a joint World Bank–NGO committee to review the SAPs.

Great controversy roars around the significance of the changes introduced by the World Bank. Some commentators think that the Bank has adopted a new orientation more beneficial to developing countries, whereas others argue that these changes are largely window dressing and do not weaken the Bank's commitment to the SAPs or the neoliberal logic behind them. Today, the World Bank is deeply committed to "world governance." Good governance has also become a concern of the United Nations (1995). *Governance*, I note, is not the equivalent of *government*. *Governance* refers, rather, to the interaction of several factors — including government and markets — in creating and sustaining order and peace in society, especially given the social and cultural consequences of globalization. Apart from governments and markets, the concept of civil society encompasses other governance-producing factors. Civil society includes professional associations, labour unions, religious institutions, schools and universities, nonprofit organizations, citizens' movements, cultural centres, and — especially in the South — foreign NGOs.

The protest movement leading up to the World Bank's 50th birthday may not have been the only reason for the Bank's new concern for global governance. The Bank shares the fear of all well-informed citizens that the globalization of the economy and the breakdown of subsistence economies, cultural cohesion, and social integration in many developing countries are producing conditions of grinding misery and social chaos that may easily explode in violence. An explosion of violence in developing countries would cause great human suffering, threaten investment and private property, inhibit production and delivery of goods, and thus impede the expansion of the free-market economy. For all of these reasons (humanitarian and economic), the World Bank has decided to encourage and support good governance, that is, the ordering and pacifying of society under conditions of poverty and dislocation.

73

In the name of good governance, the World Bank now actively intervenes in the affairs of developing countries on several levels:

❧ It puts new emphasis on role of the state;

❧ It seeks cooperation with, and offers financial support for, NGOs and other organizations of civil society; and

❧ It recognizes and encourages a role for religion, ethics, and spirituality.

THE WORLD BANK'S DIALOGUE WITH RELIGION

Good governance includes support for an ethical culture that promotes social well-being. Inwardness or spirituality has social consequences. The world religions form patterned communities that sustain people in difficult times, strengthen them in their communal efforts, and create close bonds of friendship, cooperation, and mutual aid. For these reasons, religious communities, as part of civil society, play an important role in ensuring good governance. It is not surprising that the World Bank, faithful to its new, post-1994 image, has begun to show concern for spirituality and religion. It has sponsored several international conferences on these issues in the hope that a better understanding of the Bank's aims will allow religious leaders and teachers of spirituality to make a more focused contribution to humanity's well-being. At the same time, the World Bank is willing to learn from the wisdom of the world religions.

I wish to comment on two such international conferences: the first, the 1995 Conference on Ethics and Spiritual Values, held in Washington, DC, focused on sustainable development; the second, the 1998 Conference on World Faiths and Development, held at Lambeth Palace in London, United Kingdom, focused on cooperation between religions and the World Bank.

At the opening of the 1995 Conference on Ethics and Spiritual Values, James Wolfensohn gave the keynote address, "New Partnerships," in which he made the following statement:

> Development is not just a matter of looking at increases in gross domestic product (GDP) par capita. In Africa I saw successful development in villages where people were pulling themselves out of deep poverty. Development is visible in people who, within the structure of their familial or tribal system, possess a sense of grandeur, a sense of optimism, a sense of hope; who talk with excitement in their eyes about their children's future. These people, living on next to nothing, feel a sense of progress that is more than economic. It encompasses recognition of roots and their spiritual and cultural values, which we [the World Bank] need to nurture and encourage. These values are what we should be developing ... .

The [World Bank's] central mission is to meld economic assistance
with spiritual, ethical and moral development.

It is not easy to explain to most people why I would leave a
successful business practice to come and try to make the world a
better place. ... I came [here] because of a background that had, I
believe, within my own Jewish religion some sense of ethical, spiritual and moral values that I have attempted to live by and that
guide me.

Wolfensohn (1996, p. 1)

The conference proceedings, published by the World Bank, gave
the names of the 34 men and women it had invited to address the topic.
All the speakers agreed that ethics and spiritual values must be taken
into account in formulating economic policy, especially that related to
sustainable development. Most of them lamented the indifference of
economics to ethical considerations, but, with one exception, all failed
to articulate a critique of the World Bank's economic policies. Only
Denis Goulet, a well-known, critical development economist, said in
plain language that economic globalization (as promoted by the World
Bank) undermined local economies and dissolved traditional values and
that environmentally sustainable development was therefore impossible
under the conditions created by these neoliberal policies (Serageldin and
Barrett 1996).

The Conference on World Faiths and Development, 18–19 February
1998, was hosted by George Carey, Archbishop of Canterbury, and
James Wolfensohn, President of the World Bank, and held at Lambeth
Palace, London. Participants were leaders from nine world religions
(Baha'i Faith, Buddhism, Christianity, Hinduism, Islam, Jainism,
Judaism, Sikhism, and Taoism) and included the main traditions within
these religions.

The conference at Lambeth Palace was preceded by a roundtable
conference, A Christian Response to the International Debt Crisis, on
16–17 May 1996, organized by the Anglican Community Office at the
United Nations. This earlier conference set forth the biblical and Christian foundations for ethical norms relevant to the economy. It assigned
special significance to the Jubilee year. As stated in the conference documents, the immediate purpose of the roundtable conference was "to
express uncompromising concern with the human impact of IMF and
World Bank policies" and to explore with the participants "possible
lines of practical action which might help alleviate negative effects of
[IMF and World Bank] policy on the poor and vulnerable."[7] The conference participants produced a series of policy measures that they urged
the Bretton Woods institutions to take into account.[8]

[7] See www.aco.org/united-nations/debtconf.html.

[8] A 13-page statement of these recommendations (ACOUN 1996), plus the conference
program, can be obtained from the Rt Rev. James Ottley, Anglican Observer at the
United Nations, 815 Second Avenue, New York, NY 10017, USA (e-mail:
anglican_un_office@ecunet.org).

In response to the roundtable conference, James Wolfensohn agreed to cohost, with the Archbishop of Canterbury, the 1998 Conference on World Faiths and Development. Here leaders of the world religions were engaged in sustained conversation with staff members of the World Bank. At the end of the conference, the two co-chairs made a joint statement summing up in 11 points the agreements that had been reached. I offer a brief summary:[9]

1. The religious leaders and the leading staff of the World Bank are at one in their deep moral concern for the future of human well-being and dignity.

2. Human development must have regard for spiritual, ethical, environmental, cultural, and social considerations.

3. Human well-being includes spiritual and cultural expansion and rescue from suffering that is due to poverty.

4. It is important to listen to all the actors involved in development, including especially the local community.

5. The World Bank and the major religious communities agree on the need to continue the dialogue.

6. The religious communities will be allowed to influence the thinking of the World Bank.

7. Several joint working groups will be established.

8. The World Bank staff want more education regarding the world's religions, and the religious communities want more education regarding international development.

9. The religious communities have already contributed much to development projects: they will continue to do so, with the backing of the World Bank.

10. A light and flexible steering group will monitor progress in this area.

11. Governments and international agencies will be exhorted to join the search for better understanding between religion and development.

It is difficult to know how to interpret this joint statement. It is unlikely that the churches have modified the position they have adopted and defended over the years. Nor has the World Bank moved away from its policy of imposing SAPs on developing countries or from its neoliberal approach. Critics claim that by engaging in this dialogue, the Bank

---

[9] The documentation can be obtained from the Press Office, Lambeth Palace, London, UK, SE1 7JU. It is also available on the Internet (www.worldbank.org/html/extdr/faithsdialogue).

wants to persuade the world religions to contribute to the cause of good governance and help stabilize society under the conditions of disintegration produced by the SAPs. These critics think the World Bank wants religion to save society for the globalization of the free market. In my opinion, it is too early to judge the significance of this dialogue.

THE SUBJECTIVE DIMENSION OF SOCIAL-SCIENCE RESEARCH

In this section, I touch on a topic that has been an interest of mine ever since I studied sociology. I have always been impressed by the social theorists who challenged the claim to objectivity, or value neutrality, made by the social sciences. These critical theorists had great respect for the objective methodology of these sciences, that is, the so-called scientific method: relying on empirical research, testing hypotheses, and producing a set of arguments that can be verified by other researchers. Yet, the critical theorists insisted that in social-science research there is inevitably a subjective dimension that depends on the social location, talents, and options of the researcher. I note that this claim is quite different from certain postmodern trends in sociology that deconstruct the objective methodology altogether. As the social sciences are never fully objective, or value free, the critical theorists argue that it would be more scientific if the social scientists articulated the implicit values operative in their research and offered a rational critique of them, not, indeed, "to prove" them but to defend their coherence and clarify their social implications.

In the following pages, I comment on two issues in relation to social-scientific research: its implicit sociopolitical perspectives and its dominant secularism. These are issues of concern to the Christian churches because Christianity — as well as all other religions — is linked to a particular ethic and the churches must respond to the current situation and its irrationalities in terms of this ethic. To do this, they must enter into dialogue with political scientists, economists, and other social scientists. Which of the many diverse currents in these sciences should the churches trust? To give a brief answer to this question, I say that the churches find social, political, and economic analyses trustworthy if the evaluative presuppositions operative within these analyses have an affinity with their own sets of values (Baum 1998).

THE SOCIOPOLITICAL PERSPECTIVE

That the social location of social scientists and their political options affect their analyses of society was an insight that was first articulated by Marx and then explored and developed in the sociology of

77

knowledge. I became acquainted with the sociology of knowledge through two German authors of the 1920s: Max Scheler (1980 [1924]), a conservative social thinker, and Karl Mannheim (1936 [1928]), a liberal sociologist. Today's students of sociology are introduced to this critical approach — admittedly a minority trend in sociology — through the work of Jürgen Habermas (1971 [1968]), who has systematically explored the relations between knowledge and social interest.

This paper is not the place to develop this critical theory in any detail. Simply put, we bring to our scientific study of social phenomena a perspective that expresses the relationship we have with our own society. This is part of the subjective dimension operative in social-science research. The critical approach is also very persuasive to the ordinary citizen because it explains why research institutes and think tanks — which all apply the scientific method faithfully — arrive at such diverse conclusions. Critical theory explains why a simple appeal to the social sciences cannot resolve the important social debates. Let me give a concrete example of this dilemma, drawn from an ecclesiastical document.

When the American Catholic bishops were preparing the 1986 pastoral letter, "Economic Justice for All," they sought an answer to the question of why unemployment and poverty were growing, why the gap between rich and poor was widening, and why ever larger sectors of the population were being marginalized and excluded from participation. In their first draft of the pastoral letter (ACB 1986), the bishops told us that the social and economic scientists they consulted were divided on these issues. Some of these scientists argued that major changes had taken place in the structure of capital and the orientation of the economy; for this reason, repairing the damage and overcoming present injustices would demand major structural changes. Other scientists disagreed with this. They argued, instead, that the current economic decline was not dramatic, that it indicated no significant break with the past, and that it was simply the result of unwise policies adopted by governments and certain industries. Adopting appropriate measures could therefore incrementally overcome these issues.

In this first draft, the bishops mentioned another question that remained unresolved by the scientists they had consulted. The bishops wanted to know whether the economic collapse and the widespread misery in the South were produced by developments in these countries (to which American society was simply an onlooker) or whether these conditions were in some way related to the growing wealth and power of American society. Here, again, the scientists were unable to resolve the question, even though they all followed an objective method and provided demonstrations based on empirical research.[10]

---

[10] For the two passages in the first draft of the pastoral letter, see ACB (1984, pp. 342 and 370).

Because the scientists failed to arrive at an agreement, the American bishops decided not to raise critical questions regarding liberal or neoliberal capitalism in the final version of their pastoral letter. However, not all national bishops' conferences have been as reticent. The Latin American bishops who met at Medellín in 1968 were keenly aware that economists and other social scientists are guided by a social perspective: they may operate out of an implicit identification with the established order or they may read the social reality from the perspective of society's victims, that is, the poor, the oppressed, and the marginalized. The Latin American bishops were not surprised that scientists disagreed in their analyses of society, and the bishops decided, for theological reasons, to trust those scientists who opted for the perspective of the poor (LAB 1968).

The Latin American bishops called this perspective the option for the poor. They believed that, in fidelity to Jesus, Christians want to commit themselves to this perspective. Thanks to liberation theology and the leadership of the Latin American bishops, the option for the poor has become an important principle of interpretation guiding spirituality and social ethics in both Catholic and Protestant churches. The Canadian Catholic bishops, in particular, have produced a series of pastoral statements on social and economic ethics, based on the perspective of society's victims. This has created a certain affinity between Christian thought and critical theory.

I conclude from these reflections that because all social-scientific research operates with a conscious or unconscious value-based orientation, "engaged research" — that is, research guided by a social-justice commitment — is not only perfectly scientific but also more transparent, because it willingly articulates its implicit presuppositions.

QUESTIONING THE DOMINANT SECULARISM
OF SOCIAL SCIENCE

Another implicit presupposition of the social sciences, closely related to the topic of this paper, concerns their relation to the spiritual order. The majority of social scientists recognize that, in the past, religion played an important role in society, either as a principle of order (creating "a sacred canopy") or as a source of motivation (generating a common ethos). But most social scientists have reduced religion to its social function: the study of religion does not provide them with empirical arguments for a transcendent spiritual order. Most sociologists, moreover, are convinced that in modern society, which is marked by industrialization, scientific rationality, and cultural pluralism, religion no longer fulfills any important social function. Religion no longer unites the social order or provides a universally accepted set of values. As the existence of a divine order cannot be scientifically demonstrated, many sociologists argue that religion is becoming increasingly unbelievable. Religion, they think, survives only as the purely personal conviction of certain groups of people, as a sentiment and a commitment to an imaginary universe. Religion remains wholly extrinsic to the constitution of society. The only true reality, "the really real," is here in the visible universe and human history, without any relationship to an invisible order. The traditional notion of transcendence has lost its meaning. Spirituality is at best the private interest of the few.

This secular outlook has been adopted by vast numbers of people in present-day society, and this secularism is predominant in the guild of political scientists, economists, and other social scientists. These scientists, we note, do not regard this secular outlook as the creation of a particular culture, that is to say, modern, Western, industrial culture: rather, they see this outlook as revealing the truth about the world and hence as a perspective applicable to the understanding of all other cultures. Secularism here makes its own culture-transcending claim.

The early literature on development, starting with *The Stages of Economic Growth*, by W.W. Rostow (1960), regarded the religions of peoples in the South as an obstacle to economic development, because these religions often trusted the rhythm of nature, fostered social identification with family and community, and failed to promote a culture oriented toward personal achievement and social mobility. Seen from this perspective, development had to be accompanied by a secularization of culture, that is to say, by an exclusion of religious values from public policies and the organization of production and distribution.

On a previous page, I mentioned that critical voices in Asia and Africa, as well as among native peoples of the Americas, have decried the secular presupposition implicit in economic and other social sciences and in the development projects sponsored by the industrialized West. They regard secularization as a construct of Western empire, aimed at undermining the identity of non-Western peoples. This outlook finds a parallel in work such as *Orientalism*, by Edward Said (1978), which demonstrated how the West's claim to cultural superiority has shaped the Western perception of Islamic–Arab civilization. Other authors have shown that the same is true of the Western perception of India and other Asian civilizations (see Lopez 1995). The contemporary Christian theology of African theologians is critical of the secular attitude of Western missionaries who looked on African belief in the presence of spirits as a superstition to be discarded, even though the Near Eastern world — in which Jesus himself lived — fully shared this belief.

According to Peter Berger (1966), sociologists who study religious phenomena must adopt what he called "methodological atheism." The sociologist must examine these phenomena with the presupposition that they have material and cultural causes within history. For Berger (who presents himself as a believing Christian), science must adopt the perspective of Western secularism. In response, Robert Bellah, one of

Berger's colleagues, argued instead that to appreciate religious phenomena and avoid their systematic distortion, sociologists must opt for "symbolic realism" (Bellah 1970, pp. 220–221). What does Bellah mean by this? The sociologist, he argued, must be open to the possibility that the religious symbols that define the identity of a human community have a transcendent referent; and that the sociologist's own secular presupposition is a Western cultural product rather than a universal truth. Bellah argued that without such an openness to, and empathy with, religious phenomena, sociologists are unable to appreciate the creativity of religion, its resourcefulness in helping people cope with their hardship, and its self-transforming power in new historical situations.

The question I cannot avoid asking is whether the attitude of the social-science researcher toward the existence of a transcendent order influences his or her analysis and conclusion. It seems to me that a social scientist committed to a secular outlook would be insensitive to the creative powers of religion, unless he or she reached out for a special openness. By this I do not mean, of course, that social scientists should all be theists or believers of some sort. Not belief, but empathy, is required. Max Weber insisted that sociologists stretch their imagination and learn to think themselves into the mind-set of religious people. He wanted students of sociology to read the great novels of world literature to discover that their own symbolic understanding of the universe was just one among many others. Weber also recognized that science, or formal rationality as he called it, does not reply to the riddle of the universe. Science was not a philosophy that replied to the great human questions: What is the meaning of it all? Where do we come from and where do we go? Weber regarded himself as a nonbeliever, but he was modest about it. He did not erect his unbelief into a metaphysics. He was not committed to secularism as a definitive interpretation of the universe. In his study of religion, he was open to the new and unexpected; he recognized the historical weight of religious convictions. If there is any truth in the above reflections, then development research should acquire a special sensitivity to the spiritual dimension of people's self-constitution and to the ways the secular presuppositions of contemporary Western culture threaten their identity.

Appreciating the creativity of religion has been a characteristic of the alternative development theories produced by researchers and social thinkers since the 1950s. The paradigms proposed by Louis-Joseph Lebret (1959) (and see Malley 1968) in France and Denis Goulet (1971) in the United States, based on practical experience and theoretical considerations, have always demanded that a certain cultural and religious continuity be a dimension of integral development. This is why they insisted that the local community must be recognized as a partner in any development project, be listened to by the so-called technical experts, and be allowed to exercise co-responsibility fully. Although

Western science plays an important role in such a project, the symbolic meaning and creative energy to make the project work must come from the culture and the religion of the local community. Any new attitudes or practices must find roots in the dynamic elements of the community's own tradition. As much as people are changed by participating in a development project, they want to retain their identity or, more precisely, they want to remain faithful to the past while reconstituting their identity under new conditions.

When we examined the concept of development proposed by the popes, we found that they recognized several dimensions of this process, including a religious one. Yet, they did not sufficiently emphasize, I then suggested, that to assure such an integral development, the local community must be recognized as a partner in the full sense. Development is not a process devised by Western scientists and executed by Western-trained men and women of the South. Co-responsibility means that both parties — the Western specialists and the local community — make an original contribution. This point, as we saw, was made by the 1971 World Synod of Bishops. A truly creative aspect of integral development is the summoning forth of meaning and wisdom derived from the cultural and religious tradition.

ANNEX 1: EXCERPTS FROM PAPAL ENCYCLICALS AND STATEMENTS BY THE WORLD SYNOD OF BISHOPS CONCERNING DEVELOPMENT

EXCERPTS FROM "POPULORUM PROGRESSIO"[11]

Encyclical letter of His Holiness Pope Paul VI, promulgated on 26 March 1967

> 7. ... It must certainly be recognized that colonizing powers have often furthered their own interests, power or glory, and that their departure has sometimes left a precarious economy, bound up for instance with the production of one kind of crop whose market prices are subject to sudden and considerable variation. Yet while recognizing the damage done by a certain type of colonialism and its consequences, one must at the same time acknowledge the qualities and achievement of colonizers who brought their science and technical knowledge and left beneficial results of their presence in so many underprivileged regions. The structures established by them persist, however incomplete they may be; they diminished

[11] Original footnotes omitted. Emphasis added by the author (bold).

ignorance and sickness, brought the benefits of communications and improved living conditions.

8. Yet once this is admitted, it remains only too true that the resultant situation is manifestly inadequate for facing the hard reality of modern economics. Left to itself it works rather to widen the differences in the world's levels of life, not to diminish them: rich peoples enjoy rapid growth whereas the poor develop slowly. The imbalance is on the increase: some produce a surplus of foodstuffs, others cruelly lack them and see their exports made uncertain.

. . .

14. **Development cannot be limited to mere economic growth. In order to be authentic, it must be complete: integral, that is, it has to promote the good of every man and of the whole man.** As an eminent specialist has very rightly and emphatically declared: "We do not believe in separating the economic from the human, nor development from the civilizations in which it exists. What we hold important is man, each man and each group of men, and we even include the whole of humanity."

83

15. In the design of God, every man is called upon to develop and fulfill himself, for every life is a vocation. At birth, everyone is granted, in germ, a set of aptitudes and qualities for him to bring to fruition. Their coming to maturity, which will be the result of education received from the environment and personal efforts, will allow each man to direct himself toward the destiny intended for him by his Creator. Endowed with intelligence and freedom, he is responsible for his fulfillment as he is for his salvation. He is aided, or sometimes impeded, by those who educate him and those with whom he lives, but each one remains, whatever be these influences affecting him, the principal agent of his own success or failure. By the unaided effort of his own intelligence and his will, each man can grow in humanity, can enhance his personal worth, can become more a person.

16. However, this self-fulfillment is not something optional. Just as the whole of creation is ordained to its Creator, so spiritual beings should of their own accord orientate their lives to God, the first truth and the supreme good. Thus it is that human fulfillment constitutes, as it were, a summary of our duties. But there is much more: this harmonious enrichment of nature by personal and responsible effort is ordered to a further perfection. By reason of his union with Christ, the source of life, man attains to new fulfillment of himself, to a transcendent humanism which gives him his greatest possible perfection: this is the highest goal of personal development.

17. But each man is a member of society. He is part of the whole of mankind. It is not just certain individuals, but all men who are called to this fullness of development. Civilizations are born, develop and die. But humanity is advancing along the path of history like the waves of a rising tide encroaching gradually on the

shore. We have inherited from past generations, and we have bene-
fited from the work of our contemporaries: for this reason we have
obligations towards all, and we cannot refuse to interest ourselves in
those who will come after us to enlarge the human family. The
reality of human solidarity, which is a benefit for us, also imposes a
duty.

18. This personal and communal development would be threatened
if the true scale of values were undermined. The desire for necessities is legitimate, and work undertaken to obtain them is a duty: "If
any man will not work, neither let him eat." But the acquiring of
temporal goods can lead to greed, to the insatiable desire for more,
and can make increased power a tempting objective. Individuals,
families and nations can be overcome by avarice, be they poor or
rich, and all can fall victim to a stifling materialism.

19. **Increased possession is not the ultimate goal of nations nor
of individuals. All growth is ambivalent. It is essential if man
is to develop as a man, but in a way it imprisons man if he considers it the supreme good, and it restricts his vision.** Then we
see hearts harden and minds close, and men no longer gather
together in friendship but out of self-interest, which soon leads to
oppositions and disunity. The exclusive pursuit of possessions thus
become an obstacle to individual fulfillment and to man's true
greatness. Both for nations and for individual men, avarice is the
most evident form of moral underdevelopment.

20. If further development calls for the work of more and more
technicians, even more necessary is the deep thought and reflection
of wise men in search of a new humanism which will enable modern man to find himself anew by embracing the higher values of
love and friendship, of prayer and contemplation. This is what will
permit the fullness of authentic development, a development which
is for each and all the transition from less human conditions to those
which are more human.

21. **Less human conditions:** the lack of material necessities for
those who are without the minimum essential for life, the moral
deficiencies of those who are mutilated by selfishness. Less human
conditions: oppressive social structures, whether due to the abuses
of ownership or to the abuses of power, to the exploitation of workers or to unjust transactions. **Conditions that are more human:**
the passage from misery towards the possession of necessities, victory over social scourges, the growth of knowledge, the acquisition
of culture. Additional conditions that are more human: increased
esteem for the dignity of others, the turning toward the spirit of
poverty, cooperation for the common good, the will and desire for
peace. Conditions that are still more human: the acknowledgment
by man of supreme values, and of God their source and their final-
ity. Conditions that, finally and above all, are more human: faith, a
gift of God accepted by the good will of man, and unity in the

charity of Christ, Who calls us all to share as sons in the life of the living God, the Father of all men.

...

24. If certain landed estates impede the general prosperity because they are extensive, unused or poorly used, or because they bring hardship to peoples or are detrimental to the interests of the country, the common good sometimes demands their expropriation. While giving a clear statement on this, the Council recalled no less clearly that the available revenue is not to be used in accordance with mere whim, and that no place must be given to selfish speculation. Consequently it is unacceptable that citizens with abundant incomes from the resources and activity of their country should transfer a considerable part of this income abroad purely for their own advantage, without care for the manifest wrong they inflict on their country by doing this.

25. The introduction of industry is a necessity for economic growth and human progress; it is also a sign of development and contributes to it. By persistent work and use of his intelligence man gradually wrests nature's secrets from her and finds a better application for her riches. As his self-mastery increases, he develops a taste for research and discovery, an ability to take a calculated risk, boldness in enterprises, generosity in what he does and a sense of responsibility.

26. **But it is unfortunate that on these new conditions of society a system has been constructed which considers profit as the key motive for economic progress, competition as the supreme law of economics, and private ownership of the means of production as an absolute right that has no limits and carries no corresponding social obligation.** This unchecked liberalism leads to dictatorship rightly denounced by Pius XI as producing "the international imperialism of money." One cannot condemn such abuses too strongly by solemnly recalling once again that the economy is at the service of man. But if it is true that a type of capitalism has been the source of excessive suffering, injustices and fratricidal conflicts whose effects still persist, it would also be wrong to attribute to industrialization itself evils that belong to the woeful system which accompanied it. On the contrary one must recognize in all justice the irreplaceable contribution made by the organization of labor and of industry to what development has accomplished.

...

30. There are certainly situations whose injustice cries to heaven. When whole populations destitute of necessities live in a state of dependence barring them from all initiative and responsibility, and all opportunity to advance culturally and share in social and

political life, recourse to violence, as a means to right these wrongs to human dignity, is a grave temptation.

31. We know, however, that a revolutionary uprising — save where there is manifest, long-standing tyranny which would do great damage to fundamental personal rights and dangerous harm to the common good of the country — produces new injustices, throws more elements out of balance and brings on new disasters. A real evil should not be fought against at the cost of greater misery.

32. We want to be clearly understood: the present situation must be faced with courage and the injustices linked with it must be fought against and overcome. Development demands bold transformations, innovations that go deep. Urgent reforms should be undertaken without delay. It is for each one to take his share in them with generosity, particularly those whose education, position and opportunities afford them wide scope for action. May they show an example, and give of their own possessions as several of Our brothers in the episcopacy have done. In so doing they will live up to men's expectations and be faithful to the Spirit of God, since it is "the ferment of the Gospel which has aroused and continues to arouse in man's heart the irresistible requirements of his dignity."

33. **Individual initiative alone and the mere free play of competition could never assure successful development.** One must avoid the risk of increasing still more the wealth of the rich and the dominion of the strong, whilst leaving the poor in their misery and adding to the servitude of the oppressed. Hence programs are necessary in order "to encourage, stimulate, coordinate, supplement and integrate" the activity of individuals and of intermediary bodies. It pertains to the public authorities to choose, even to lay down the objectives to be pursued, the ends to be achieved, and the means for attaining these, and it is for them to stimulate all the forces engaged in this common activity. But let them take care to associate private initiative and intermediary bodies with this work. They will thus avoid the danger of complete collectivization or of arbitrary planning, which, by denying liberty, would prevent the exercise of the fundamental rights of the human person.

34. This is true since every program, made to increase production, has, in the last analysis, no other raison d'être than the service of man. Such programs should reduce inequalities, fight discriminations, free man from various types of servitude and enable him to be the instrument of his own material betterment, of his moral progress and of his spiritual growth. **To speak of development, is in effect to show as much concern for social progress as for economic growth. It is not sufficient to increase overall wealth for it to be distributed equitably. It is not sufficient to promote technology to render the world a more humane place in which to live.** The mistakes of their predecessors should warn those on the road to development of the dangers to be avoided in this field. **Tomorrow's technocracy can beget evils no less**

redoubtable than those due to the liberalism of yesterday. Economics and technology have no meaning except from man whom they should serve. And man is only truly man in as far as, master of his own acts and judge of their worth, he is author of his own advancement, in keeping with the nature which was given to him by his Creator and whose possibilities and exigencies he himself freely assumes.

...

40. In addition to professional organizations, there are also institutions which are at work. Their role is no less important for the success of development. "The future of the world stands in peril," the Council gravely affirms, "unless wiser men are forthcoming." And it adds: "many nations, poorer in economic goods, are quite rich in wisdom and able to offer noteworthy advantages to others." Rich or poor, each country possesses a civilization handed down by their ancestors: institutions called for by life in this world, and higher manifestations of the life of the spirit, manifestations of an artistic, intellectual and religious character. When the latter possess true human values, it would be grave error to sacrifice them to the former. A people that would act in this way would thereby lose the best of its patrimony; in order to live, it would be sacrificing its reasons for living. Christ's teaching also applies to people: "What does it profit a man to gain the whole world if he suffers the loss of his soul."

41. **Less well-off peoples can never be sufficiently on their guard against this temptation which comes to them from wealthy nations. For these nations all too often set an example of success in a highly technical and culturally developed civilization; they also provide the model for a way of acting that is principally aimed at the conquest of material prosperity.** Not that material prosperity of itself precludes the activity of the human spirit. On the contrary, the human spirit, "increasingly free of its bondage to creatures, can be more easily drawn to the worship and contemplation of the Creator." However, "modern civilization itself often complicates the approach to God, not for any essential reason, but because it is excessively engrossed in earthly affairs." Developing nations must know how to discriminate among those things that are held out to them; they must be able to assess critically, and eliminate those deceptive goods which would only bring about a lowering of the human ideal, and to accept those values that are sound and beneficial, in order to develop them alongside their own, in accordance with their own genius.

42. What must be aimed at is complete humanism. And what is that if not the fully-rounded development of the whole man and of all men? A humanism closed in on itself, and not open to the values of the spirit and to God Who is their source, could achieve apparent success. **True, man can organize the world apart from God, but "without God man can organize it in the end only to**

87

man's detriment. An isolated humanism is an inhuman humanism." There is no true humanism but that which is open to the Absolute and is conscious of a vocation which gives human life its true meaning. Far from being the ultimate measure of all things, man can only realize himself by reaching beyond himself. As Pascal has said so well: "Man infinitely surpasses man."

...

47. But neither all this nor the private and public funds that have been invested, nor the gifts and loans that have been made, can suffice. It is not just a matter of eliminating hunger, nor even of reducing poverty. The struggle against destitution, though urgent and necessary, is not enough. It is a question, rather, of building a world where every man, no matter what his race, religion or nationality, can live a fully human life, freed from servitude imposed on him by other men or by natural forces over which he has not sufficient control; a world where freedom is not an empty word and where the poor man Lazarus can sit down at the same table with the rich man. This demands great generosity, much sacrifice and unceasing effort on the part of the rich man. Let each one examine his conscience, a conscience that conveys a new message for our times. Is he prepared to support out of his own pocket works and undertakings organized in favor of the most destitute? Is he ready to pay higher taxes so that the public authorities can intensify their efforts in favor of development? Is he ready to pay a higher price for imported goods so that the producer may be more justly rewarded? Or to leave his country, if necessary and if he is young, in order to assist in this development of the young nations?

48. **The same duty of solidarity that rests on individuals exists also for nations:** "Advanced nations have a very heavy obligation to help the developing peoples." It is necessary to put this teaching of the Council into effect. Although it is normal that a nation should be the first to benefit from the gifts that Providence has bestowed on it as the fruit of the labors of its people, still no country can claim on that account to keep its wealth for itself alone. Every nation must produce more and better quality goods to give to all its inhabitants a truly human standard of living, and also to contribute to the common development of the human race. Given the increasing needs of the under-developed countries, it should be considered quite normal for an advanced country to devote a part of its production to meet their needs, and to train teachers, engineers, technicians and scholars prepared to put their knowledge and their skill at the disposal of less fortunate peoples.

...

52. There is certainly no need to do away with bilateral and multilateral agreements: they allow ties of dependence and feelings of bitterness, left over from the era of colonialism, to yield place to the happier relationship of friendship, based on a footing of constitutional and political equality. However, if they were to be fitted into

the framework of worldwide collaboration, they would be beyond all suspicion, and as a result there would be less distrust on the part of the receiving nations. These would have less cause for fearing that, under the cloak of financial aid or technical assistance, there lurk certain manifestations of what has come to be called neo-colonialism, in the form of political pressures and economic suzerainty aimed at maintaining or acquiring complete dominance.

. . .

57. Of course, highly industrialized nations export for the most part manufactured goods, while countries with less developed economies have only food, fibers and other raw materials to sell. As a result of technical progress the value of manufactured goods is rapidly increasing and they can always find an adequate market. On the other hand, raw materials produced by under-developed countries are subject to wide and sudden fluctuations in price, a state of affairs far removed from the progressively increasing value of industrial products. As a result, nations whose industrialization is limited are faced with serious difficulties when they have to rely on their exports to balance their economy and to carry out their plans for development. The poor nations remain ever poor while the rich ones become still richer.

89

58. In other words, the rule of free trade, taken by itself, is no longer able to govern international relations. Its advantages are certainly evident when the parties involved are not affected by any excessive inequalities of economic power: it is an incentive to progress and a reward for effort. That is why industrially developed countries see in it a law of justice. But the situation is no longer the same when economic conditions differ too widely from country to country: prices which are "freely" set in the market can produce unfair results. One must recognize that it is the fundamental principle of liberalism, as the rule for commercial exchange, which is questioned here.

59. The teaching of Leo XIII in Rerum Novarum is always valid: if the positions of the contracting parties are too unequal, the consent of the parties does not suffice to guarantee the justice of their contract, and the rule of free agreement remains subservient to the demands of the natural law. What was true of the just wage for the individual is also true of international contracts: **an economy of exchange can no longer be based solely on the law of free competition, a law which, in its turn, too often creates an economic dictatorship. Freedom of trade is fair only if it is subject to the demands of social justice.**

. . .

71. We are happy that experts are being sent in larger and larger numbers on development missions by institutions, whether international or bilateral, or by private organizations: "**they ought not conduct themselves in a lordly fashion, but as helpers and**

co-workers." A people quickly perceives whether those who come to help them do so with or without affection, whether they come merely to apply their techniques or to recognize in man his full value.

Their message is in danger of being rejected if it is not presented in the context of brotherly love.

72. Hence, necessary technical competence must be accompanied by authentic signs of disinterested love. Freed of all nationalistic pride and of every appearance of racism, experts should learn how to work in close collaboration with all. **They realize that their competence does not confer on them a superiority in every field. The civilization which formed them contains, without doubt, elements of universal humanism, but it is not the only civilization nor does it enjoy a monopoly of valuable elements. Moreover it cannot be imported without undergoing adaptations.** The men on these missions will be intent on discovering, along with its history, the component elements of the cultural riches of the country receiving them. Mutual understanding will be established which will enrich both cultures.

...

76. Excessive economic, social and cultural inequalities among peoples arouse tensions and conflicts, and are a danger to peace. As We said to the Fathers of the Council when We returned from Our journey of peace to the United Nations: "The condition of the peoples in process of development ought to be the object of our consideration; or better: our charity for the poor in the world — and there are multitudes of them — must become more considerate, more active, more generous." To wage war on misery and to struggle against injustice is to promote, along with improved conditions, the human and spiritual progress of all men, and therefore the common good of humanity. **Peace cannot be limited to a mere absence of war, the result of an ever precarious balance of forces. No, peace is something that is built up day after day, in the pursuit of an order intended by God, which implies a more perfect form of justice among men.**

EXCERPTS FROM "SOLLICITUDO REI SOCIALIS"[12]

Encyclical letter of the Supreme Pontiff John Paul II, promulgated in 1987 on the 20th anniversary of "Populorum Progressio"

9. ... Unfortunately, from the economic point of view, the developing countries are much more numerous than the developed ones; the multitudes of human beings who lack the goods and services

[12] Original footnotes omitted. Emphasis in the original (italics) and added by the author (bold).

offered by development are *much more numerous* than those who possess them.

We are therefore faced with a serious problem of *unequal distribution* of the means of subsistence originally meant for everybody, and thus also an unequal distribution of the benefits deriving from them. And this happens not through the *fault* of the needy people, and even less through a sort of *inevitability* dependent on natural conditions or circumstances as a whole.

The Encyclical of Paul VI, in declaring that the social question has acquired worldwide dimensions, first of all points out a *moral fact*, one which has its foundation in an objective analysis of reality. In the words of the Encyclical itself, "each one must be conscious" of this fact, precisely because it directly concerns the conscience, which is the source of moral decisions.

In this framework, the *originality* of the Encyclical consists not so much in the affirmation, historical in character, of the universality of the social question, but rather in the *moral evaluation* of this reality. **Therefore political leaders, and citizens of rich countries considered as individuals, especially if they are Christians, have the moral obligation, according to the degree of each one's responsibility, to *take into consideration*, in personal decisions and decisions of government, this relationship of universality, this interdependence which exists between their conduct and the poverty and underdevelopment of so many millions of people.** Pope Paul's Encyclical translates more succinctly the moral obligation as the "duty of solidarity"; and this affirmation, even though many situations have changed in the world, has the same force and validity today as when it was written.

On the other hand, without departing from the lines of this moral vision, the *originality* of the Encyclical also consists in the basic insight that the *very concept* of development, if considered in the perspective of universal interdependence, changes notably. **True development *cannot* consist in the simple accumulation of wealth and in the greater availability of goods and services, if this is gained at the expense of the development of the masses, and without due consideration for the social, cultural and spiritual dimensions of the human being.**

...

15. ... We should add here that in today's world there are many other *forms of poverty*. For are there not certain privations or deprivations which deserve this name? The denial or the limitation of human rights as for example the right to religious freedom, the right to share in the building of society, the freedom to organize and to form unions, or to take initiatives in economic matters — do these not impoverish the human person as much as, if not more than, the deprivation of material goods? And is development which

91

does not take into account the full affirmation of these rights really development on the human level?

In brief, modern underdevelopment is not only economic but also cultural, political and simply human, as was indicated twenty years ago by the Encyclical Populorum Progressio. **Hence at this point we have to ask ourselves if the sad reality of today might not be, at least in part, the result of a *too narrow idea* of development, that is, a mainly economic one.**

16. It should be noted that in spite of the praiseworthy efforts made in the last two decades by the more developed or developing nations and the International Organizations to find a way out of the situation, or at least to remedy some of its symptoms, **the conditions have become *notably worse*.**

Responsibility for this deterioration is due to various causes. Notable among them are undoubtedly grave instances of omissions on the part of the developing nations themselves, and especially on the part of those holding economic and political power. Nor can we pretend not to see the responsibility of the developed nations, which have not always, at least in due measure, felt the duty to help countries separated from the affluent world to which they themselves belong.

Moreover, one must denounce the existence of economic, financial and social *mechanisms* which, although they are manipulated by people, often function almost automatically, thus accentuating the situation of wealth for some and poverty for the rest. These mechanisms, which are manoeuvred directly or indirectly by the more developed countries, by their very functioning favor the interests of the people manipulating them. But in the end they suffocate or condition the economies of the less developed countries. Later on these mechanisms will have to be subjected to a careful analysis under the ethical–moral aspect.

Populorum Progressio already foresaw the possibility that under such systems the wealth of the rich would increase and the poverty of the poor would remain. A proof of this forecast has been the appearance of the so-called Fourth World.

. . .

28. At the same time, however, the *"economic"* concept itself, linked to the word development, has entered into crisis. In fact there is a better understanding today that the *mere accumulation* of goods and services, even for the benefit of the majority, is not enough for the realization of human happiness. Nor, in consequence, does the availability of the many *real benefits* provided in recent times by science and technology, including the computer sciences, bring freedom from every form of slavery. **On the contrary, the experience of recent years shows that unless all the considerable body of resources and potential at man's disposal is guided by a *moral***

understanding and by an orientation towards the true good of the human race, it easily turns against man to oppress him.

A *disconcerting conclusion* about the most recent period should serve to enlighten us: side-by-side with the miseries of under-development, themselves unacceptable, we find ourselves up against a form of *superdevelopment*, equally inadmissible, because like the former it is contrary to what is good and to true happiness. This superdevelopment, which consists in an excessive availability of every kind of material goods for the. bene-fit of certain social groups, easily makes people slaves of "posses-sion" and of immediate gratification, with no other horizon than the multiplication or continual replacement of the things already owned with others still better. This is the so-called civilization of "consumption" or "consumerism," which involves so much "throwing-away" and "waste." An object already owned but now superseded by something better is discarded, with no thought of its possible last-ing value in itself, nor of some other human being who is poorer.

All of us experience firsthand the sad effects of this blind sub-mission to pure consumerism: in the first place a crass materialism, and at the same time a *radical dissatisfaction*, because one quickly learns unless one is shielded from the flood of publicity and the ceaseless and tempting offers of products that the more one possesses the more one wants, while deeper aspirations remain unsatisfied and perhaps even stifled.

The Encyclical of Pope Paul VI pointed out the difference, so often emphasized today, between "having" and "being," which had been expressed earlier in precise words by the Second Vatican Coun-cil. To "have" objects and goods does not in itself perfect the human subject, unless it contributes to the maturing and enrichment of that subject's "being," that is to say unless it contributes to the real-ization of the human vocation as such.

Of course, the difference between "being" and "having," the danger inherent in a mere multiplication or replacement of things possessed compared to the value of "being," need not turn into a *contradiction*. One of the greatest injustices in the contemporary world consists precisely in this: that the ones who possess much are relatively *few* and those who possess almost nothing are *many*. It is the injustice of the poor distribution of the goods and services orig-inally intended for all.

This then is the picture: there are some people — the few who possess much — who do not really succeed in "being" because, through a reversal of the hierarchy of values, they are hindered by the cult of "having"; and there are others — the many who have little or nothing — who do not succeed in realizing their basic human vocation because they are deprived of essential goods.

The evil does not consist in "having" as such, but in possess-ing without regard for the *quality* and the *ordered hierarchy* of the goods one has. *Quality and hierarchy* arise from the

93

subordination of goods and their availability to man's "being" and his true vocation.

This shows that although *development* has a *necessary economic dimension*, since it must supply the greatest possible number of the world's inhabitants with an availability of goods essential for them "to be," it is not limited to that dimension. If it is limited to this, then it turns against those whom it is meant to benefit.

The characteristics of full development, one which is "more human" and able to sustain itself at the level of the true vocation of men and women without denying economic requirements, were described by Paul VI.

29. Development which is not only economic must be measured and oriented according to the reality and vocation of man seen in his totality, namely, according to his *interior dimension*. There is no doubt that he needs created goods and the products of industry, which is constantly being enriched by scientific and technological progress. And the ever greater availability of material goods not only meets needs but also opens new horizons. The danger of the misuse of material goods and the appearance of artificial needs should in no way hinder the regard we have for the new goods and resources placed at our disposal and the use we make of them. On the contrary, we must see them as a gift from God and as a response to the human vocation, which is fully realized in Christ.

. . .

32. ... Collaboration in the development of the whole person and of every human being is in fact a duty of all towards all, and must be shared by the four parts of the world: East and West, North and South; or, as we say today, by the different "worlds." If, on the contrary, people try to achieve it in only one part, or in only one world, they do so at the expense of the others; and, precisely because the others are ignored, their own development becomes exaggerated and misdirected.

Peoples or *nations* **too have a right to their own full development, which while including as already said the economic and social aspects should also include individual cultural identity and openness to the transcendent. Not even the need for development can be used as an excuse for imposing on others one's own way of life or own religious belief.**

33. Nor would a type of development which did not respect and promote *human rights* — personal and social, economic and political, including the *rights of nations and of peoples* — be really *worthy of man*.

Today, perhaps more than in the past, the *intrinsic contradiction* of a development limited *only* to its economic element is seen more clearly. Such development easily subjects the human person and his deepest needs to the demands of economic planning and selfish profit.

The *intrinsic connection* between authentic development and respect for human rights once again reveals the *moral* character of development: the true elevation of man, in conformity with the natural and historical vocation of each individual, is not attained *only* by exploiting the abundance of goods and services, or by having available perfect infrastructures.

When individuals and communities do not see a rigorous respect for the moral, cultural and spiritual requirements, based on the dignity of the person and on the proper identity of each community, beginning with the family and religious societies, then all the rest — availability of goods, abundance of technical resources applied to daily life, a certain level of material well-being — will prove unsatisfying and in the end contemptible. The Lord clearly says this in the Gospel, when he calls the attention of all to the true hierarchy of values: "For what will it profit a man, if he gains the whole world and forfeits his life?" (Mt 16:26).

95

True development, in keeping with the *specific* needs of the human being man or woman, child, adult or old person implies, especially for those who actively share in this process and are responsible for it, a lively *awareness* of the *value* of the rights of all and of each person. It likewise implies a lively awareness of the need to respect the right of every individual to the full use of the benefits offered by science and technology.

On the *internal level* of every nation, respect for all rights takes on great importance, especially: the right to life at every stage of its existence; the rights of the family, as the basic social community, or "cell of society"; justice in employment relationships; the rights inherent in the life of the political community as such; the rights based on the *transcendent vocation* of the human being, beginning with the right of freedom to profess and practice one's own religious belief.

. . .

In order to be genuine, development must be achieved within the framework of *solidarity* and *freedom*, without ever sacrificing either of them under whatever pretext. The moral character of development and its necessary promotion are emphasized when the most rigorous respect is given to all the demands deriving from the order of *truth* and *good* proper to the human person. Furthermore the Christian who is taught to see that man is the image of God, called to share in the truth and the good which is *God himself*, does not understand a commitment to development and its application which excludes regard and respect for the unique dignity of this "image." In other words, true development must be based on the *love of God and neighbor*, and must help to promote the relationships between individuals and society. This is the "civilization of love" of which Paul VI often spoke.

34. Nor can the moral character of development exclude respect *for the beings which constitute* the natural world, which the ancient Greeks — alluding precisely to the order which distinguishes it — called the "cosmos." Such realities also demand respect, by virtue of a threefold consideration which it is useful to reflect upon carefully.

The first consideration is the appropriateness of acquiring a growing awareness of the fact that one cannot use with impunity the different categories of beings, whether living or inanimate — animals, plants, the natural elements — simply as one wishes, according to one's own economic needs. On the contrary, one must take into account *the nature of each being* and of its *mutual connection* in an ordered system, which is precisely the "cosmos."

The *second consideration* is based on the realization which is perhaps more urgent that *natural resources* are limited; some are not, as it is said, *renewable*. Using them as if they were inexhaustible, with *absolute dominion*, seriously endangers their availability not only for the present generation but above all for generations to come.

The *third consideration* refers directly to the consequences of a certain type of development on the *quality of life* in the industrialized zones. **We all know that the direct or indirect result of industrialization is, ever more frequently, the pollution of the environment, with serious consequences for the health of the population.**

Once again it is evident that development, the planning which governs it, and the way in which resources are used must include respect for moral demands. One of the latter undoubtedly imposes limits on the use of the natural world. The dominion granted to man by the Creator is not an absolute power, nor can one speak of a freedom to "use and misuse," or to dispose of things as one pleases. The limitation imposed from the beginning by the Creator himself and expressed symbolically by the prohibition not to "eat of the fruit of the tree" (cf. Gen 2:16–17) shows clearly enough that, when it comes to the natural world, we are subject not only to biological laws but also to moral ones, which cannot be violated with impunity.

. . .

37. This *general analysis*, which is religious in nature, can be supplemented by *a number of particular considerations* to demonstrate that among the actions and attitudes opposed to the will of God, the good of neighbor and the "structures" created by them, two are very typical: on the one hand, the *all-consuming desire for profit*, and on the other, the *thirst for power*, with the intention of imposing one's will upon others. In order to characterize better each of these attitudes, one can add the expression: "at any price." In other words, we are faced with the *absolutizing* of human attitudes with all its

possible consequences. Since these attitudes can exist independently of each other, they can be separated; however in today's world both are *indissolubly united*, with one or the other predominating.

Obviously, not only individuals fall victim to this double attitude of sin; nations and blocs can do so too. And this favors even more the introduction of the "structures of sin" of which I have spoken. **If certain forms of modern "imperialism" were considered in the light of these moral criteria, we would see that hidden behind certain decisions, apparently inspired only by economics or politics, are real forms of idolatry: of money, ideology, class, technology.**

I have wished to introduce this type of analysis above all in order to point out the true *nature* of the evil which faces us with respect to the development of peoples: it is a question of a *moral evil*, the fruit of *many sins* which lead to "structures of sin." To diagnose the evil in this way is to identify precisely, on the level of human conduct, *the path to be followed* in order *to overcome it*.

38. ... In the context of these reflections the decision to set out or to continue the journey involves, above all, a *moral* value which men and women of faith recognize as a demand of God's will, the only true foundation of an absolutely binding ethic.

One would hope that also men and women without an explicit faith would be convinced that the obstacles to integral development are not only economic but rest on *more profound attitudes* which human beings can make into absolute values. **Thus one would hope that all those who, to some degree or other, are responsible for ensuring a "more human life" for their fellow human beings, whether or not they are inspired by a religious faith, will become fully aware of the urgent need to change the *spiritual attitudes* which define each individual's relationship with self, with neighbor, with even the remotest human communities, and with nature itself; and all of this in view of higher values such as the *common good*** or, to quote the felicitous expression of the Encyclical Populorum Progressio, the full development "of the whole individual and of all people."

...

It is above all a question of *interdependence*, sensed as a *system determining* relationships in the contemporary world, in its economic, cultural, political and religious elements, and accepted as a *moral category*. When interdependence becomes recognized in this way, the correlative response as a moral and social attitude, as a "virtue," is *solidarity*. This then is not a feeling of vague compassion or shallow distress at the misfortunes of so many people, both near and far. On the contrary, it is a *firm and persevering determination* to commit oneself to the *common good*; that is to say to the good of all and of each individual, because we are *all* really responsible for *all*. This determination is based on the solid conviction that what is hindering full development is that desire for profit and that thirst for power already mentioned. These attitudes and "structures of sin" are only conquered — presupposing the help of divine grace — by a *diametrically opposed attitude*: a commitment to the good of one's neighbor with the readiness, in the Gospel sense, to "lose oneself" for the sake of the other instead of exploiting him, and to "serve him" instead of oppressing him for one's own advantage (cf. Mt 10:40–42; 20:25; Mk 10:42–45; Lk 22:25–27).

39. The exercise of solidarity *within each society* is valid when its members recognize one another as persons. Those who are more influential, because they have a greater share of goods and common services, should feel *responsible* for the weaker and be ready to share with them all they possess. Those who are weaker, for their part, in the same spirit of *solidarity*, should not adopt a purely *passive* attitude or one that is *destructive* of the social fabric, but, while claiming their legitimate rights, should do what they can for the good of all. The intermediate groups, in their turn, should not selfishly insist on their particular interests, but respect the interests of others.

Positive signs in the contemporary world are the *growing awareness* of the solidarity of the poor among themselves, their *efforts to support one another*, and their *public demonstrations* on the social scene which, without recourse to violence, present their own needs and rights in the face of the inefficiency or corruption of the public authorities. By virtue of her own evangelical duty the Church feels called to take her stand beside the poor, to discern the justice of their requests, and to help satisfy them, without losing sight of the good of groups in the context of the common good.

The same criterion is applied by analogy in international relationships. **Interdependence must be transformed into *solidarity*, based upon the principle that the goods of creation are *meant for all*.** That which human industry produces through the processing of raw materials, with the contribution of work, must serve equally for the good of all.

Surmounting every type of *imperialism* and determination to preserve their *own hegemony*, the imperial and richer nations must have a sense of moral *responsibility* for the other nations, so that a *real international system* may be established which will rest on the foundation of the *equality* of all peoples and on the necessary respect for their legitimate differences. The economically weaker countries, or those still at subsistence level, must be enabled, with the assistance of other peoples and of the international community, to make a contribution of their own to the common good with their treasures of *humanity* and *culture*, which otherwise would be lost for ever.

Solidarity helps us to see the "other" — whether a *person, people or nation* — not just as some kind of instrument, with a work capacity and physical strength to be exploited at low cost and then discarded when no longer useful, but as our "neighbor," a "helper" (cf. Gen 2:18–20), to be made a sharer, on a par with ourselves, in the banquet of life to which all are equally invited by God. Hence the importance of reawakening the *religious awareness* of individuals and peoples.

Thus the exploitation, oppression and annihilation of others are excluded. These facts, in the present division of the world into opposing blocs, combine to produce the *danger of war* and an excessive preoccupation with personal security, often to the detriment of the autonomy, freedom of decision, and even the territorial integrity of the weaker nations situated within the so-called "areas of influence" or "safety belts."

...

In this way, the solidarity which we propose is the *path to peace and at the same time to development.* For world peace is inconceivable unless the world's leaders come to recognize that *interdependence* in itself demands the abandonment of the politics of blocs, the sacrifice of all forms of economic, military or political imperialism, and the transformation of mutual distrust into *collaboration.* This is precisely the *act proper* to solidarity among individuals and nations.

The motto of the pontificate of my esteemed predecessor Pius XII was Opus iustitiae pax, peace as the fruit of justice. Today one could say, with the same exactness and the same power of biblical inspiration (cf. Is 32:17; Jas 3:18): Opus solidaritatis pax, peace as the fruit of solidarity.

The goal of peace, so desired by everyone, will certainly be achieved through the putting into effect of social and international justice, but also through the practice of the virtues which favor togetherness, and which teach us to live in unity, so as to build in unity, by giving and receiving, a new society and a better world.

...

42. Today more than in the past, the Church's social doctrine must be open to an *international outlook*, in line with the Second Vatican Council, the most recent Encyclicals, and particularly in line with the Encyclical which we are commemorating. It will not be superfluous therefore to reexamine and further clarify in this light the characteristic themes and guidelines dealt with by the Magisterium in recent years.

Here I would like to indicate one of them: the *option or love of preference* for the poor. This is an option, or a *special form* of primacy in the exercise of Christian charity, to which the whole tradition of the Church bears witness. It affects the life of each Christian inasmuch as he or she seeks to imitate the life of Christ, but it applies equally to our *social responsibilities* and hence to our manner of living, and to the logical decisions to be made concerning the ownership and use of goods.

Today, furthermore, given the worldwide dimension which the social question has assumed, this love of the preference for the poor, and the decisions which it inspires in us, cannot but embrace the immense multitudes of the hungry, the needy, the homeless, those

99

without medical care and, above all, those without hope of a better future. It is impossible not to take account of the existence of these realities. To ignore them would mean becoming like the "rich man" who pretended not to know the beggar Lazarus lying at his gate (cf. Lk 16:19-31). ...

43. The motivating concern for the poor — who are, in the very meaningful term, "the Lord's poor" — must be translated at all levels into concrete actions, until it decisively attains a series of necessary reforms. Each local situation will show what reforms are most urgent and how they can be achieved. But those demanded by the situation of international imbalance, as already described, must not be forgotten.

In this respect I wish to mention specifically: the *reform of the international trade system*, which is mortgaged to protectionism and increasing bilateralism; the *reform of the world monetary and financial system*, today recognized as inadequate; the *question of technological exchanges* and their proper use; the *need* for a *review of the structure of the existing International Organizations*, in the framework of an international juridical order.

The *international trade system* today frequently discriminates against the products of the young industries of the developing countries and discourages the producers of raw materials. There exists, too, a kind of *international division of labor*, whereby the low-cost products of certain countries which lack effective labor laws or which are too weak to apply them are sold in other parts of the world at considerable profit for the companies engaged in this form of production, which knows no frontiers.

The *world monetary and financial system* is marked by an excessive fluctuation of exchange rates and interest rates, to the detriment of the balance of payments and the debt situation of the poorer countries.

Forms of technology and their transfer constitute today one of the major problems of international exchange and of the grave damage deriving therefrom. There are quite frequent cases of developing countries being denied needed forms of technology or sent useless ones.

In the opinion of many, the *International Organizations* seem to be at a stage of their existence when their operating methods, operating costs and effectiveness need careful review and possible correction. Obviously, such a delicate process cannot be put into effect without the collaboration of all. This presupposes the overcoming of political rivalries and the renouncing of all desire to manipulate these Organizations, which exist solely for the *common good*.

...

44. **Development demands above all a spirit of initiative on the part of the countries which need it.** Each of them must act in accordance with its own responsibilities, *not expecting everything* from the more favored countries, and acting in collaboration with

others in the same situation. Each must discover and use to the best advantage its *own area of freedom*. Each must make itself capable of initiatives responding to its own needs as a society. Each must likewise realize its true needs as well as the rights and duties which oblige it to respond to them. The development of peoples begins and is most appropriately accomplished in the dedication of each people to its own development, in collaboration with others.

...

In order to take this path, *the nations themselves* will have to identify their own *priorities* and clearly recognize their own needs, according to the particular conditions of their people, their geographical settling and their cultural traditions.

...

45. ... An essential condition for global *solidarity* is autonomy and free self-determination, also within associations such as those indicated. But at the same time solidarity demands a readiness to accept the sacrifices necessary for the good of the whole world community.

46. Peoples and individuals aspire to be free: their search for full development signals their desire to overcome the many obstacles preventing them from enjoying a "more human life."

Recently, in the period following the publication of the Encyclical Populorum Progressio, a new way of confronting the problems of poverty and underdevelopment has spread in some areas of the world, especially in Latin America. This approach makes *liberation* the fundamental category and the first principle of action. The positive values, as well as the deviations and risks of deviation, which are damaging to the faith and are connected with this form of theological reflection and method, have been appropriately pointed out by the Church's Magisterium.

It is fitting to add that the aspiration to freedom from all forms of slavery affecting the individual and society is something *noble* and *legitimate*. This in fact is the purpose of development, or rather liberation and development, taking into account the intimate connection between the two.

Development which is merely economic is incapable of setting man free; on the contrary, it will end by enslaving him further. Development that does not include the *cultural, transcendent and religious dimensions* of man and society, to the extent that it does not recognize the existence of such dimensions and does not endeavor to direct its goals and priorities towards the same, is *even less* conducive to authentic liberation. Human beings are totally free only when they are completely *themselves*, in the fullness of their rights and duties. The same can be said about society as a whole.

Excerpt from "Justitia in Mundo"

World Synod of Bishops, Second General Assembly, 30 November 1971

> 71. (8) In order that the right to development may be fulfilled by action:
> (a) people should not be hindered from attaining development in accordance with their own culture;
> (b) through mutual cooperation, all peoples should be able to become the principal architects of their own economic and social development;
> (c) every people, as active and responsible members of human society, should be able to cooperate for the attainment of the common good on an equal footing with other peoples.

REFERENCES

ACB (American Catholic Bishops). 1984. Pastoral letter: economic justice for all. Origins: National Catholic Documentary Service, 14(1884), 338–383.

ACOUN (Anglican Community Office at the United Nations). 1996. A Christian response to the international debt crisis. Conference programme and recommendations of the Round Table Conference, May 16–17, 1996. ACOUN, New York, NY, USA. 13 pp.

Baum, G. 1998. Sciences sociales et option pour les pauvres. Relations, Mar, pp. 46–49.

Bellah, R. 1970. Beyond belief. Harper and Row, New York, NY, USA. 298 pp.

Berger, P. 1966. The sacred canopy: elements of a sociological theory of religion. Doubleday, Garden City, NY, USA. 230 pp.

Drache, D. 1995. Celebrating Innis: the man, the legacy, our future. In D. Drache, ed., Harold Innis: staples, markets and cultural change. McGill–Queen's University Press, Montréal, PQ, Canada. pp. xiii–liii.

ECA (Economic Commission for Africa). 1989. African alternative framework to structural adjustment programmes for socio-economic recovery and transformation. ECA, Addis Ababa. UN Ref. No. E/ECA/CM.15/6/Rev.3.

Fabella, V. 1997. Ecumenical Association of Third World Theologians (EATWOT). In Dictionary of mission. Orbis Books, Maryknoll, NY, USA. pp. 117–120.

George, S. 1976. How the other half dies: the real reasons for world hunger. Penguin Books, New York, NY, USA. 352 pp.

Goulet, D. 1971. The cruel choice: a new concept in the theory of development. Athenaeum, New York, NY, USA. 362 pp.

Gutierrez, G. 1973. A theology of liberation. Orbis Books, Maryknoll, NY, USA. 323 pp.

Habermas, J. 1971 [1968]. Knowledge and human interest. Beacon Press, Boston, MA, USA. 256 pp.

Hargreaves, J. 1975. Sport, power and culture. St Martin's Press, New York, NY, USA. 258 pp.

John Paul II. 1987. Sollicitudo rei socialis. Libreria Editrice Vaticana, Vatican City, Italy. 102 pp.

LAB (Latin American Bishops). 1968. Medellin documents: justice, peace, family and demography, poverty of the Church. *In* Gremillion, J., presenter, The gospel of peace and justice. Orbis Books, Maryknoll, NY, USA. pp. 445–476.

Lebret, L.-J. 1959. Pour une civilisation solidaire. Les Éditions Ouvrières, Paris, France. 141 pp.

Lopez, D. 1995. Curators of Buddha: the study of Buddhisms under colonialism. University of Chicago Press, Chicago, IL, USA. 298 pp.

Malley, F. 1968. Le Père Lebret : l'économie au service des hommes. Les Éditions du Cerf, Paris, France. 254 pp.

Mannheim, K. 1936 [1928]. Ideology and utopia. Harcourt, Brace and Co., New York, NY, USA. 319 pp.

Martin, H.-P.; Schumann, H. 1997. The global trap: globalization and the assault on democracy and prosperity. Black Rose, Montréal, PQ, Canada. 269 pp.

Mihevc, J. n.d. The market tells them so: the World Bank and economic fundamentalism in Africa. Zed Books, London, UK. 320 pp.

O'Brien, D.; Shannon, T., ed. 1992. Catholic social thought: the documentary heritage. Orbis Books, Maryknoll, NY, USA. 668 pp.

Orbis Books. 1997. Dictionary of mission. Orbis Books, Maryknoll, NY, USA. 518 pp.

Paul VI. 1967. Populorum progressio: on the development of peoples. *In* Gremillion, J., presenter, The gospel of peace and justice. Orbis Books, Maryknoll, NY, USA. pp. 387–415. Internet: listserv.american.edu/catholic/church/papal/paul.vi/p6popp.txt

Rostow, W.W. 1960. The stages of economic growth: a non-communist manifesto. University Press, Cambridge, UK. 178 pp.

Said, E. 1978. Orientalism. Pantheon Books, New York, NY, USA. 368 pp.

SBSGA (Synod of Bishops, Second General Assembly). 1971. Justitia in mundo: justice in the world. *In* Gremillion, J., presenter, The gospel of peace and justice. Orbis Books, Maryknoll, NY, USA. pp. 513–529.

Scheler, M. 1980 [1924]. Problems of the sociology of knowledge. Routledge and Kegan Paul, London, UK. 239 pp.

Serageldin, I.; Barrett, R., ed. 1996. Ethics and spiritual values: promoting environmentally sustainable development. International Bank for Reconstruction and Development–World Bank, Washington, DC, USA. Environmentally Sustainable Development Proceedings Series, No. 12. 54 pp.

United Nations. 1995. Our global neighborhood. Oxford University Press, New York, NY, USA. 410 pp.

Wolfensohn, J. 1996. New partnerships. *In* Serageldin, I.; Barrett, R., ed., Ethics and spiritual values: promoting environmentally sustainable development. International Bank for Reconstruction and Development–World Bank, Washington, DC, USA. Environmentally Sustainable Development Proceedings Series, No. 12. p. 1.

CHAPTER 3

Rediscovering the Resources of Religion

Azizan Baharuddin

INTRODUCTION

The era of independence in the South has been characterized by decades of "development." Lessons learned, especially in recent years, make it timely for the developing world to take stock of its accomplishments and mistakes. Costs of advances in science and technology (S&T) are steadily mounting, and the ideals of scientific progress are not without their flaws (Sardar 1988). The dramatic and lopsided impact of rapid change, together with the disruptions of traditional values, requires the South to reevaluate the meaning of "progress." Technology, research processes, and entire patterns of economic structuring have been transplanted and adopted from the West. The intelligentsia of the South is increasingly realizing that it has derived its definition of modernity from values implicit in S&T and that these are largely products of one civilization's worldview and historical experience. Many are beginning to see that for true development to occur, material progress must be accompanied by, and pursued in accordance with, intangible, yet essential, human and moral values (Sardar 1988).

As in other disciplines, the discourse on development has been highly compartmentalized. This results from a reductionistic frame of mind that prevents the individual from transcending narrow, often jealously guarded, boundaries of thought or academic territories and achieving comprehensive solutions. Compartmentalization characterizes much of the modern approach to the various dimensions of life (Capra 1985); it is common to consider human activities, such as commerce, education, art, politics, and religion, as separate spheres. The result is that human beings are not thinking and perceiving, and thereby acting and living, in holistic or healthy ways. The dichotomy between scientific knowledge and religious values has also separated development from religion and spirituality. Within the development field itself, the dichotomy between theory and practice has put "people-centred" development — loudly touted of late — in danger of becoming a cliché (UNDP 1997).

One might suggest that the mind-set of this compartmentalizing and reductionistic approach to living contributes to the problems multiplying all over the world.[1] To ensure human progress, and perhaps even survival, we must integrate the various spheres of knowledge and endeavour. Intellectual investigation must be joined with a range of discourses articulating human meaning; development, then, would be the product of both science and values. Religion is a fundamental source of ancient wisdom and values; its insights, tested over generations, can galvanize large numbers of people to act on the promptings of their highest ideals and from the centre of their sense of self and community.

But from which perspective should one reflect and speak on the interrelated themes of science, religion, and development (SRD) — from that of an academician, politician, scientist, or theologian? Each viewpoint has valuable contributions to make but can only speak in a certain context and in limited ways about particular aspects of development. No one perspective presents the entire picture. Thus, despite our best intentions, as soon as we attempt to enter into the question of how the fields of SRD should be related, we immediately encounter the problem of the compartmentalization of knowledge. Among the resulting set of problems, and not the least of them, is the challenge of convincing people from various sectors to work toward a common goal; to this should be added the issue of dissimilar meanings assigned by various parties to the same concepts. To clarify my understanding of these concepts, I will start by making some general observations about SRD; in these observations, I will identify various assumptions and questions that I feel need to be addressed. I hope to show that experts working in any of the three areas must not only transcend their own boundaries to incorporate concepts and questions from the other components of the SRD triangulation but also reexamine old assumptions and try to see the precepts of their respective fields as others do. It is perhaps not too impertinent to

106

[1] For example, Fritjof Capra (1985, pp. 118–119) described how the influence of the Cartesian paradigm on medical thought resulted in the "biomedical model," in which the human body is conceptualized as a machine that can be analyzed in terms of its parts: "By concentrating on smaller and smaller fragments of the body, modern medicine often loses sight of the patient as a human being, and by reducing health to mechanical functioning, it is no longer able to deal with the phenomenon of healing."

suggest that it is especially important for agents of development, particularly governments and policymakers, to integrate elements of the
relevant fields into their thinking.

One must seriously ask whether the sharp separation of religion
from science and development is the result of weakness and lack of
clarity in efforts to apply religious awareness to real life issues. For
example, mosques used to be centres of learning and venues for the
discussion of politics and trade; today, they often serve only for daily
obligatory prayers, for which the congregational numbers are ever
dwindling. Several authors and commentators have indicated that the
coming millennium will see a kind of religious revival. But as John
Naisbitt and Patricia Aburdene (1990) pointed out in their book, *Megatrends* 2000, religiosity will not be the same as before. Individuals will
want to be in control of their own spirituality, instead of depending on
persons traditionally vested with religious authority. It is increasingly
common that individuals desire to know the transcendent directly and
to experience its reality personally. It is not difficult to see the connection between this orientation and another trend observed by Naisbitt
and Aburdene: the ascendancy of the individual. In my initial remarks,
I will be touching briefly on the need for a quiet but concrete revival-
ism within the institutions of religion so that the traditional authorities
learn to be more democratic in their treatment of their *ummah* (or flock).

> The Qur' an says that God deliberately created human beings
> into different races and tribes so that they might
> get to know one another.
> (Q 10:99 and Q 13:18, 29)

My paper begins with general comments on science, religion, and
development, followed by a brief discussion of Islam and Islamic metaphysics. I will attempt to tell my own story of how religion became
something real to me, despite my early training in science, with its
attendant sceptical and agnostic outlook. One of my main concerns will
be to share the perspective of a practicing believer. I want to persuade
the secular humanist and nonbeliever to consider the rationality of my
point of view, just as I am interested in, and try to empathize with, the
reasons for the unbeliever's agnosticism. I feel that all the proponents of
a more just, humane form of development have a great need for genuine,
mutual empathy and acceptance. The fact of the matter is — and herein
lies the difficulty — we exist in a sea of cultural, philosophical, and religious plurality; indeed, the need for nonviolent modes of discourse, in
which our differences contribute to strength rather than fostering dis-
sension, is extremely urgent.

It is important for nonbelievers to see how and why believers think
as they do, if we are to open the door for religion to contribute to

107

deliberations on science and development. The "reasons for religion" must appeal to secular-humanist scientists and development practitioners. Many scientists, scholars, and philosophers — including A.N. Whitehead (1985 [1925]) and Bertrand Russell (1976) — have spoken of the need for convergence. For such a convergence to take place, religion has to speak in a "language" that is intelligible to the secular humanist, including language derived from *natural theology* (the understanding of religious beliefs in terms of empirical scientific discourse) and *the theology of nature* (the understanding of religion by the use of scientific facts obtained from nature). I have come to believe strongly that science and religion are complementary ways of looking at reality; we may often ascertain the real value of religious understanding and increase its impact by coupling it with the way science understands actual situations in life. I would like to share with others what the endeavour to understand the complementarity between religious understandings and scientific findings might mean in terms of a new cosmology.

In the section entitled "Islam," I will turn my attention to a brief explanation of what Islam can bring to SRD discourse and the steps already taken in this direction. From the outset, I reject any claims to comprehensiveness; suffice it to say that this is a new area of discourse, even though researchers have called for the "Islamization of knowledge," especially science, since the early 1980s (see al-Faruqi and al-Faruqi 1986). Even earlier, in the 1960s, scholars such as S.H. Nasr (1968) began to consider the ramifications of the loss of spirituality in modern human beings.

In the past few decades, the Muslim world has been steadily reawakening to an S&T that thrived during the 8th to 11th centuries and was based on the worldview and ethics of Islam, and this has been in no small measure a result of exposure to Western thinkers and modes of life. People in the Muslim world are realizing that the significance of this legacy lies not merely in the recovery of the technological answers of the past but also in the fact that it offers guidelines on how to incorporate values into current human efforts toward progress and development. Muslims, especially Muslim scientists, are realizing that values shared by scientists and nonscientists must determine the direction, control, and purpose of S&T, as it is clear that no amount of technical hardware can, of and by itself, resolve dilemmas that require moral choice.

Muslim writers and scholars are recognizing that development is not a fixed package to be received in its entirety; they can draw on their own distinctive perspectives and experience in history to shape moral and ethical values to help guide the course of development. For example, publications such as *The Touch of Midas: Science, Values and the Environment in Islam and the West* (Sardar 1988) include articles on issues related to science, values, and development in Islam. Muslim intellectuals are also entering into dialogue with others, earnestly trying to alter the perceptions of those who see the awakening of Islamic consciousness as nothing more than fundamentalist reaction and isolation. In the words of a Muslim political leader, Muslims genuinely feel that

> if they are to control their destiny in the future, then they must find a way of expressing their moral being, according to their *ethos* whilst at the same time still being able to be interdependent and interconnected with others as they live in one world with others and face dilemmas and problems that understand no boundaries.
>
> Sardar (1988, p. iv)

Muslims are acknowledging that bringing a diversity of viewpoints to the debate can help everyone discern the essentials, allowing the most basic and intransigent problems to be seen in a fresh light.

109

SCIENCE

It is often unclear to the creators of science (and even more so to the consumers of S&T) that the impact of science is closely related to the way one thinks about and approaches the world; worldviews are fundamentally linked to scientific research and the application of science. "Science" as the method of obtaining data from nature through empirical observation may be neutral, but its purpose, direction, and application are value laden. Two philosophies implicit in much of today's "science" are the following:

❦ *Scientism* — the hegemony of the modern scientific worldview and modes of knowledge;[2] and

❦ *Reductionism* — the principle that complex entities and systems can be fully understood in terms of their isolated parts.

Scientism and reductionism are also linked to a mechanical picture of the world. Newton based his work on the notion of a mechanistic universe, set in motion by a "clockmaker" God, who then left it to run on its own via the operation of fixed laws instituted into the body of the universe.[3] Given the incorporation of scientism and reductionism into

---

[2] Also, it represents the belief that the methods used in studying natural sciences should be employed in investigating all aspects of human behaviour and conditions, for example, in philosophy and the social sciences.

[3] This encouraged deism, or a belief in the existence of God that is based on reason rather than on revelation. Deism is still widely prevalent today and, to my mind, is one of the reasons behind religion's loss of relevance, for it suggests that God is no longer involved in the world (Brooke 1979). For a fuller treatment of this issue, see Lindberg (1986).

modern life, it should not be surprising that these philosophies also underlie the secular worldview. Willis Harman noted that this picture of the universe and the approaches it gives rise to have been undeniably useful:

> The scientific view has been, in its way, outstandingly successful — yielding both technological and predictive successes — and hence has gained tremendous prestige. It has been broadly accepted as the nearest we can come to a "true" picture of knowledge. But it is nonetheless also true that the cosmos described by modern science is devoid of meaning and largely lacks relationship to the profound spiritual insight of thousands of years of human experience.
>
> Harman (1988, p. 13)

> Few would gainsay the accomplishments of reductionistic science. For the purpose toward which it evolved — prediction, manipulation and control of the physical environment — it is superb. The issue is whether it needs to be complemented by another kind of science that can deal more adequately with wholes, with living organisms, and particularly with human consciousness.
>
> Harman (1988, p. 16)

The physicist David Bohm supports this view and believes that one's way of thinking of the totality, that is, one's general worldview, is crucial to the overall operation of the mind itself. If we think of the totality as comprising independent fragments, then that is how our minds will tend to operate, and the products of our minds will tend to reflect this assumption. If, however, we can see everything included in a coherent and harmonious whole, then our minds will tend to move in a similar way (Bohm 1981). Bohm disagreed with scientists who use science as a mechanism simply to predict and control phenomena. As Bertrand Russell explained, this is the attitude of those who become interested in science only insofar as it provides power, first to control nature and then other human beings (Russell 1976).

Scientism inappropriately raises science and its methods to the status of unquestionable truth, a hegemony that seems to have imposed itself on development strategy and to have helped to create its current inadequacies. Developmentalism — the belief that economic and even human progress as a whole depends on an expanding consumer society — derives from scientism. Developmentalism is the motivating force behind the traditional model of development. It is "expressed in such words as industrialisation, modernisation, consumerism, growth, etc., and measured by monetary aggregates. Developmentalism defines the principal social objectives of all countries as consumption and accumulation" (Ekins 1992, pp. 204–205).

It is impossible to create a well-working society on the basis of scientism, reductionism, and ultimately developmentalism — knowledge bases that are "fundamentally inadequate, seriously incomplete, and mistaken in basic assumptions" (Harman 1988, p. 20). Many sectors of society have come, or are coming, to the conclusion that the global dilemmas we face stem from our modern picture of reality. Even at the practical level, it can be shown that science itself is demanding a new, holistic worldview, because the fragmentary view is fundamentally flawed and cannot adequately explain the complicated web of interconnections among, for example, biology, physics, ecology, medicine, and agriculture as manifested in the systemic problems our globe faces today (Capra 1985).

We have to acquire a holistic, ecological worldview, and from this reorientation will flow the realignment of our economic and development concepts. But the challenge is to find the means to achieve this. Scientist–philosophers, such as David Bohm, Fritjof Capra, and Muhammad Iqbal, have pointed out that one way of articulating the proper worldview is to consider a philosophy of nature or cosmology that combines the religious and scientific perspectives on the universe.

111

DEVELOPMENT

In this section, I briefly examine a few issues I feel are crucial to the meaning of development. Writing from the perspective of their own countries and experiences, figures like Aung San Suu Kyi (Nobel Peace Prize laureate and head of the Burmese prodemocracy movement) have highlighted the close interdependence of peace and development. Her concerns centre around the uncertainty about the extent to which democracy is indispensable for peace and therefore essential to human development (Aung San Suu Kyi 1997).

The concept of indigenousness, or indigenous culture, is frequently raised in discussions of democracy, and outsiders sometimes give it too much credence. Culture indisputably provides fundamental guidance and security, yet there is also ample evidence that some societies use "culture" as a pretext to resist calls for human rights and democracy. Culture is normally defined as dynamic and flexible, but when it is bent on serving narrow interests it becomes static and rigid: exclusivity comes to the fore and culture assumes coercive overtones; national culture can even become a bizarre graft of selected historical facts and social norms, intended to justify the policies of those in power, who insist on seeing development in the outmoded sense of simple economic growth (Aung San Suu Kyi 1997). Aung San Suu Kyi argued that it is not unknown for some governments to use the argument that democracy is a Western concept, unacceptable in the context of indigenous values, or that democratic rights must be pushed aside for the sake of economic development.[4] What use is development in the materialistic sense if, in the end, basic liberties have to be sacrificed at its altar?

Democracy and people's empowerment must become an integral component of any concept or strategy of development. Although every democracy needs to acquire a character of its own, it is imperative that, in each, people be sufficiently and truly empowered. National governments, Aung San Suu Kyi said, urgently need to find new ways to empower their people. Otherwise, the people's mounting aspirations may clash with those of the ruling elite. The results of this clash may ultimately serve as a setback to development (Aung San Suu Kyi 1997). In Asia, it is widely believed that rapid economic transformation is most likely to succeed in a context of peace, political stability, and public order, rather than that of upheavals and turbulence. However, a real danger is that this insight will be taken to mean that these ideals are not valuable ends in themselves but are desirable only for facilitating economic transformation. This is an example of how economic hegemony can corrupt even the most basic requirements of civil life.

In many countries of the South, the record of development has been unsatisfactory, and this has led to the search for the fuller meaning of the term. Francis Perroux (1983), in his book *A New Concept of Development: Basic Tenets*, stated that if development is taken to mean a growth in awareness, intellectual capacity, personal development, and the freedom to fulfill one's potential in accordance with one's own values, then not only has development not taken place but it has not even been clearly perceived (Aung San Suu Kyi 1997). Even though international economists and administrators, including the United Nations Development Programme itself, are focusing on people's participation, many developing countries still see the market economy as the primary way to make material progress. In such countries economic measures are deemed to be all that is needed to resolve problems. Historical developments suggest that when economics is regarded as the most important ingredient in a society's life, human worth will gradually also be gauged by nothing more than a person's "effectiveness as an economic tool" (Aung San Suu Kyi 1997, p. 2). Surely this is contrary to the idea that economic structures, as well as social and political institutions, should be the servants of humans rather than having humans serve their ideologies (Aung San Suu Kyi 1997). In indigenous societies, for example, many have lamented the breakdown of the old familiar and cohesive

---

[4] We also need to consider who has the power and how much power any sector should have to determine the norms and definitions ultimately governing our lives. Bertrand Russell (1976) remarked that when those in charge can even make the people say that the sun is cold (because those who said otherwise would be liquidated), one wonders if Zeus could have done any better! Again, in such societies, I hope that religion can play the dual role of empowering the weak — for example, the negotiator and activist roles played by some Christian groups in the Philippines — and making secular political leaders more understanding and respectful of religious–spiritual sanctions.

social fabric; the decline in the spirit of voluntarism, courtesy, and manners; and the rise in divorce rates, child abuse, baby-dumping, incest, rape, and disrespect for elders and the infirm. And yet, these manifestations of dissatisfaction, alienation, and greed only reflect changes in social norms occurring in rapidly developing countries as people abandon — often without satisfactory alternatives — traditional ways of life and adopt externally generated values and goals without examining them carefully (Jeyaraj 1997a, b).

Leading development proponents must convince political leaders in the South of the need for a paradigm shift, away from the economically oriented worldview currently dominant. Not surprisingly, many leaders are unable to understand the need for this change: they have been schooled in the old mechanistic–reductionistic way of thinking. They find the need for change difficult to accept, let alone to act on. Given this resistance, we may have to have more experts like Herman Daly (1996) speak out; we require contributions from thinkers with economic–scientific insights that are synthesized with religious values into consistent and (if need be, controversial) well-thought-out theses (Ryan 1998). The need is acute, for even among leaders aware of the inadequacy of the materialist–scientific model there are many who fear the political consequences of making political and social decisions relating to, for example, control of natural resources or the equitable distribution of wealth and income (Ryan 1998).

Under these circumstances, it is in everyone's interest to reexamine the definitions of culture and development so that they are not used to thwart basic democratic institutions, basic rights, and the fulfillment of basic needs. In countries where religion is a strong actor in civil society (for example, Buddhism in Thailand, Christianity in the Philippines, and Islam in Malaysia), religious leaders and institutions should be brought into the efforts to deal with this task to lend it credibility among the people and within the government and to help ensure its success.

113

RELIGION

In my opinion, despite the growing interest in personal spirituality, religion has for a long time suffered from a gradual decay in its influence.[5] A.N. Whitehead observed that religion in Western civilization tends to degenerate into "a decent formula wherewith to embellish a

---

[5] Many Muslims, for example, feel that it is no longer sufficient that the *imams* or *ulama* tell them what the Qur'an or God says. They want to read and, what is more important, see the meaning of scripture for themselves. "Meaning" entails seeing the relevance of the Qur'anic teachings in everyday experience — business, family and social situations, the environment, and politics. Having seen this relevance, people would then automatically "live religion out," and it would be integrated into systems such as science and development.

comfortable life" (1985 [1925], p. 233). I want to examine two reasons for this decline: the inability of religion to deal with social and, in particular, scientific change; and the perception that the symbols and roles assigned to religion are psychologically unsatisfying.

RELIGION AND CHANGE

Like science, religion must be willing to respond to new data or changes in human life. Religious ideas and interpretations can never be static (Whitehead 1985 [1925]). No generation can merely reproduce the interpretations of its ancestors; no society can live on borrowed faith. Religious ideas, A.N. Whitehead suggested, can avoid fading away into meaninglessness or outdated formulas if they are transformed by the urge of critical reason, by the vivid evidence of universal experiences of the emotions, and by the sureness of empirical — that is, scientific — perception.

> When it is said to them: "Follow what Allah hath revealed."
> They say, "Nay! We shall follow the ways of our fathers."
> What! Even though their fathers were void of wisdom and guidance?
>
> (Q 2:170)

I take care to point out that neither I nor any of the scholars cited here are suggesting that revelation be changed to adapt to new human knowledge. The essential message, or *shariah*,[6] of Islam does not change; what needs to be modified periodically, even as it was done in the past, is the **human interpretation** (the *fiqh*, or jurisprudence) of the *shariah*. This tradition of *tajdid* (or renewal) goes back to the earliest periods of Islam (Iqbal 1930). But the process is deemed to have stopped in the 12th or 13th century with the announcement of the closure of the doors of *ijtihad* (the independent analysis and interpretation of Islamic law in the face of new situations).

The longstanding and ongoing debate between science and religion illustrates the need for religion to be open to change. Whitehead pointed out that on each opportunity for convergence with scientific and rational mind-sets, religious thinkers have been unprepared. With each challenge from science, principles once deemed vital were, after much stress and conflict, modified or otherwise interpreted by religions. The result of a succession of such undignified retreats has been a general loss

114

---

[6] The laws set out by God. But *law* is too rigid a term to explain the nature of the *shariah*. Epistemologically, it means "the way," which I think does better justice to the concept. In connection with it, then, Muslims have derived "ways" or "laws" for doing things. The word *law* in Arabic is *hakm*, or "good," that is, all the "things," "ways," and "laws" that God has prescribed for humans are supposed to be of maximum "good" for them because those laws correspond best to the natural state of human beings (*fitrah*). Logically, who knows creation better than the Creator?

of the intellectual credibility of religious thinkers (Whitehead 1985 [1925]). If one looks into the history of Western societies in the 16th and 17th centuries, for example, one finds that the decreasing influence of religion is not the result of deficiencies in spiritual statements about reality but of the unwillingness of religious leaders and interpreters "to disengage their spiritual message from associations with particular imageries" (Whitehead 1985 [1925], p. 233). We can take, for instance, the Roman Catholic Church's rejection for 200 years of Nicolaus Copernicus's heliocentric (sun-centred) model of the universe in favour of a geocentric (Earth-centred) one. But such a position by religious authority is hardly unique. In the Islamic world, one can see a similar struggle with science in the 18th to 21th centuries.

Thinkers suggesting ways to reconcile science and religion have, likewise, encountered objections from religious authorities: the writings of the social reformists and theologian–philosophers Sayyid Ahmad Khan (1817–98), Jamal al-Din al-Afghani (1838–97), and Muhammad Iqbal (1878–1938) met with resistance from traditional religious teachers and clerics who were unprepared to deal with the new challenges posed by the rapidly secularizing trends of modern science and colonization. Muhammad Iqbal, a poet–philosopher, never questioned the status of scripture. Instead, based on the new discoveries in science at the turn of the century and their ensuing *Weltanschauung,* Iqbal argued that religious experience is also empirical and that a rational account of it could be given. His theological and intellectual endeavours to bring science and religion into closer alignment had two objectives: to provide a new theology for the increasingly Westernized, materially and scientifically oriented Muslim of the 20th century; and to naturalize what had been considered supernatural, by arguing that religious experience is comprehensible in terms of a religious psychology accessible to all. He was also motivated by the lack of development and the political apathy of his people. The closed doors of *ijtihad* never restricted his endeavours because he thought and acted the esoteric alongside the exoteric dimensions of religion.

In reconstructing Islamic religious thought, Iqbal's efforts were not unprecedented in the history of Islam. Iqbal's own predecessor in this process of explaining religion in terms of reason and science was the renowned Sufi Shah Wali Allah (d. 1762), who visualized scientific knowledge as emanating in the form of a light reflected in the West (Halepota 1974). In his *Hujjat al-Balighah* (Matured Arguments), Wali Allah wrote "then my lord influenced me with the idea that the time has nearly arrived when the laws concerning life by the *shariah* could be given exposition via the extensive and commodious garb of reasoning and scientific method" (Halepota 1974, p. 228). In other words, modern (even secular[7]) and scientific knowledge each had a role in the

---

[7] In Islam the term *secular* actually does not exist, as knowledge is always understood as the unity of both the worldly and the religious.

interpretation of Islam. Therefore, long before Iqbal and others of his generation, Wali Allah had adopted a positive attitude toward scientific knowledge. In his lecture on freedom and immortality, Iqbal (1930, p. 97) reiterated the same message, saying that "the only course open to us is to approach modern knowledge with a respectable but independent attitude and to appreciate the teachings of Islam in the light of that knowledge, even though we may be led to differ from those who had gone before us."

"Religion today requires," Iqbal said, "a method physiologically less violent and more suited to a coherent type of mind. In the absence of such a method the demand for a scientific form of religious knowledge is only natural" (Iqbal 1930, p. v). Like theologian–scientists of other faiths, Iqbal thought that the scientific and religious processes are in a sense parallel but different methods for moving toward the final aim of reaching "the most real." Through science, we try to understand the external behaviour of reality, whereas through religion we try to understand its inner nature. Both are descriptions of the same reality, with the difference being that in the scientific process the self is excluded as much as possible, whereas in the religious experience the self is fundamentally integrated into the process. For Iqbal, it was important that, just as Hume had helped to objectify science, so too the student of mystical or religious experience can help to render an objective account of it by studying and describing the common elements of such experience.[8]

In the West, Whitehead pointed out that the process of change in science could offer religion valuable models for dealing with change. When Einstein introduced theories that modified our entire perception of the universe, for example, it was considered another step in scientific insight rather than an invalidation of science, even though it proved that previous theories were inadequate (Whitehead 1985 [1925]). Whitehead felt that religion could learn from science and face change in a similar spirit. He emphatically insisted (and Muslim scholars would support him here) that if religion is a sound expression of truth, the modification of meanings attributed to statements of belief as they come into contact with scientific facts can only benefit religion; such changes serve to show ever more clearly the essence of those teachings. As science advances so too can interpretations of religious revelation become deeper and more multilayered (Whitehead 1985 [1925]).[9] Thus, the evolution

[8] We can say that no two individuals experience spirituality or the presence and working of God in exactly the same way, but these experiences share a number of commonalities that can be documented and verified by others. Also, in Islam, inner spiritual experience is preceded and accompanied by psychological, physical, and moral purification; these processes are observed by all Muslims and, as such, are also points at which the spiritual experience can be studied "objectively."

[9] The exercise described here is an example of *natural theology* and *theology of nature*. In the Qur'an, for instance, a verse describes the development of the embryo from the point of fertilization to the time of birth. A 20th-century Muslim would understand this verse much more clearly than a 7th- or 8th-century Muslim, because of the confirmation and explanation of the processes through science (see also Baharuddin 1994).

of religious thought requires a disengagement of its foundational ideas from what Muslim writers call accretions, which have crept into doctrine by virtue of how individuals in a particular society at a particular time see the world. This process allows religion to draw from, and yet change along with, expanding human science. The principles of religion are eternal, but the expression of those principles requires a growing and continuous development, that is, a focusing, sharpening, and deepening of meanings.

EXPERIENTIAL PROCESSES IN RELIGION

The fading interest in religion presents another challenge, that of reconsidering the symbols and the roles assigned to religion. Consider the following, for example:

117

&- Religion has exploited the fear of an all-powerful, arbitrary tyrant who is behind the unknown forces of nature. Such appeals to human fears and insecurities are losing their power because science has taught people to analyze catastrophes critically in terms of cause and effect (Whitehead 1985 [1925]).

&- Some advocate the view that religion is valuable for ordering human life and society; this is what Goulet (1992) might call the instrumental use of religion. Religion functions as a guide to right conduct, but without true engagement with principles its rules can become hollow social conventions. Conduct is and should be a natural by-product of religion, but it is not the main point of it. Many religious teachers have spoken against the reduction of religion to a mere sanction for rules of conduct. The Qur'an denounces those who are externally pious but internally possess no heart or compassion for their fellow human beings.

What is needed is to accept the fuller meaning of religion, one that charts out the human relationship not only to the cosmos but also, and more importantly, to transcendent being. This is the relationship emphasized in Sufism (the Islamic mystical tradition), although it is not easy to explain. Iqbal was emphatic that humans should try to inquire into this relationship, saying "we have to find out an effective method of inquiry into the nature and significance of this extraordinary experience" (Iqbal 1930, p. 183). Psychology he found unsatisfactory because, instead of giving real insight into the essential nature of religion and its meaning, it provides a plethora of new theories and misunderstands the nature of religion as revealed in its higher manifestations. On the whole, the implication of these theories is that

religion does not relate the human ego to any objective reality beyond itself. [The psychological] view only saw religion as a kind of device calculated to build barriers of ethical nature around

human society in order to protect the social fabric against the otherwise unresistable instincts of the ego.

Baharuddin (1989, p. 328)

To Iqbal, the psychological approach misses the whole point of
higher religion because the ultimate purpose of religious life is to steer
individuals in directions far more important to their fulfillment than
can be dictated by reference solely to the moral health of the social fabric of their present environment, although one must recognize that the
health of the social fabric plays an undeniably important role in such
fulfillment. Higher religious experience offers the self contact with the
source of life, or God. Through this contact, the ego has the opportunity and capacity for true freedom and change; this contact transforms
the human being into a stronger and more creative person who has a
new capacity to effect change in oneself and others. Iqbal was certain
(Baharuddin 1989, p. 328) that the ultimate human religious experience "is the revelation of a new life process, original, spontaneous," and
he felt that the moment the individual "reaches this revelation he recog-
nises it as the ultimate root of his being without hesitation." Iqbal is at
pains to convince his audience that such an experience has nothing
mysterious about it; it is a perfectly natural phenomenon, possessing
cognitive value for the recipient, as well as biological significance to the
self.

Bergson (1985 [1903], p. 83) said, "even though the certitude of
mystical experience cannot be simply converted into philosophical wisdom, the mystics have changed the philosophical perspective, that is,
we cannot philosophise about God, love and creation without reference
to their experience." Mysticism, he thought, could perhaps form the
basis for a "universal religion." "Genuine mysticism," he said, "is the
guiding force of dynamic religion; it appears very infrequently in the
history of religion but it is able to move a real, if hidden, layer in our
minds and gradually transform or ennoble conservative religion"
(Bergson 1985 [1903], p. 83). He believed that "mysticism culminates
in a 'contact' and therefore partial coincidence with the creative effort
that life reveals. This effort is of God if not God Himself" (Bergson
1985 [1903], p. 29).

The difficulties of translating mystical experience into a philosophy that can guide practical life become immediately apparent through
an examination of mystical texts. The Qur'an and other Islamic
religious texts, for example, use metaphorical language to describe mystical knowledge. The Qur'an explains,

God is the Beginning and the End, the Invisible and the Manifest,
the Internal and the External; He is closer to man than his jugular
vein is to his neck. ... His closeness is without distance; There is
not a single atom, nor a leaf that falls that He does not know about.

(Q 50:16)

118

And from the sayings of the Sufi prophet (Hadith) (Stoddart 1976, pp. 78–80), one reads

> My Heaven cannot contain Me, nor can My earth, but the heart of the believers ... can contain Me.

> Whoso seeketh to approach me one cubit, I approach him two fathoms; and whoso walketh towards Me, I run towards Him.

> Whoso knoweth himself, knoweth His Lord.

Whitehead has similar difficulties in precisely describing the amorphous, all-encompassing, and paradoxical nature of mystical experience:

> The vision of something which stands beyond, behind, and within, the passing flux of immediate things; something which is real and yet waiting to be realised, something which is a remote possibility and yet the greatest of present facts; something that gives meaning to all that passes and yet eludes apprehensions; something whose possession is the final good, and yet is beyond all reach; something which is the ultimate ideal ... the fact of the religious vision and its history of persistent expansion is our ground for optimism. Apart from it, human life is a flash of occasional enjoyments lighting up as a mass of pains and misery, a bagatelle of transient experience. The vision claims nothing but worship and worship is a surrender to the claim for assimilation, urged with the motive force of mutual love. The vision ... is always there, and it has the power of love presenting the one purpose whose fulfilment is eternal harmony. ... Evil is the brute motive force of fragmentary purpose, disregarding the eternal vision. Evil is overruling, retarding, hurting. The worship of God ... is an adventure of the spirit.
>
> Whitehead (1985 [1925], p. 237)

119

For Iqbal, this difficulty of language is part of the problem of understanding mystical experience, that is, we lack the necessary psychological language to explain the observations of reality couched in visions, revelations, and illuminations — genuine mystical experience reported in every religious tradition. Iqbal's challenge to psychology is to develop an independent method calculated to discover a new technique better suited to the temper of our times (Baharuddin 1989). Fortunately, as writers such as Iqbal, Bergson, Whitehead and, more recently, Fritjof Capra (1983) have pointed out, experience traditionally termed "mystical" can now be imagined and articulated through the understanding and analogies provided by atomic reality.

My point is that despite the attendant difficulties of translation, we must take religious experiences of a "mystical" nature seriously and find ways to appreciate the knowledge they offer. They can provide windows onto transcendence that humankind seems to be demanding and, I believe, a convergence of inner and outer experience that humankind can no longer afford to defer. Within this view, a whole realm of experience — one of the cardinal principles of which seems to be that the nature of reality is unity and wholeness rather than fragmentation and separation — awaits articulation and integration into philosophical and, finally, social and political systems and processes. In fact, a number of scientists and philosophers are trying to express the nature of such an integrated reality: see David Bohm's (1981) *Wholeness and the Implicate Order*, Fritjof Capra's (1983) *The Tao of Physics: An Exploration of the Parallels between Modern Physics and Eastern Mysticism*, and Stanislav Grof's (1996) *Beyond the Brain: Birth, Death, and Transcendence Psychotherapy*. Although not engaged in the praxis of psychology, these thinkers are working from within their own legitimate fields of science to create a more comprehensive and holistic worldview.

120

ISLAM

Among Westerners and those involved in the development community there is a great deal of misunderstanding about Islam and its message. This lack of clarity might be said to begin with Muslims themselves, especially those educated in the secular humanistic mode, either at home or abroad, without exposure to traditional Islamic culture and community. Lack of understanding, coupled with the militant activism fostered in certain groups, not surprisingly gives rise to the common stereotypical view among non-Muslims that Islam is a fatalistic religion with an antidevelopment posture or, at best, with little to say on the subject of development.

As mentioned earlier, there is a strong belief that the Western model of development provides the only legitimate path. To a certain degree, this belief arises in the developing world from a feeling of inferiority, which becomes especially pronounced when outsiders call into question original and indigenous perspectives on development issues. Yet, even though the West still exerts a powerful political and economic influence, forums and opportunities are available for non-Westerners to become seriously engaged in fruitful dialogue with the West and to intellectually confront problems commonly faced by diverse peoples and by all religions. Muslim intellectuals have yet to share with others their belief that the Qur'an has great wisdom to offer the whole of humanity.

UNDERSTANDING ISLAM AND THE REALITY OF THE MUSLIM FAITH

The discussion of what Islam can bring to the discourse on SRD requires a brief overview of some basic features of Islam, Islamic metaphysics, and the Islamic worldview. Muslims believe that Islam is a religion that was divinely revealed more than 1400 years ago; its essence is contained in the Qur'an, as well as in the traditions (sayings and habits) of the

Prophet Muhammad. It has an orthodox dimension, generally associated with the *shariah*, as well as an esoteric dimension, usually referred to as Sufism (Nasr 1993a). The fundamental message of Islam is the acceptance of, and submission to, the one true God. The word *Islam* means to surrender to the will of God (Nasr 1993b). Muslims believe in all the prophets sent before Muhammad, as well as the religious texts revealed before the Qur'an.

In addition to providing ethical and moral norms, Islam encompasses schools of law, theology, philosophy, and a variety of arts and sciences, as well as a distinctive educational system and political, economic, social, and family structures. It is not meant to be a monolithic system but one in which believers can continue to adhere to its precepts while performing *ijtihad* (fresh interpretations); these interpretations are not supposed to stray from the essence of the law. *Ijtihad*, however, remains more an ideal than a reality in many situations.

The spread of Islam around the world (for example, into Africa, Europe, the Middle East, and Southeast Asia) and into vastly different cultures has resulted, to cite Nasr, in various modes of development. Similarly, the Muslim encounter with Westernism, modernism, secularism, and colonialism has produced a wide range of responses within Islam. Nasr (1993a) described the various modes and degrees of Muslim religiosity within the following categories (which are likely to have parallels in other religions):

❦ Those who never miss their daily prayers and live as much as they can by the *shariah* (these people consider their manner of following Islam to be the only way);

❦ Those who do not follow all the injunctions of the *shariah* and do not perform the obligatory daily prayers yet definitely consider themselves Muslims;

❦ Those who do nothing specifically Islamic except to follow a vaguely Islamic, humanistic ethic, who nonetheless identify themselves as Muslims and would protest vehemently if called anything else; and

❦ Those who perform the Islamic rituals meticulously and claim to be devout even while they break many of the moral injunctions of the *shariah*, including the obligation to be honest in business.

These distinctions show that the portrayal of Islam as a stagnant religion or a "uniform wave of fundamentalism" is stereotypical and unrealistic (Nasr 1993a).

Despite the varying degrees of fidelity to their religion on the part of Muslims, scholars such as Nasr believe that Islam remains intact in the Islamic world today. For most Muslims, religion informs all their relationships — among themselves, with others, and with God. This is a reality they live with and strive to make manifest in their day-to-day affairs. They make use of religious precepts not only in solving family problems and achieving economic goals but also in exercising political power (Nasr 1993a). Of course, it is equally true that the fears and desires of Muslim communities (*ummah*) have been used by those whose motives were anything but Islamic — a misuse that has served to discredit the religion.

Apart from the modernists, the traditionalists, and the fundamentalists — and this Nasr is correct to point out — there is another group in the contemporary Islamic world that is often ignored by Western analyses. This group would like to revive the Islamic tradition from within. It comprises those who have fully encountered the modern world and are completely aware of its complexities and problems. With the philosophical, scientific, and social issues clear in their minds, they have chosen to return to the heart of the Islamic tradition to find answers and to revive the *ummah*. They long to enliven the spiritual reality of religion and to prove that it has a place in today's world. Their numbers are seldom large, and their "theatres of action" are not mass meetings or political gatherings. They are minds and souls that usually interact with each other in small circles. They do not reject traditional Islam, not even its esoteric dimension, which they consider "the heart of the whole body" of the religion; the *shariah* governs the limbs of this body, and the blood from the heart animates the body entire (Nasr 1993a).

This group seeks answers in Islamic metaphysics to problems raised by such ideologies as rationalism and materialism. People in this group see the revival of Islam as a revival within believers themselves; thus, they disagree with the modern dictum that emphasizes the reform of the world but not the individual human being. They believe in and, beginning with themselves, strive to manifest inner revival (*tajdid*) and to avoid mere external reform (*islah*) (Nasr 1993a). The attitude of this group stems from its awareness of a transcendental presence. It is not an attitude of passive acceptance in the face of the myriad problems afflicting society, both Muslim and non-Muslim, but one of realistic application of religious precepts as guiding principles for action. This approach has engendered some of the most meaningful Islamic responses to the modern world, in terms of both religion and development. Examples of these efforts are more fully described in Annex 1.

PERSONAL EXPERIENCES WITH RELIGION

I was brought up as a Muslim, with substantial Sufi influence early in my life. My father is a Sufi, who teaches his *murid* (students), and the subject he most emphasizes in his theological discussions with his audiences is *Tauhid*, or the oneness of Allah (God). In this understanding of reality, God is the beginning and the end, the seen (*zahir*) and the unseen (*batin*), the *raison d'être* of one's being. From a very early age, I also had instilled in me the belief that the constant remembrance (*dhikr*) of God would be the only true source of strength for me to rely on in my spiritual life and, by implication, in my physical, social, emotional, and intellectual life.

When I was an undergraduate training as a biologist in the West (Australia), the methods of science enabled me to see the workings of nature in all its complexity and to feel the tremendous sense of awe that nature can invoke. The philosophy of that science, however, was secular and reductionistic, and one who adhered to it might, at best, claim to be an agnostic. So convincing was the logic of the science I was studying at that time that I underwent my first spiritual crisis in my second undergraduate year. Was God real? How does one know? In the face of so much evidence to the contrary, how can one believe? Is there a universally verifiable "method," like the scientific method, to use to answer these questions? It was at this point that I decided to find out whether science and religion were truly alien to one another.

In Islam, the heart (or *Qalbu*) is a valid source of knowledge, as well as of reason; the heart is the medium through which we discover the reality of God. My assumption, then, was that God, being omnipotent, omniscient, and omnipresent, should know my questions and the confusion I was experiencing. If God was real — as my religion had taught to me — then God would be the best teacher to demonstrate that existence. All I needed to do was to allow God to enter my heart. Thus began an earnest period of communication with God through prayer and invocation, whereby I gained insight into religious truth in my own work and experience. I have since had the opportunity to confirm the validity of this process with religious teachers. In a more formal sense, the "method" of acquiring faith involves consciously cleansing "evil" from one's heart and mind, doing good, and being in a state of constant remembrance of, and communication with, God. For example, one can invoke God through the names that express his attributes. Later, in the works of authors like William James, Muhammad Iqbal, and A.F. Schumacher, who explain religious experience in naturalistic terms commensurate with human experience, I found a language to articulate my thoughts.

Before undertaking my experiment with this method, the problem for me, as I am sure it is for many other Muslims, was that God is portrayed as outside and totally other than oneself. In fact, God is very close to humans, although this does not mean that God is human or that humans are God. According to Islam, humans do not possess anything by or of themselves. When one divorces oneself from God, one does not have anything substantial — either integrated knowledge or a solid sense of purpose, for example. I would say that before my experiment, this was the situation in which I found myself.

After a time, I became aware that the process I had been going through is universally accessible, as it involves only the capacities all humans possess. The method and the experiment reminded me of those in science, and I understood Iqbal's comparison of the state of the scientist in the contemplation of nature with the state of prayer. It was important to me to see the universal applicability, or truthfulness if you like, of the principles of my religion; without this conviction, it would be difficult for me to be true to what I profess.

How has this changed what I do? These understandings did not change my desire to be a biologist, but they made me see my work in a new light. My studies of microscopic organisms in Tasmanian lakes, for instance, provided me with numerous examples of God's design in nature. A certain kind of plankton found in these lakes displays striking patterns — intricate, geometrical, symmetrical, and beautiful. In their form, I also saw the intricacy of God's design and the wisdom of the 99 names attributed to God, for example, "the Alive," "the Maker," "the Creator." Another life form in these lakes is a tiny insect. I must have discovered 10 species and had to describe the peculiarities of each. I found that the distinguishing characteristic of each species was the shape and size of the left posterior leg of the male, which played an important role in reproduction. These creatures measure only about 1 mm. Most people would think that they are just dots in the water, but, in fact, they are beautiful and unique. Their intricacy, despite their size, convinced me of the value and purpose of all living beings. Simply put, God's reality showed itself to me through my work, even though my work concerned only a tiny speck of the whole of creation. For me, that tiny speck held an entire world of its own.

The heaven and the earth and all beings therein declare His glory:
There is not a thing but celebrates His praise: And yet
ye understand not how they declare His glory.
(Q 16:48–49)

I suppose that these realizations have made me aware of the role that assumptions and worldviews, whether acknowledged or not, play in everything human beings do. We all operate on the basis of certain assumptions about ourselves and the way the world works. For example, Western worldviews often come with the assumption that the maximization of profit is an unchallengeable good. Islam offered me another set of assumptions and goals, based on the *shariah*; these are the principles I tested in my experiments, and I found that they are, in fact, a true representation of the way the world works. Moreover, they have given me real happiness, peace, and acceptance of life. Thus, I now do things with motives and intentions (*niat* in Islam) connected with God's "will" as explained in the Qur'an and the *shariah*. But this does not mean that I act without foundation in fact or without reason. I have found that the principles set out in the Qur'an and *shariah* provide a true picture of the world; this picture can be described equally in terms of the socioanthropological principles of social science or the natural laws of physical science. I have been able to understand the Qur'an and appreciate its relevance to all aspects of my life and in what I perceive to be the whole of life; I can now see the "scientific" nature or reasonableness of what the *shariah* asks of humans. Later in this paper, for example, I explain the concept of *zakat*, or tithe, as a means of redistributing the imbalances of wealth and preventing social inequities. I have also come to see that being religious is not merely a matter of thought or remembrance of God; these must be accompanied by action. Acting from these motivations gives me the courage to face misunderstandings and setbacks, even denigration and hatred, because I feel confident that I am acting from a valid picture of reality — one that integrates and ensures justice for all humans and the environment.

I understand that real tranquility and peace can be achieved through the remembrance of God, for even though one has an obligation to act and to act with the best of motivations, ultimately reality is far too complex for any one human being to be in complete understanding or control of it. Rather than attempting the impossible — trying to manage all the consequences of my actions and controlling all contingencies — I now accept that only God alone, in his infinite wisdom and knowledge, can possibly know everything. I have also come to see what Iqbal and Bergson meant when they talked about the "discovery" stage of religion, when one adheres to religious principles willingly and without feelings of compulsion because one understands the reasons for the tenets of one's religion and how they contribute to a just society. What, however, are the rewards of this approach, other than those I have already mentioned — personal peace, well-being, and a sense of doing good in your community and society? If one believes in the afterlife, the reward will be an ongoing life in the presence of God. In the here and now, this approach offers an opportunity to become, in Iqbal's words, "co-partners with God in creation itself" (Sheikh 1971, p. 75).

Before closing this section on my personal reflections about my religion, I would like to share some reflections on the often controversial issue of women in Islam. From the "right practices" and "right interpretations" concerning women that I have studied and observed, I am convinced that neither Islam nor God discriminates against women. Allah expects the same from men and women, as seen from the following Qur'anic verse:

> For believing men and women
> For devout men and women
> For true men and women
> For men and women who are
> Patient and constant, for men

And women who humble themselves
For men and women who guard their chastity
And for men and women who engage
Much in Allah's praise
For them has Allah prepared
Forgiveness and great reward.

(Q 33:55)

Muhammad, the Prophet,[10] introduced Qur'anic laws to elevate the status of women, including

&- A ban on the practice of burying daughters alive;

&- The maintenance of women's property rights and their right to keep their names after marriage;

&- Women's right to choose their own husbands;

&- Women's access to education and careers outside the home;

&- Women's access to positions of leadership; and,

&- Women's right to buy and sell.

Cultural practices and influences existing before or concurrently with Islam have had a negative influence on men's treatment of women. Such attitudes and practices persist, despite the Qur'anic injunctions.

METAPHYSICS AND ITS ROLE

Nasr (1993b, p. 506) pointed out that metaphysics in Islam is not a branch of philosophy but the "supreme science of the Real." He considered metaphysics a science, acting as the centre of human existence, found at the heart of all orthodox and authentic religions, and attainable through human intellect. Metaphysics deals with both the domains of nature and the realms of the human psyche — art, thought, and community. The establishment of a metaphysical tradition tied to appropriate spiritual methods within the fold of religion could help to rejuvenate theology; Nasr suggested that, combined with philosophy, a theology of nature would provide the criteria for regulating the sciences. Metaphysics gives fundamental unity to any Muslim perspective on issues of science and development and provides the conceptual tools

---

[10] It is interesting to note that a rich widow, Siti Khadijah, proposed to Muhammad when he was 25 and she was 40 years old. He was working as a trader of her goods to places outside of Mecca. They were together for 25 years, and the Prophet only took other wives after the age of 55. These later marriages have been attributed to missionary and political purposes. Although polygamy is technically sanctioned by the Qur'an, in fact, it is very difficult, if not impossible, to meet the conditions set out, because they require a man to be absolutely equal to his wives in every sense — financially, emotionally, and socially.

needed to understand why, historically, Muslim societies were able to wed religion and development. In view of the current intellectual climate, Nasr has emphasized the need to create the space for such a science while critically analyzing the "totalitarian claims of modern science or at least of positivism and scientism that today claim a monopoly over knowledge" (Nasr 1993a, p. 11).

Scholars such as Syed Muhammad Naquib Al-Attas referred to Islam, not merely as a religion, but as (to use the Qur'anic term) *din*, which involves the totality of life, if not reality itself. The difference that this perspective makes in one's understanding is hard to over-emphasize. Nasr also commented on the all-encompassing nature of Islam:

> In the Islamic perspective, religion is not seen as a part of life or a special kind of activity along with art, thought, commerce, social discourse, politics, and the like. Rather, it is the matrix and world-view within which these and all other human activities, efforts, creations, and thoughts take place or should take place. ... Islam does not even accept the validity of a domain outside of the realm of religion and refuses to accord any reality to the dichotomy between the sacred and ... secular or the spiritual and temporal.
>
> Nasr (1993b, pp. 439–440)

127

> According to Islam, religion is not only a matter of private conscience, although it certainly includes this dimension, but it also is concerned with the public domain, with humans' social, economic, and even political lives. There is no division between the Kingdom of God and the kingdom of Caesar in the Islamic perspective.
>
> Nasr (1993b, p. 442)

I use the concept of *zakat* (or tithe) to illustrate this integrated perspective. Muslims believe that all forms of income, benefits, and harvests are gifts from God. The Qur'an teaches that the poor have a right to the resources of the Earth, which God created for all humans. Accordingly, a portion of the property of the rich belongs to the poor. Many Muslims give 2.5% of the value of their property to various groups specified in the *shariah*, such as the economically disenfranchised and orphans. Thus, on the one hand, *zakat* is a religious duty, but, on the other, it helps to ensure justice in the distribution of resources in a community, thereby preventing a huge gap between rich and poor and maintaining social stability. Also, the principle of interconnectedness suggests that very rarely, if ever, is any process of change uniquely positive or neutral. The structures of society allow negative effects to visit themselves on the poor and other marginalized groups disproportionately, and, for this reason, *zakat* is not merely charity but a means to ensure justice.

In his book, *Islam: The Concept of Religion and Foundations of Ethics and Morality*, Al-Attas (1992), a renowned Sufi, analyzed the concept of *din* to provide an understanding of human submission to God, a foundational precept in Islam that constitutes the basis for its idea of development. Al-Attas explained the connections between *din* and such concepts as submissiveness, judicious power, and natural inclination. He showed how these concepts are all connected to the basic tenet of humankind's creation and sustenance by God and its indebtedness for these gifts.

Verily God has purchased of the Believers their selves.
(Q 9:111)

Din is derived from the verb *dana*, according to Al-Attas, which means to be indebted. Finding oneself in debt — that is, *a da'in* — one is under the obligation (*dayn*) to yield to the laws and ordinances governing debts. Being in debt and under obligation also involves reckoning and judgment, *daynuyah*. In Islamic metaphysics, even before individuals exist as human beings, they realize that they have to acknowledge God as their Creator, cherisher, and sustainer of their very selves, their souls. The nature of the debt of creation is so tremendous that the moment humans are called into existence, they are in a state of utter loss; they possess nothing themselves, as they see that everything about them, in them, and from them comes from the Creator.

Verily man is in loss.
(Q 103:2)

According to Al-Attas, as humans own absolutely nothing to repay the debt, except their consciousness of themselves as the very substance of the debt, they must repay it with themselves, by returning themselves to God. Returning the debt means to give themselves in service (*khidmah*), sincerely and consciously, by living out the dictates of God's law, or way. Thus, the concept of *din* also alludes to a "return" to the spiritual and physical nature inherent in being human, and this return is therefore beneficial to the individuals themselves.

He who enslaves himself gains.
(Q 13:18, 29)

Muslims believe that the love and service they give other humans is given to God. The act of service to God is called *ibadah*, and the service itself is called *ibadat. Ibadat* refers to all conscious and willing acts of service for the sake of God alone, including prescribed worship. This service feels normal to humans because it is a natural inclination. Muslims also refer to the tendency to serve and worship God as *din*, which has connotations of custom, habit, and disposition. The natural state of being is *fitrah*, the pattern according to which God has created all things (for example, it is the *fitrah* of the moon to move around the Earth). Everything is best suited to the pattern created for it and is set in its proper place. This is the *shariah* of God: submission to it brings harmony, as it means the realization of one's true nature. Opposition to it brings discord because it means the realization of something alien that causes suffering to one's true nature. *Shariah* is cosmos, as opposed to chaos; justice, as opposed to injustice. Submission in this sense does not entail the loss of freedom but the achievement of freedom, the freedom to fulfill one's true nature. Humans who submit to God in this way are living out the *din*.

Al-Attas suggested that the concept of *din* also reflects the idea of a kingdom, or a cosmopolis, for it is only in organized societies, in towns or cities (*mudun* or *mada'in*) involved in commercial life, that the implications of *din* are realized. Towns and cities have judges, rulers, or governors (*adayyan*), and thus the picture of societal life that emerges is one of law, order, justice, and authority. *Din* is conceptually connected with another verb, *maddana*, which means to refine, to build (as in the founding of cities), and to civilize, and these processes fit well in a vision of development. At least in theory, then, the civilizing inspiration or "developmental push" for Muslims is commerce and trade and its various implications as inherent in the concept of *din*. It is not surprising that the Qur'an so persistently depicts worldly life through the metaphors and analogies of commerce. It describes the cosmopolis as bustling with commercial activity and "the traffic of trade." From a spiritual perspective, humans are metaphorically engaged in a form of trade (*al-tijarah*) in which their selves are both subject and object, the trader and the traded: "He is his own capital and his loss and gain depends upon his own sense of responsibility and exercise of freedom. Depending on how he exercises his will and deeds his trade will either prosper or suffer loss" (Qur'an). Human beings realize that they are not just animals that eat, drink, and gain sensual pleasure; they must transcend themselves so as to redeem themselves from the obligation of their very existence.

The concept of *din* presupposes in humans the emergence of higher beings "capable of lofty aspirations towards self-improvement" (Qur'an); this is the actualization of the desire and latent capacity to become perfect (*insan kamil*). In Islam, believers are conscious that they are microcosms of the macrocosm — that is, they are the kingdom in miniature. Each human manifests the attributes of the Creator, because God created human beings in his own image. Muslims believe that humans, being both physical and spiritual, have two souls: the lower, animal soul and the higher, rational soul. In the context of submission,

129

it is the animal soul that has to return itself to the rational soul. The statement of the Prophet Muhammad, "Die before ye die," refers to the submission of this lower soul to the higher soul, or the subjugation of one's self to one's true self. This process of knowing the self leads ultimately to God.

> *He who knoweth his self knowest his Lord.*
> Hadith (quoted in Waly 1991, p. 6)

In Al-Attas's analysis, the ideal human being lives a civilized life in a community with clearly defined foundations of social order and codes of conduct. Human obedience to the Divine Way is the means to "realising true justice and striving after right knowledge and cardinal virtues" (Qur'an). From this conduct, humans may hope to experience a state of supreme peace, even in this world, and eternal blessedness. One's ultimate bliss would be to behold the countenance of God in his kingdom. Thus, although the ultimate goal of the Muslim is in the afterlife, the journey toward that life begins here, that is, Muslims must start by development in the here and now.

These concepts provide the very foundation and motivation for the Islamic approach to science and development.

WHAT IS ISLAMIC SCIENCE AND DEVELOPMENT?

With these thoughts in mind, I will now turn to the question of how Islam interacts with science and development. I will approach this question in the following way. First, I address a fundamental challenge faced by all religions: Does the promise of an otherworldly salvation thwart attempts to achieve justice in the here and now? I then identify four themes arising from the discussion throughout my paper that might be called the "value perspectives" that Islam brings to science and development and attempt to show how they apply in practice.

Denis Goulet, the economist and development theorist, noted that Marx handed a fundamental challenge to religion when he decried that it places human destiny outside history and thereby turns humans away from the task of working for justice on Earth. This otherworldly orientation, he argued, negates true humanism and perpetuates injustice. On this basis, Goulet asked whether any religion can supply men and women with a convincing rationale for building this world while striving to bear witness to transcendence. His answer was that the "coefficient of secular commitment" contained to some degree in all religions (that is, religious commitment to worldly affairs) needed to be analyzed, awakened, and maximized (Goulet 1996, p. 226). The ability of believers to "see" religion in real life and to apply its values and tenets in solving worldly problems can be strengthened only if they have a fluidity or dynamism in their thinking and practice; they should not see religion as a monolithic, isolated entity, but as a flexible, practical system of knowledge, well integrated into every facet of their lives.

> *People should work as if they will live forever*
> *and worship as if they will die the next day.*
>
> Hadith 40 (quoted in Rahman 1998, pp. 343, 345)

Yet, this runs contrary to the generally accepted approach. In the Islamic world, many secular leaders have confined the role of religion to the personal lives of individuals, relevant only to the afterlife. The religious sector, for its part, has tried not to become involved in "worldly affairs." The administrative structures and governance systems inherited from colonialization have reduced the areas in which religion is allowed to exercise authority to those of family and personal law. Many governments of modern Muslim countries are only now beginning to incorporate religion into their systems. A first step in this process would be to develop an adequate system of education that combines religious and secular knowledge. As yet, the *ulama* (clergy), ruling groups (politicians), and intelligentsia (academics) have not been able to organize themselves to work together and produce this type of synthesis, even though they are all practicing Muslims. There are exceptions, of course: nongovernmental organizations (NGOs), working in concert with, and receiving support from, all three groups, have often managed to produce practical results.

131

> *Part of the meaning of Islam is that we worship God as if we "see"*
> *Him or, if we do not "see" Him, to know that He sees us.*
>
> Razak and Lathief (1980, p. 48)

In tackling the issue of how to rejuvenate religion, one may find it useful to distinguish three phases of religious practice — faith,[11] thought, and discovery — as recognized in the work of both Iqbal and Bergson. In the faith phase, one unconditionally accepts religious commands, without understanding them. In the second phase, thought, there is perfect submission to discipline based on a rational understanding of that discipline. In this phase, religious life seeks its foundation in

---

[11] For example, at least much of the Muslim community assumes that *taqlid*, or blind acceptance, is sufficient and workable. But I would argue that this type of faith is the most susceptible to doubt, confusion, and disillusionment, especially when one confronts information from science, technology, and secular education that is seemingly contradictory to religion. It is not surprising that many Muslims now find themselves quite at a loss to know how to be loyal to their religion, given the prevalence of a totally secular and reductionistic outlook.

a kind of metaphysics, that is, a logically consistent view of the world, with God as part of that view. In the third phase, discovery, metaphysics is displaced by what might be termed a psychological state of being in which the one living a religious life develops a desire or ambition to come into direct contact with God. Individuals in this phase achieve a "free" personality, not because they are released from the dictates of the law or dogma but because they discover the ultimate source of the law within the depths of their consciousness (Iqbal 1930; Baharuddin 1989). Does this mean that ordinary dogmatic religion is not important? Perhaps this is not the right question. As Iqbal explained, no religion is without dogma, but religions often fail to emphasize that it is the third phase that makes the dogma understandable and practicable.

> A Muslim mystic asserted that no understanding of the Holy Book is possible until it is actually revealed to the believer, just as it was revealed to the Prophet.
>
> Baharuddin (1989, p. 324)

In maximizing the coefficient of secular commitment, what is important, according to Goulet (1996), are the precise links postulated between religiously inspired commitment to human tasks (this-worldly existence) and the transcendent reality that is the object of religious faith. He suggested that where there is a high coefficient, these links are intrinsic and essential, rather than extrinsic or accidental. Iqbal and others in the Muslim world would agree with Teilhard de Chardin, who argued that those who believe in transcendence see a world that is open and infinite; they love the world no less than secular humanists, but they work in the here and now to make this reality purer and finally to escape from it. This escape is not an alienating flight from reality, but a means to reach a more complete reality, one providing this world and human efforts within it full and final meaning (Goulet 1996). For those equipped for it, the esoteric path[12] allows the "window" to transcendence to be clarified and even traversed. But the intimate connection between this world and the next demands human effort in the here and now; de Chardin would also argue that no spiritual excuse can justify

---

[12] But in Islam, as in Christianity and other religions, esoterism can be and has been abused: its insights, for example, are not susceptible to objective verification; they can be validated but frequently only through personal practice and implementation — hence some people's suspicion of, and attacks on, esoteric practices. But true esoterism, or mysticism, in Islam (as well as in other religions) is the **internal** component or content of the unity that is Islam, as the meaning of *esoterism* indicates. Any internal aspect must be accompanied by an external one, or an outer covering; this is the law, or *shariah*, from which Islamic esoterism is never divorced. Everything a Muslim does embraces both the esoteric and the exoteric realms. In giving *zakat*, for example, the exoteric meaning is that you assist marginalized people in your society; the esoteric meaning is that it expands the quality of the giver's heart.

inertia in religious believers confronted with "an array of pressing secular tasks to accomplish, knowledge and wisdom to be gained, greater justice to be forged, creativity and creation to be unleashed, political fraternity to be instituted, and comprehensive human development to be progressively achieved" (Goulet 1996, p. 227).

Even for people not inclined to esoteric lines of thinking, Islam's coefficient of secular commitment is still clearly present in a number of arenas. As described above, the very metaphysics of Islam dictates that progress toward the afterlife is contingent on development of the self and on actions performed in the here and now. According to the renowned theologian and philosopher–scholar Imam al-Ghazali (d. 111 AD), the knowledge–belief–action (*ilm–iman–amal*) triad of being in Islam requires of Muslims two types of knowledge:

133

❀ *'lm fardhu 'ain*, or knowledge related to individual obligations — Individuals must be taught and learn the knowledge of God (that is, God's attributes and the human relationship to God); the angels (that is, what they are, their role and function in relation to God and humans); the afterlife and creation; human duties to themselves, to society, and to God; *solat*, or prayers (meant to provide strength, growth, and a means of tapping energy from the Creator); and the significance of giving alms and tithes, fasting (the physical, psychological, and spiritual reasons behind it), pilgrimage (a physical, intellectual, social, and emotional journey toward purification and universal brotherhood), and several other principles by which life takes on meaning. Such knowledge provides a purpose, a code of ethics, a basis for ritual, and the courage to live with oneself, society, nature, and God. Without this type of knowledge, individuals are in danger of being in a state of error and injustice in regard to both themselves and others.

❀ *Ilm fardhu kifayah*, or knowledge related to social and collective obligations — This type of knowledge deals with matters such as the establishment of Islamic society, politics, economics, business, trade, law, medicine, and development (Salleh 1998). Each community must have at least a certain number of individuals with the knowledge to enable the community to cope with life's exigencies and flourish. This type of knowledge applies in various areas according to the needs of the given community: fishing, sailing, agriculture, building and engineering, medicine, economics, and science. The list continues to grow as human endeavours expand. To the extent that the community lacks the knowledge and know-how it requires to live properly it remains in a state of injustice and "backwardness."

Am I guilty of some form of caste systemization when I emphasize the significance of esoterism? It is not my intention to make a value judgment on the different approaches to faith. Teamwork is of the utmost importance in endeavours to develop society. The concept of *ilm–iman–amal* (knowledge–belief–action) shows us that each group and individual in society functions with different inclinations, knowledge, and strengths. Society is the product of their teamwork. That is why in Islam the societal factor, or the *ummah* (community), is important, as the community provides the environment for the "blooming" or development of individuals into their complete selfhood. But even though development falls into the category of social knowledge, we cannot forget the importance of the individual realm; society and the individual are inseparable and must evolve together (Salleh 1998). Ideally, the *ummah* not only is nurturing but also acts to rectify mistakes and sins in a spirit of love and mutual acceptance. In fact, the ideal product of development would be *masyarakat madani*, a God-centred civil society, one in which the ruler and the ruled are equally and mutually accountable to one another before God, who dwells both outside the community (transcendent) and within it (immanent).[13]

In Islam, human beings are seen as God's servants and the *khalifah* (or vicegerents) of God on Earth; development, by fulfilling these functions, is a means to worship God. "In this sense, development is just a means to another end, not an end in itself. It is a means to worship and seek the pleasure of [God], so that humans beings attain happiness in this world and the hereafter" (Salleh 1998, p. 18). In Islam and in other faiths, religion has as its primary goal the attainment of salvation, no matter how this may be envisaged. In this Earthly life, salvation is development. In religion, doctrine–theory and practice–method are inseparable. Doctrine concerns the mind, whereas practice concerns the will; religion must therefore engage both the mind and the will of believers. Thus, the mechanisms for, and of, development can ideally be seen as manifestations of religious theories and methods. Believers act as channels for the Spirit to manifest itself through matter, that is, for God to act through humans.

Islam exhorts Muslims to be firmly of this world and act in it, even while they recognize the transcendent. It puts a subtle but definite emphasis on worldly development and intertwines it with the "inner" personality of the individuals who embody the individually required knowledge (*'lm fardhu 'ain*). They are to do all this in the constant awareness of God. As Goulet suggested, a system of transcendent

[13] In 1996–97, the Malaysian Institute for Development Studies (MINDS), a local NGO, organized a series of conferences at the national and state levels (Malaysia has 14 states). These conferences were intended to promote the idea of a spiritually based civil society, or *masyarakat madani* (in Malay). A series of working papers describing the possibilities for various aspects of this civil society were prepared by a group of local NGO activists and academicians. I prepared a paper on city development and the environment and helped to edit the volume of papers that subsequently emerged. This volume, *Masyarakat Madani*, was published by MINDS in 1998. Its target audience comprised policymakers, NGOs, and the public at large.

meaning (such as Islam) can be a powerful developmental force; the human tasks required in development can draw from a transcendent orientation a "new dignity, urgency, and depth" (Goulet 1996, p. 229).

Islamic value perspectives on science and development

Here, I identify four main Islamic value perspectives that, if creatively and thoroughly applied, could change the direction, goals, and processes of science and development:

1. All human activity is "religious," even and especially economics, development, and science, and therefore cannot be pursued in isolation from the goals and values inherent in the religious worldview, such as justice, unity, vicegerency, and recognition of God. For example, Islam pays particular attention to economics and the market — we have seen how Islam expresses itself in market metaphors; it has developed its own guidelines and rules to limit human greed, selfishness, and avarice. It has injunctions relating to "how transactions should be carried out, the hoarding of wealth as well as its distribution, religious taxation, endowment ... economic treatment of the poor, the prohibition of usury" (Nasr 1993b, p. 443). Islam consigns many resources, such as forests and certain types of water supplies, to the public sector but also emphasizes the right to own private property, as long as moral and ethical guidelines are followed (Nasr 1993b). (An example of how these ideas might be extended to development paradigms is provided in the comments on Chapra in Annex 1.)

135

You will find me with Me.
Hadith Qudsi (quoted in al-Palembangi 1953, p. 105)

2. Islam has always preserved the nexus between rational thought, mystical intuition, and revelation and offered models for integrating these interrelated processes of the mind, which have long suffered the effects of separation. Willis Harman, for example, described a "participatory" research method[14] in which the researcher gains knowledge by identifying with what he or she observes:

> [The] intuitive approach is not antithetical to that of objective science; rather, it is complementary to it. The rational/analytical

---

[14] Harman's approach to "participation" must be distinguished from the meaning of "participatory" research in international development discourse. Harman uses the term to refer to research in which the researcher gains knowledge by identifying with the observed, thus engaging the subject–object of research through "compassionate consciousness" (Harman 1988, p. 15).

and the intuitive/compassionate are, in a sense, aspects of each other. Morris Berman ... makes a strong case that an adequate science cannot be based on attempting to know nature from the outside through controlled experiments in which phenomena are examined in abstraction from their context. With participatory research we understand that nature is revealed only in our relations with it, and phenomena can be known only in context (that is, through participant observation).

Harman (1988, p. 16)

A particularly Islamic example of this integration is offered by the Islamic perspective on nature (see point 4 below).

3. Islam emphasizes humility before God and responsibility. This important perspective should stand alongside traditions stressing the individual and envisaging a more anthropocentric universe. Remembrance of humility and responsibility would be helpful in refocusing our goals and processes in economics, science, and development toward human well-being and sustainability and balancing the assumptions of scientism, reductionism, and materialism embedded in the current processes and goals of these disciplines.

4. Islam offers a particular vision of the relationship between the environment, humans, and God:

    It emphasizes that all natural phenomena are signs (*ayat*) of God, that nature shares in the Qur'ánic revelation, and that humans, as God's vicegerents (*khalifahs*) on earth, are responsible before God for not only themselves but all creatures with which they come into contact.

    Nasr (1993b, p. 529)

As an example of the integration of diverse modes of thought, the Islamic approach to nature, as set out in the Qur'an, upholds the view that nature provides lessons and signs for humans so that through observation they may know themselves and thence God. Such signs include the water cycle, the habits and characteristics of flora and fauna, and the movements of the planets. Each of these phenomena discloses God's will and attributes to humans. Scholars such as Ismail Al-Faruqi (1986) even go as far as to see every Muslim as having been "born a scientist," because understanding the content of scripture requires the serious contemplation of nature. Muslims who do not use their faculties to penetrate the truths disclosed by nature are deemed to have missed a fundamental point of their existence.

*I was a hidden Treasure. I desired to be known.
I created creation, that I might be known.*
Hadith (quoted in al-Palembangi 1953, p. 105)

A theology of nature is an attempt to comprehend nature in the context of a religious interpretation obtained from revelation and religious experience. But most theology does not discuss nature or its relation to humanity directly, and thus science can help perfect the understanding of scripture and religious experience in terms of the environment. For example, a scientific understanding of the world points to continuous creation, as well as the effects of God's action in the here and now. Other thinkers, notably Nobel laureate and biologist George Wald, have come to similar conclusions about the nature of matter and consciousness:

> Our growing scientific knowledge ... points unmistakably to the idea of a pervasive mind intertwined with and inseparable from the material universe. This thought may sound pretty crazy, but such thinking is not only millennia old in the Eastern philosophies but arose again and again among the monumental generation of physicists [Eddington, Schrödinger, and Pauli, among others] in the first half of this century.
>
> Wald (cited in Harman 1988, p. 18)

I would take these ideas further by recalling that religion encompasses all aspects of life. I think these value perspectives suggest the need to articulate a universal philosophy of nature. By this, I mean an attempt to draw a coherent, logical, necessary system of general ideas for interpreting all elements of our experience; a philosophy of nature would provide us with a holistic basis of thought and action for societal and resource problem-solving, and these are, in a sense, the goals of development. This philosophy would attempt to provide us with a coherent view of reality based on the exploration and interpretation of all types of experience so that we may know and love ourselves, others, nature, and God. Such a philosophy would, by necessity, take into account and render coherent both the scientific and the theological understandings of reality, a reality that includes the environment, not merely human beings (Baharuddin 1994).

CONCLUSION

Earlier in the paper, I referred to a definition of development put forward by Francis Perroux (1983). Its essential features are a growth in awareness and intellectual capacity, personal development, and the freedom to fulfill one's potential in accordance with one's own values. If these features are part, or are becoming part, of the goals of development, my observations in this paper can bring me to but one conclusion: our present course will fail to achieve the desired goals. In other words, we will not achieve these goals without processes that recognize and thus work toward them. The aims we wish to attain have always belonged to the arena of religious experience and spiritual existence, and therefore I feel that this ancient realm of experience must become an explicit part of the objects of scientific study.

Of course, incorporating religion into every human endeavour calls for "checks and balances" to prevent the misuse of authority and guarantee the preservation of individual self-determination. The approach one takes to religion, I believe, acts as a major balancing influence. Without a doubt, people in positions of authority have often used the doctrines and precepts of religion to consolidate their power. But, clearly, this is an instrumental use of religion, using it as a means to an end. As an end in and of itself, religion involves an internalization of its precepts — a process that includes evaluation and comparison with experience — and then a manifestation of these ideals in thought and action. Such an approach demands commitment, sacrifice, humility and, above all, an openness to change.[15] The mystical aspects of religion enable the individual to maintain a connection with God and rely on the internal guidance that is characteristic of this connection.

Other checks and balances include a strong commitment to education — nationally, locally, and personally — and a deep sense of responsibility toward democracy, peace, and equality for all. Islam places great emphasis on knowledge and education and regards knowledge as crucial to faith. Its orientation to education supports a commitment to democracy, peace, and equality. People must be in a position to know their rights, that is, what is due to them from those in power, and to understand their responsibilities to others and society. And they must live in a context that allows them to exercise those rights and discharge those responsibilities. In an environment that strives toward these balancing influences, religion and spirituality could be indispensable partners with science in its search for a better understanding of the physical and social reality; and with development in its search for a better understanding of human well-being.

ANNEX 1:
ISLAMIC SCHOLARS AND ORGANIZATIONS
INVOLVED IN SCIENCE, RELIGION, AND DEVELOPMENT

In this annex, I briefly describe the projects and efforts of several Muslim academicians and NGOs to effect changes that integrate SRD.

---

[15] Consider the difference between the person who says "this is what I think my tradition and my self-development demand of me and what I feel I can do to act in accordance with those beliefs" and the person who says "this is what the tradition says and this is how you should think and act."

SEYYED HOSSEIN NASR

S.H. Nasr and his works are well known, and I have cited some of his views in this paper. Originally from Iran, Nasr received his early training in the United States in geology and the history of science. In the 1960s, he began to write about the relationship between science, religion, and the environment and about the problems pertaining to them. As we have seen earlier in the document, his main thesis is that modern humans need to rediscover the lost science of metaphysics, which, together with an extended and rejuvenated form of theology and philosophy, could serve to make science and its use a more balanced affair. Like George Sarton (1927), Nasr has been instrumental in reminding Muslims of the accomplishments of Islamic civilization during the Middle Ages, triggering, among the intelligentsia, a new set of debates and discussions on SRD issues in general. Nasr still writes prolifically regarding the contributions that Muslims can make in contemporary society. Although not everyone would agree with his well-known traditionalist stance, he stands out among Muslim writers for his vast knowledge of Islamic theology, history, and philosophy.

139

ZIAUDDIN SARDAR

Ziauddin Sardar is another figure whose works are popular among Muslim scientists and intelligentsia in the areas of development and the future of the *ummah* (flock). Trained in Manchester, United Kingdom, and currently based in London, Sardar has a background in science, including the history and philosophy of science. A prolific writer,[16] he works closely with Western scholars and Muslim leaders in various parts of the world on projects to enable scientists and policymakers in Muslim societies to more fully understand Islamic philosophy of science, especially its ethical dimension.

Policymakers in the Muslim world are increasingly showing an interest in Islamic science, both its history and its contemporary application. Sardar's (1988) *The Touch of Midas: Science, Values and the Environment in Islam and the West* is the fruit of symposiums he organized in Stockholm (1981) and Granada (1982) that brought together Muslim and non-Muslim scholars to discuss the range of issues suggested by the book's title. The meetings resulted in a rapprochement between the Muslim and non-Muslim participants; they agreed that the symposiums had provided an opportunity for genuine dialogue and had succeeded in identifying a system of values of use in understanding the crisis of science and in shaping S&T policies to reflect Islamic cultural and

---

[16] His works include *The Future of Muslim Civilization* (Sardar 1979a), *Islam, Outline of a Classification Scheme* (Sardar 1979b), *Arguments for Islamic Science* (Sardar 1985a), and *Islamic Futures: The Shape of Ideas to Come* (Sardar 1985b).

religious imperatives. These value concepts derive from a set of principles forming a paradigm for development and progress within an ideal Islamic society: *tauhid* (unity); *khalifah* (trusteeship); *ibadah* (worship); *ilm* (knowledge); *halal* (praiseworthy) and *haram* (blameworthy); *adl* (social justice) and *zulm* (tyranny); *istislah* (public interest); and *dhiya* (waste) (Sardar 1988).[17] Researchers frequently cite Sardar's 10-point value system, indicating the need felt by researchers for a framework of action.

MUHAMMAD UMER CHAPRA

Chapra is an economic adviser to the Saudi Arabian Monetary Agency. He has written extensively on Islamic economics and finance, and his most important work is *Towards a Just Monetary System: A Discussion of Money, Banking, and Monetary Policy in the Light of Islamic Teachings* (1985). He received the Islamic Development Bank Award in Islamic Economics for his contributions in this area. Unlike the others we have seen so far, Chapra is one of the few Muslim economists who seems confident enough in what Islam has to offer to explain at length how economics, development, and religion might interact. Chapra's ideas are set out in a work of some 400 pages, *Islam and the Economic Challenge*[18] (Chapra 1992). In the context of today's economic uncertainties, Chapra earnestly appeals to Muslim countries to try out what he calls the goals of the *shariah* (*Maqasid-al-shariah*) as a means of avoiding disintegration (by this he means social upheavals and recolonization by multinational corporations). A recent example is offered by events in Indonesia, sparked by the currency and debt crisis that hit all the economies of Asia. Through mass demonstrations, the people — many poor and jobless — demanded the removal of the incumbent leaders. Observing the huge disparities in wealth between the various sectors of Indonesian

---

[17] *Tauhid* — usually understood to mean the unity of God — is extended here to refer to an all-embracing value that includes the unity of humankind, human beings and nature, and knowledge and spiritual principles. *Khalifah* (vicegerency, trusteeship) means that humans are responsible to God for their scientific and technological activities. The vision of humans conquering and having dominion over nature has no place in this framework; nor are they passive observers. Nature is a trust. It is also the medium through which humans perform their *ibadah*. Although contemplation is an *ibadah* (good deed) in itself, it also leads to an awareness of unity with nature and of human vicegerency. The pursuit of knowledge (*ilm*), as in science, is another way to perform *ibadah* (worship). Islam recognizes many categories of knowledge: a particular scientific knowledge or specific technology could be *haram* if it is destructive (physically or otherwise) for humans or the environment. If, on the other hand, it is of benefit to humans or the environment then it is *halal*. *Halal* finds parallels in *adl* (justice), as *haram* does in *zulm* (tyranny). One knows *zulm* science and technology if it destroys human, environmental, or spiritual resources or generates waste. Such a science is often called *dhiya*, or wasteful. Scientific and technological activity that ensures justice (*adl*) also promotes the public interest (*istislah*) (Sardar 1988).

[18] See also his *Towards a Just Monetary System* (Chapra 1985).

society, they understandably felt that their leaders were corrupt and thinking only of themselves. The leaders forgot their duties as vicegerents (*khalifah*) of God, because they neglected the people.

The goals of the *shariah* are, first and foremost, human well-being (*falah*) and a good life (*hayat tayyibah*). To Chapra, the *shariah* is the basis of development because, in its emphasis on socioeconomic justice, it aims to satisfy both the spiritual and the material needs of human beings. Chapra derives inspiration from al-Ghazali, whom he quotes as saying "the very objective of the *shariah* is to promote the welfare of the people, which lies in safeguarding their faith, their life, their intellect, their posterity and their wealth. Whatever ensures the safeguarding of these five, serves public interest and is desirable" (Chapra 1992, p. 1).

Chapra also agrees with al-Ghazali in putting faith at the top of the list of the *Maqasid* because it is the most crucial ingredient in human well-being. Faith places human relations on a proper foundation, enabling human beings to interact in a balanced and mutually caring manner for the well-being of all (Chapra 1992). Faith also acts as a moral filter to keep the allocation and distribution of resources in line with requirements for unity and socioeconomic justice. Without the element of faith in human economic decisions — in the household, the corporate boardroom, and the market — we cannot possibly realize efficiency and equity in the distribution of resources; efficiency and equity are prerequisites for avoiding macroeconomic imbalances, economic instability, crime, conflict, and the many symptoms of anomie (Chapra 1992).

Chapra emphasizes that, if we are to achieve equilibrium between scarce resources and the various claims on those resources, we need to focus on human beings, rather than on the market or the state. It is imperative, therefore, to reinstate the human being as the foundation of the economic system. Humans must be motivated to pursue self-interest within the constraints facing the world (Chapra 1992). Truly believing in the possibility of a just and sane economic system, Chapra sets out the various stages for achieving such a system.

Like others, Chapra begins with a critique of the present situation, followed by a reevaluation of principles embedded in the religious metaphysics of Islam. Choosing the three well-known principles of *tauhid* (unity), *khalifah* (vicegerency, trusteeship), and *adl* or *adalah* (justice), he delineates a strategy for a more enlightened economic system. In his treatment, he deals with all the details and complexities of the modern economic system and integrates religious principles and economics throughout.

Chapra (1992) speaks of *tawhid*, *khalifah*, and *adalah* as being connected with, and translatable into, ideas about universal fellowship, resources as a trust, humble lifestyles, human freedom, needs fulfillment, equitable distribution of income and wealth, growth, and stability. He suggests reviving systems laid out in the Qur'an, such as the *zakat* (or tithe) system, and other principles pertaining to wealth. He deals clearly with an entire complex of ideas, starting with the role of the *ulama* (clergy), the restructuring of policies, land and labour reforms, education and training, access to finance, and the size of land holdings, and he moves then to the restructuring of the financial and investment systems, just and efficient taxation, tariffs and import substitution, and priorities in spending. To do justice to Chapra's ideas, however, I urge readers knowledgeable in economics to read his writings and engage with his ideas more directly.

Chapra (1992) concludes his treatise by reiterating that imbuing economics with religious values would imply a serious effort to raise (along Islamic lines) the spiritual and material well-being of all people. On the spiritual side, inner happiness can be achieved only by drawing nearer to God; on the material side, Islamization requires the just and efficient allocation of resources so that the good life can be achieved (*hayat tayyibah*). Islamization is not against liberalization; rather, Islamic liberalization involves passing public- and private-sector economic decisions through the filter of moral values before they affect the market. Without the Islamization of Muslim societies (including a fundamental sector like the economy), that is, without integrating SRD, it will be virtually impossible for Muslim countries to achieve development. Chapra observes, however, that there seems to be little evidence that Muslim policymakers have been inspired to translate Islam's economic ideals into development policies. Chapra predicts that, even if attitudes change, the task will be arduous and time consuming; he urges policymakers to read the signs of the times quickly.

INTERNATIONAL INSTITUTE OF ISLAMIC THOUGHT

The International Institute of Islamic Thought (IIIT) was founded in 1981. Its main aims are to revive and encourage Islamic thought and promote the Islamization of knowledge in contemporary disciplines. It also explores the potential for packaging knowledge so that it integrates *tauhid* (the concept of oneness) and the *shariah*. It addresses problems relevant to the development of the Muslim community and economic development in general through the values and principles of the Islamic religious paradigm.

IIIT's primary appeal has thus far been to academicians. To achieve its goals it promotes research in the social sciences, especially in the methodology and philosophy of science. Moreover, it organizes seminars and conferences and sponsors the publication of specialized works. It awards scholarships and offers guidance to research students. Currently, it is planning to establish special programs of higher studies to strengthen Islamic culture. Although based in the United States, it receives technical and monetary support from countries such as Malaysia. More information about IIIT is available on the Internet (www.iiit.org).

MALAYSIAN ACADEMY OF ISLAMIC SCIENCE

In 1977, Muslim scientists in Malaysia got together to revive the tradition of an Islamic science. This group, which includes many top scientists and engineers working in key sectors, aims to Islamicize attitudes and practices in S&T in ways that follow the ideas explored in this paper. They are also interested in promoting S&T among Malaysians. What may be of particular interest from the viewpoint of SRD, however, is how they focused their efforts on the issues of science, Islam, and development in the recent National Science Policy Seminar. Like a number of other countries, Malaysia has been trying to telescope a few centuries of development into a few decades. Its current statement of general policy — called Vision 2020 — states that Malaysia should strive to be, among other things, a producer of its own S&T and not merely a user of technologies imported from abroad. Despite the honourable and bold intentions expressed in this document, not much thought has been given to implementing its goals. Thus, even though Malaysia has a national science policy, there is no widespread, substantial awareness of it, let alone a healthy critique. Nor is there an ongoing debate about the role and character of science in the country's development in general. Anxious to prove that an Islamic ideal could be universal, however, the Malaysian Academy of Islamic Science (MAIS) has undertaken to explore a developmental model based on science and religion. Its work is promising, as it has thus far managed to garner the support and participation of some Malaysian policymakers.

143

The two most active proponents of MAIS ideas are Shaharir Mohamad Zain (a professor of mathematics) and Wan Daud (a professor of chemistry). Zain and Daud looked at the approaches and ideas of other Muslims on SRD before establishing their own perspectives. Below I have briefly summarized the main tenets of their approach to defining a Malaysian model for the integration of SRD. They presented these at a seminar in September 1998 (Daud and Zain 1998):

1. Development in Islam is the holistic development of humans themselves; material development is merely a by-product or effect of human development. Humans develop on the basis of *ta'dib* (a civilizing factor), the cleansing of the heart and mind (*tazkiyah*), and education (*tarbiyah*). The goal of human development is the good human, of which the highest form is the perfect individual, or *insan kamil*. Such individuals are in a state of total acceptance of God; and God, of them.

2. Capital should be gained and increased through labour and not merely through investment. In the secular model, the accumulation of capital through investment requires savings. In Islam, savings alone cannot give rise to profit because usury (*riba*) in the form of charging interest is prohibited. Instead, Islam encourages

people to save through a medium or simple lifestyle and the avoidance of waste. To avoid usury, the banks neither pay interest to depositors nor charge it to borrowers. Because they need to operate as sustainable economic enterprises, however, the banks receive a share of the borrower's profits and distribute a portion of these profits to depositors; this spreads the risk out across borrowers and depositors. Accumulated capital is taxed through the "alms tax" and tithe so that wealth flows back and can be distributed to the poor.

3. Under this proposed system, economics in Islam would not be as liberal as in the current *laissez-faire* system, because the institution of *hisbah* would watch and regulate the market; *hisbah* is an institution akin to a district governorship, possessing judicial and policing power and having access to all government records. The *hisbah* was once a living institution in the Islamic civilization (al-Faruqi and al-Faruqi 1986). The *muhtasib* (a person in charge of the *hisbah*) deals with cheating and usury, as well as other *haram* acts.

4. Proposed development models must be based on the good (*maslahah*) of society and not only on the motive of gain for the investor.

5. In economic terms, science helps to increase profits through the use of labour- and resource-saving technologies. MAIS is inspired by Ibn Khaldun (d. 1404), the famous Muslim sociologist from Tunis. In his treatise *Muqadimah* (literally, The Introduction), Khaldun not only wrote on the importance of S&T in human life but also suggested a model of Islamic development for the achievement of a high civilization (*umran*); from a concrete historical perspective, this goal began with the Prophet and the city of Madinah. The first believers were strong in their faith because their *ta'dib* and *tazkiyah* took place in the hands of the Prophet himself. Thus, they possessed a genuine feeling of unity (ideally faith is incomplete unless believers love the next person as they love themselves); this is called *'asabiyyah*. Khaldun observed that the downfall or disintegration of a nation occurs, not so much because of a breakdown in its economic system, but more because of the breakdown of the political power of the ruling elite, beginning with the loss of *'asabiyyah*.

6. In the modern view, economic development involves industrialization, basically using resources, labour, and technology to produce an assortment of products and services in large quantities so as to be cost-effective. This process is, in principle, acceptable because the Qur'an mentions the use of resources (*tashkir*). Human dominion over nature is not an absolute fact, however; it is based on the condition that humans use nature only in accordance with the limits, purposes, and ethics prescribed by the Qur'an.

7. Technology as a means of controlling nature or gaining political power is rejected. In the religious perspective, technology is a branch of the practical sciences used to achieve a practical end. Both the means and the purpose of the technology, however, must conform to principles such as those outlined by Sardar so that the effect is harmonious and balanced with humans and nature.

8. Local people must have the freedom to innovate or improvise on imported technologies. Such indigenization is required at every level of technological development (that is, conception, form and design, production, and application). Usually, however, developing countries are only passive receivers and users of technologies imported from developed countries. Giant corporations own these technologies and exercise their right of ownership to maximize their profits; the motive of assisting developing nations is not part of the scenario. The Southern users of technology have little opportunity to innovate or indigenize the technology to make it truly theirs. Technology transfers often involve patent and copyright conditions preventing any indigenous innovation. This framework serves to ensure the continuous dependency of the South on the North, which some characterize as an ongoing form of colonialism.

9. An ironic situation exists in some developing countries, where the local population may be proud of the tallest buildings, the latest sophisticated transport systems, television satellites, and cybertechnologies, but the truth is that these are almost completely imported technologies. Some see globalization as a pretext for ensuring the dependency of Southern countries. Efforts should be made to strengthen local knowledge and capacity in S&T.

10. The negative effects of current development interventions on both humans and the environment are lamentable. Many developing nations prefer to hasten their development projects by imposing laws, for instance. But development is not a transparent process; the context of land acquisition for project implementation provides us with an example of the unintended consequences of legal measures. In some cases, they include no requirement to inform landowners, let alone consult them, regarding the project to be implemented; planners and politicians make the decisions. In addition, people are rarely provided with cost–benefit and risk–benefit analyses so that they can participate in the decision-making that will affect their lives so acutely. Compensation hardly removes the suffering caused by the loss of land, nor can it provide the security of livelihood provided by land ownership.[19]

145

---

[19] Personally, I feel that problems such as this can be linked to the lack of empowerment in general among people in developing countries. This question, in turn, is linked to a poor grasp of the meaning of religious principles such as *khalifah*, *amanah*, and humans' being accountable to God for all their actions.

REFERENCES

Al-Attas, S.M.N. 1992. Islam and the concept of religion and the foundation of ethics and morality. Dewan Bahasa dan Pustaka, Kuala Lumpur, Malaysia. 50 pp.

al-Faruqi, I.R.; al-Faruqi, L.L. 1986. The cultural atlas of Islam. Macmillan Publishing, New York, NY, USA. 512 pp.

al-Palembangi, A.S., Sheikh. 1953. Sirrus Salikin. Maktabah Wamatbaah Walmuarif, Penang, Malaysia.

Aung San Suu Kyi. 1997. Towards a culture of peace and development. JUST Commentary, New Series No. 6 (Nov), 1–4.

Baharuddin, A. 1989. Islam and science: some neglected perspectives. University of Lancaster, Lancaster, UK. PhD dissertation. 520 pp.

——— 1994. Science and religion as the basis of a universal philosophy of nature. In Baharuddin, A., ed., Science and belief: discourses on new perspectives. Institute for Policy Research, Kuala Lumpur, Malaysia. 233 pp.

Bergson, H. 1985 [1903]. Introduction to metaphysics. In Kolakowski, L., ed., Bergson. Oxford University Press, New York, NY, USA. 115 pp.

Bohm, D. 1981. Wholeness and the implicate order. Routledge and Kegan Paul, London, UK. 224 pp.

Brooke, J.H. 1979. Natural theology in Britain from Boyle to Paley. Milton Keynes; Open University, London, UK.

Capra, F. 1983. The Tao of physics: an exploration of the parallels between modern physics and Eastern mysticism. Fontana Paperbacks, London, UK. 384 pp.

——— 1985. The turning point: science, society and the rising culture. Fontana Paperbacks, London, UK. 464 pp.

Chapra, M.U. 1985. Towards a just monetary system: a discussion of money, banking, and monetary policy in the light of Islamic teachings. Islamic Foundation, Leicester, UK. 292 pp.

——— 1992. Islam and the economic challenge. Islamic Foundation and International Institute of Islamic Thought, Leicester, UK. 428 pp.

Daly, H.E. 1996. Beyond growth: the economics of sustainable development. Beacon Press, Boston, MA, USA. 253 pp.

Daud, W.R.W.; Zain, S.M. 1998. Islamisation and Malaysianisation of science and technology in the context of the National Science Policy. Paper presented at the National Seminar on National Science and Technology Policy, 16–17 Sep 1998, Kuala Lumpur, Malaysia. Academy of Islamic Sciences (Malaysia), Kuala Lumpur, Malaysia. 24 pp.

Ekins, P. 1992. A new world order: grassroots movements for global change. Routledge, New York, NY, USA. 248 pp.

Goulet, D. 1992. Development: creator or destroyer of values? World Development, 20(3), 467–475.

——— 1996. Development: historical task or opening to transcendence? Cross Currents, 46(2), 221–230.

Grof, S. 1996. Beyond the brain: birth, death, and transcendence in psychotherapy. State University of New York Press, New York, NY, USA. 466 pp.

Halepota, A.J. 1974. Shah Waliyullah and Iqbal: philosophers of the modern age. Islamic Studies, 13(4), 7–11.

146

Harman, W. 1988. The transpersonal challenge to the scientific paradigm: the need for a restructuring of science. Revision, 11(2), 13–21.

Iqbal, M. 1930. The reconstruction of religious thought in Islam. Ashraf, Lahore, India. Ashraf Publication 19. 128 pp.

Jeyaraj, S. 1997a. Downside of urban spiral. Sunday Magazine, Kuala Lumpur Sun, 30 Nov, pp. 4–5.

————— 1997b. Modern sickness. Sunday Magazine, Kuala Lumpur Sun, 30 Nov, pp. 6–8.

Lindberg, D.C., ed. 1986. God and nature: historical essays on the encounter between Christianity and science. University of California Press, Berkeley, CA, USA. 516 pp.

Naisbitt, J.; Aburdene, P. 1990. Megatrends 2000: the new directions for the 1990's. Avon Books, New York, NY, USA. 384 pp.

Nasr, S.H. 1968. Man and nature: the spiritual crisis of modern man. Unwin Paperbacks, London, UK. 151 pp.

————— 1993a. The need for a sacred science. Curzon Press, Surrey, UK. 187 pp.

————— 1993b. Islam. In Sharma, A., ed., Our religions. HarperCollins Publishers, New York, NY, USA. pp. 427–532.

Perroux, F. 1983. A new concept of development: basic tenets. Croom Helm; United Nations Educational, Scientific and Cultural Organization, Paris, France. 212 pp.

Rahman, M.A. 1998. Hadith. Dewan Pusataka Fajar, Shah Alam, Malaysia.

Razak, H.A.; Lathief, H.R. 1980. Translation of Hadith Sahih Muslim (vol. 1). Pustaka Al-Husna, Jakarta, Indonesia.

Russell, B. 1976. The impact of science on society. Unwin Paperbacks, London, UK. 127 pp.

Ryan, W.F. 1998. The book that the World Bank wouldn't publish. Review of Herman Daly, Beyond growth: the economics of sustainable development. Catholic New Times, 12 Apr, p. 18.

Salleh, M.S. 1998. Globalisation, development and Islam. Institute of Comparative Culture, Sophia University, Tokyo, Japan. ADMP Series, No. 28. 50 pp.

Sardar, Z. 1979a. The future of Muslim civilization. Croom Helm, London, UK. 288 pp.

————— 1979b. Islam, outline of a classification scheme. C. Bingley, London, UK. 81 pp.

————— 1985a. Arguments for Islamic science. Centre for Studies in Science, Aligarh, India. 63 pp.

————— 1985b. Islamic futures: the shape of ideas to come. Mansell, London, UK. 308 pp.

—————, ed. 1988. The touch of Midas: science, values and the environment in Islam and the West. Pelanduk Publications, Kuala Lumpur, Malaysia. 253 pp.

Sarton, G. 1927. Introduction to the history of science (vol. 1). Williams & Wilkins Co., Baltimore, MD, USA. For the Carnegie Institution of Washington.

Sheikh, M.S., ed. 1971. Studies in Iqbal's thoughts and art. Bazm-e-Iqbal, Lahore, India. 271 pp.

Stoddart, W. 1976. Sufism: the mystical doctrine and methods of Islam. Thorsons Publishers, Wellingborough, UK. 91 pp.

UNDP (United Nations Development Programme). 1997. Human development report 1997. Oxford University Press, New York, NY, USA. 245 pp.

Waly, K.H.M. 1991. The essence of the wisdom in *Tauhid* and *Tasauf*. Pustaka Nasional, Singapore.

Whitehead, A.N. 1985 [1925]. Science and the modern world. Free Association Books, London, UK. 265 pp.

CHAPTER 4

Promoting a Discourse on Science, Religion, and Development

Farzam Arbab

ON PERSONAL EXPERIENCE

It seems to me essential that, at the outset of a research program on the theme of science, religion, and development, one should acknowledge candidly the privileged role science must play as the source of methodology. The issues surrounding the choice of scientific methods, however, are in themselves complex, and a few words here on the subject may be in order.

Science in its broadest sense, embracing a wide range of phenomena in both nature and society, admits a variety of approaches and methods, each suitable to the character of a specific object of inquiry. In the study of innumerable systems and processes, questions related to the existence of God or the spiritual dimension of life simply do not arise; proper method must necessarily exclude them from consideration, if for no other reason than the preservation of scientific rigour. Yet, when such exclusion becomes a rule to be applied dogmatically across the board, an inflexibility sets in that robs science of some of its powers. Rigidly "scientific" approaches make it difficult to weigh science's own assumptions in balance with belief systems lying outside it. They allow the study of religion, but usually as a psychic or social phenomenon created by the interactions of human beings among themselves and with their environment, interactions that, in the final analysis, are thought to occur among aggregates of atoms and molecules, each behaving in strict compliance with the measure of complexity accorded it by nature. That this is not the view of the vast majority of humanity, who, everyone agrees, will have to participate fully in the process of social transformation and whose cultures, beliefs, and values are to be incorporated into the design and implementation of development activity, poses a contradiction that severely limits the usefulness of development studies carried out according to narrow definitions of the "scientific method."

I take it to be a premise of our research program that it is possible to rigorously explore issues of religious belief without trivializing them or explaining them away, relegating matters of faith to the private and isolated world of the individual, or confining religious practice to the domain of ritual, legitimized by the needs of humanity as a social species. This, of course, is not a new premise: it underlies the work of social scientists and theologians of various schools. Unfortunately, it has not had a significant influence on the kind of thinking that has shaped the field of development in the past few decades.

Furthermore, it appears unavoidable that to deal properly with the difficulties of methodological choice, our approach to this research should remain measured and judicious. Thus, I hope that for some time to come the emphasis will continue to be on the formulation of a discourse on the theme of science, religion, and development, rather than shifting to elaborate studies or the articulation of hypotheses. Naturally, to be scientific, our discourse would have to fulfill certain conditions. For example, its language must strive to be rational, unambiguous, and objective. The challenge before us is to achieve this when the object of inquiry touches so intimately on each participant's own faith.

I find quite inadequate the approach to the study of religion that divides the researcher into two separate entities, the scientist and the believer, the first bound to the rules of academia and the second obliged to ignore the absurdities this duality introduces into his or her belief system. That so untenable an approach should have widespread acceptance is due to the impositions of secularism acting as a kind of fundamentalist creed. As a result, much of the reality of science, religion, and the forces that transform society has ended up hidden behind a veil created by false objectivity.

The alternative to the prevailing situation is not apologetics or sectarian controversy. What is called for is a new look at the interpenetration of reason and faith, as well as a systematic exploration of rational approaches that are not tied to materialism. Although such a thorough exploration is not part of the mandate of this project, acknowledgment of its absolute necessity is important to our frame of reference.

An immediate consequence of this realization, it could be argued, is to require the researcher in certain fields to make explicit the relevant aspects of his or her own belief and experience. To do so in a meaningful way, one must be convinced that it is possible to be firm in one's convictions without being judgmental. Although the statement "if I believe something to be right, then he whose opinions differ from mine must be wrong" passes the tests of formal logic and although it is applicable in countless situations, its usefulness vanishes once the object of discussion becomes relatively complex. It is not that "A" and "not A" can both be true, but that the vastness of truth does not allow most matters of belief, if there is any depth to them at all, to be reduced to such comparisons. The only options this simplistic posture finally leaves open are either religious and ideological fanaticism or the brand of relativism that does away with faith, embraces scepticism, and idolizes doubt. It is instructive to note how the assaults of such relativism on belief, initially launched against religion, have been directed in the postmodern era to the very foundations of science.

It is for the reasons expressed above, and not because of an urge to defend a set of religious beliefs, that I will incorporate in this paper brief explanations of certain elements of my own faith. In this introductory section, I will try to describe how my personal experience and belief system determine the way I address issues in the subsequent sections.

MY INTRODUCTION TO DEVELOPMENT

I was first introduced to the field of development in 1971, when I was invited to join the deliberations of an interdisciplinary group concerned with integrated approaches to rural development. At the time, I was a visiting professor at the Universidad del Valle in Colombia, helping to reorganize its department of physics to meet the standards of universities in North America and Western Europe. Our project was part of the Rockefeller Foundation's intensive effort to improve higher education in several universities around the world and turn them into efficient instruments of modernization.

To contribute to the formation of a generation of scientists who would lay a firm foundation for progress in their country was an exciting prospect and one that indeed had drawn me to Colombia. Yet, I was uncomfortable with the distance that separated our formal academic endeavour from the lives of the millions of people whose needs and aspirations demanded immediate attention. Participation in the deliberations of the interdisciplinary group at the university was a welcome opportunity to pursue my search for a more direct use of science in systems and processes relevant to the social reality of the masses of humanity. After all, science, the source of technology, was for me the most crucial force moving at the very heart of modernization, that

magical process that I had been taught to cherish and revere all through
the various stages of my education.

As it turned out, my enthusiasm for the group's intellectually
stimulating discussions on the nature of social and economic development lasted for about a year. In keeping with our original motivation
for moving to Latin America, my wife and I were simultaneously
becoming involved in the activities of the Colombian Bahá'í community, especially in a rural region near Cali known as Norte del Cauca.
The gap between the reality of life we encountered there and the elaborate constructs of the interdisciplinary group uncovered contradictions
that I found difficult to ignore.

By the time I had joined the interdisciplinary group, my colleagues had already decided on a series of definitions about development
and were committed to constructing a model to guide their future activities. According to this model, well-being resulted from the convergence of several factors such as health, housing, education, employment,
family life, community organization, and other elements that could be
grouped together under the general heading of "culture." Integrated
development implied the simultaneous and united action of various
governmental organizations to improve these factors. The role of the
university was to coordinate these interventions and provide the necessary theoretical framework.

The exercise in which our group was engaged was by no means
unique. Those were the years when the field of development was beginning to focus on the poor, and the World Bank, under the leadership of
Robert McNamara, was promoting growth with equity, attention to
basic needs, and integrated rural development. We were often in contact
with world experts, some of whom visited us and brought us the latest
in development thinking. With their help our theoretical elaboration
became increasingly more sophisticated; we discovered new factors,
refined our definitions, saw new relationships, and contemplated the
effects of a change in one factor on the workings of the others.

If I remember correctly, the subject that presented the greatest
challenge to us was "participation," a theme that, at the time, was gaining prominence in development discourse. It was my dissatisfaction
with the way this challenge was faced that helped crystallize in my
mind a series of objections to the premises underlying the approach our
group had taken. My response was gradually to distance myself from the
group and, with the help of a few other colleagues, begin to formulate
the framework for the activities of a small organization of our own:
Fundación para la Aplicación y Enseñanza de las Ciencias (FUNDAEC,
Foundation for the Application and Teaching of the Sciences).[1] Some of
the questions we asked ourselves at that time — and some of the
answers we found over the years as the scope of our actions increased and

---

[1] More information on FUNDAEC's principles and activities can be found at its website
(www.bcca.org/services/lists/noble-creation/fundaec1.html).

FUNDAEC became a well-established development organization — seem highly relevant to the present inquiry on the theme of science, religion, and development.

THE INSIDE–OUTSIDE DICHOTOMY

The first question was cast, initially, in the language of the previous group: What was the role of the villagers themselves in interdisciplinary, multi-institutional development intervention? The analyses we found in the literature on participation, though thought provoking, were not entirely satisfactory. No matter how hard we tried, we could not escape an uneasy feeling that by adopting any of the prevalent approaches, we would be asking a people to participate in our plans and follow our models. That we would do everything possible to give them a voice in the endeavour, especially at the level of implementation, would do little to change this underlying message, which, we had no doubt, would be picked up by the people themselves.

153

What was curious about these deliberations on the theme of participation was that the more one thought in terms of "we" and "they," the farther away seemed the people one wished to serve. The pendulum seemed to swing from extreme to extreme, from the paternalism of the previous decades to the glorification of cultural autonomy and self-determination. Why were so many development organizations taking on with such tenacity the role of an outsider? Are human beings doomed to be outsiders to every group except a single one, a subculture narrowly defined by nationality, ethnicity, social class, religion, and occupation?

My experience with the Bahá'í community presented a sharp contrast to the efforts of most development projects I had come to know. Here, I was a member of a community — in this case consisting mostly of people of little material means — morally bound to participate in its plans, to follow the guidance of its elected institutions, and to contribute my talents and resources to its spiritual and material advancement. Although learning the subtleties of a new culture would take time, I was, by definition, part of the collectivity from the very beginning: I was not an outsider.

Becoming acquainted with a people as an agent of a development organization or bearer of charity is profoundly different from working among friends for a common purpose. In the latter case, one's perception of reality is not shaped simply by academic theories that describe, from the outside, the needs and aspirations of the great masses of humanity. Although the gravity of social injustice is felt and understood, the integrity and capacity for joy of its victims offer protection against some of the emotions that afflict external observers of poverty: pity, fear, sanctimonious indignation, ambivalence, and the inordinate desire to direct others to irrelevant paths laid out in accordance with one's own accomplishments or frustrations. For me, what was most striking about my new community was not material poverty per se but the wealth of talent that went uncultivated, together with the dreams of noble futures that went unfulfilled, as injustice systematically blocked the development of potentialities.

Over the years, I have become increasingly convinced that what I originally perceived as a matter of personal choice — to learn to see the world from inside the population I wish to serve and become a participant in their endeavours to transform the world — represents in fact a fundamental issue inadequately addressed in development theory. That so many development programs are interventions managed from the outside, while the praise of participation is confidently sung, is a manifestation of a social structure that has accepted separation as the norm — the dividing of people into groups of "we" and "they" who fight, who compete, who negotiate, who cooperate, or who help each other from across the boundaries that define their separateness. This tendency reinforces, and is reinforced by, an intellectuality that sees as the hallmark of intelligence the ability to identify differences, to divide, and to relativize, all in the name of being scientific. Such an approach is a gross misrepresentation of science, for although it is true that science analyzes, it also integrates and points to underlying patterns of oneness.

Religion, of course, has done its full share to contribute to the consolidation of separateness. Yet, it would be a mistake to imagine that a posture of superiority, often assumed by one religious group in relation to another, is inherent to religion. Belief in the unity of humankind, with its implications of equity and selfless love, is, after all, ultimately a religious conception of reality. Viewed from the angle of oneness, development ceases to be something one does for others. A vision begins to emerge according to which the rich and the poor, the illiterate and the educated, are all to participate in building a new civilization, one that ensures the material and spiritual prosperity of the entire human race.

HOW THE POOR ARE PERCEIVED

The second of our questions — which remains as relevant today as it was to us in the early 1970s — had to do with the way development programs tend to view the essential nature of the masses of humanity whose participation they seek to secure. From the beginning, my colleagues and I at FUNDAEC identified ourselves with approaches that later came to be known as people-centred development. But we felt uncomfortable with the images that were being evoked by the phrase "the poorest of the poor," used so extensively in development literature in those days.

When, after World War II, development economists began to promote growth policies among the nations of the world, the technical talk about industrialization, capital accumulation, planning, foreign aid, and transfer of know-how carried connotations that were not of material poverty alone but of peoples' backwardness. This was especially true when referring to the inhabitants of rural areas, who were described, no matter how politely, as ignorant, unmotivated, lazy, and superstitious. It was even assumed that up to 50% of them lived virtually unproductive lives and could readily be moved to the cities to provide cheap labour to accelerate industrialization. Perhaps to mitigate the moral implications of such an assumption, the highest compliment was then bestowed on these masses: they were called the hidden capital of the developing nations. The first stages of migration from rural to urban areas, now so sorely lamented, were not accidents of history: they were inspired and driven by the flawed perception development thinkers held of their fellow human beings.

The pioneers of the Green Revolution argued against this view of peasants but without abandoning most of the other cherished premises of development economics. It was not the peasant, they pointed out, but the state of technology that was the cause of equilibrium at a low level of production. Villagers were indeed clever and efficient in the use of the tools at their disposal. The solution to the problem lay, therefore, in the transformation of traditional agriculture. Like their other colleagues, these pioneers revered what they saw as modern rationality. Thus, they went on to proclaim that peasants, too, belonged to the species *Homo economicus,* an article of faith that underpinned their elaborate — and admirable — efforts to modernize agricultural and animal production.

The Green Revolution was only partially successful. Food production increased notably, and millions were almost certainly saved from pending starvation. But the gap between the rich and the poor also increased both in the villages and in the cities that received a constant stream of migrants in search of a better life. In the meantime, development thinking had moved ahead to emphasize the needs of the poor and their share and participation in economic growth. But there was still no fundamental change in the way the poor were perceived. The new image, which has persisted since the early 1970s, is that of the materially poor as a bundle of problems and needs; people suffering from malnutrition and lack of sanitation; people with little education, living in inadequate quarters, lacking capital, with no access to modern technology, and unable to enjoy any reasonable level of consumption. How such aggregates of problems are expected to become active protagonists in development is not easy to understand.

The problem runs very deep. Efforts to free development thinking from such paternalistic views tend all too often to fall into ideological traps, at the heart of which is a misconception of human nature. In the cherished notions of these ideologies, the liberated agents of change are either competitive, tireless labourers and entrepreneurs busily accumulating wealth or politicized social actors focused single-mindedly on matters of individual and group power. Neither the excessive

155

individualism of the former nor the consecration to conflict of the latter, of course, supposedly serves only the self. Through some alchemy never quite explained, these labours and struggles result in social forces that will modernize underdeveloped nations and usher humanity into an age of prosperity. At the altars of such tragic misconceptions of human nature the lives of the masses of humanity have been sacrificed for decades.

It is difficult to see how development theory and practice can undergo fundamental change unless the corresponding discourse admits a reexamination of the nature of the human being. Such exploration cannot be effected simply through speculation and arbitrary expressions of uninformed opinion. The serious discussion of this vital matter inevitably calls for a new level of dialogue between science and religion.

Conceptions of human nature

So much of what I will present in the following sections is based on my view of human nature that I should make a few comments on the subject. Ideas of the kind I express here run the danger of being dismissed as utopian. But, then, the instinctive rejection of noble aspirations in the name of realism has become habitual with approaches to social issues that have failed both to uplift the human race and to acknowledge their impotence. The prevailing — presumably realistic — views of human nature are confusing and self-contradictory. On the one hand, we dream of, and labour for, a world of peace and prosperity; on the other, what passes for scientific theory depicts us as slaves to self-interest, incapable of rising to the heights of nobility we must achieve to meet our challenges. We work, then, for objectives lying forever beyond our selfish means. It is such contradictions that have led to the paralysis of will that today pervades all strata of society.

To liberate ourselves from these paralyzing contradictions, we must first ask if the history of the human race, with all its follies, substantiates any such theories as original sin, the innocent being corrupted by civilization, the human who is only one step away from being a god, or the animal who is driven by a collection of insatiable needs. When the operations of love, of the will to conquer the ego, of transcendence, and of beauty are examined — along with the cruelty that has afflicted humanity in its arduous evolutionary path — the picture that emerges is of a human being with a dual nature, and a set of complementary forces that shape and reshape that nature.

We cannot deny that we have inherited from millions of years of animal evolution attributes that belong to those origins. In the animal, such characteristics are neither good nor bad; they are merely traits required for individual or collective survival. But they do not constitute a realistic base upon which human society can be constructed. There is ample historical and experiential evidence that we also possess a higher nature, a spiritual one that has gradually made it possible for us to understand and satisfy material needs within appropriate limits while rising above the exigencies of animal existence. None of the usual attitudes toward our physical nature — rejection, guilt, passive acceptance, or loving fixation — is conducive to transcendence. The challenge is to overcome the limitations urged on us by the demands of survival, to learn to control the appetites of the animal, and to develop the qualities of the higher nature that struggles for expression. This is a personal task to be tackled by every individual and, at the same time, an imperative in the collective evolution of the human race.

The primary force propelling this, now conscious, evolutionary process is knowledge, a knowledge that is created and constantly re-created on the basis of a sound understanding of one's self, of those promptings that lead to abasement and of those that lead to dignity and honour. The two repositories of this knowledge are religion and science. With their aid we discover in ourselves the powers of nobility, freedom, and oneness and learn to apply these powers in building an ever-advancing civilization. "Thou art even as a finely tempered sword," says Bahá'u'lláh, "concealed in the darkness of its sheath and its value hidden from the artificer's knowledge. Wherefore come forth from the sheath of self and desire that thy worth may be made resplendent and manifest unto all the world" (BPT 1994, 2:72). Only belief in its inherent nobility can equip humanity to respond to the demands of this crucial historical moment. Far from the familiar expression of unbridled individualism, the freedom that is a corollary of such belief is a gift received through obedience to the laws of spiritual reality, a fruit of the recognition of the principle of oneness and interconnectedness that governs the universe.

THE URGE TO BE SCIENTIFIC

Another set of issues to which my colleagues and I at FUNDAEC gave a great deal of attention — one that again is highly relevant to the present discourse — concerns the scientific nature of the development enterprise. My first reaction to the way science was being discussed in the interdisciplinary group that started me in the field had been one of astonishment. Why was there — in a still-emerging area of human knowledge — so much emphasis on creating elaborate models, on making precise measurements, and on finding "witness" populations, as if science was reducible to a simplistic application of a few rigidly defined methods? My attitude was somewhat surprising to the group that expected the newly acquired physicist to bring rigour to its endeavours. What it received, instead, was a plea for flexibility, for the gradual consolidation of a set of facts, and for seeking insights, rather than formulating grand theories and complex models.

157

Having observed a wide range of policies and programs for many years, I am now convinced that the field of development suffers at various levels from an inadequate understanding of science. First, in the absence of a consistent conceptual framework acceptable to most practitioners, it falls prey to the impositions of competing disciplines — economics, agricultural science, public health, anthropology, management, and so on — each of which, while acknowledging a role for other disciplines, insists on fashioning the field according to underlying ideological premises of its own. Second, lacking a clear interpretation of the connections between science and technology, development thinking overemphasizes the latter and does not pay the necessary attention to the advancement of the scientific culture of peoples. Third, by focusing on certain tools and procedures — for planning, for reporting, for evaluating — it loses sight of the exigencies of systematic and structured learning, an essential characteristic of any approach that claims to be scientific.

By arguing the above, I do not wish to suggest that the very complex set of social, cultural, political, and economic interactions necessary to bring about change should be scientific. But neither is it reasonable to assume that social transformation is an engineering problem to be managed by technocrats and moved in directions set by political and economic power. What we have the right to expect is systematic learning about development through which some kind of ascertained knowledge can be gradually accumulated in communities and institutions.

Reflections such as these led FUNDAEC to dedicate its first efforts to the creation of what was called the rural university, an institution defined as the "social space" in which the inhabitants of a given rural region would learn about the path of their own development. Within this context, we focused our attention on various spheres of activity in rural life — production, marketing, decision-making, education, socialization, and the like — for each of which we set in motion a learning process that consisted of research, action, and training carried out with the growing participation of the people of the region as they gained a sense of ownership of the rural university.

That development is not a package the "developed" deliver to the "underdeveloped" but a process in which entire populations must, in one way or another, participate is a realization that came about simultaneously in many organizations and agencies. Early in our experience of the rural university, we learned that such a view of development, while freeing the field from simplistic formulas, raises new challenges. The process is not advanced by the mere application of technology, even when it is supported by political will, and must be intimately connected to structured scientific learning. But while science can offer the methods and tools of inquiry and learning, it alone cannot set the direction; the goal of development cannot come from within the process itself. The path of development must be illumined by the light of moral and spiritual principles emanating from religion, but religion willing to submit its proposals to the scrutiny of science.

THE RURAL–URBAN BALANCE

My experience in development began with intense involvement in the life of a relatively small rural population and only gradually grew to embrace issues in a global context. Throughout, the immediate future of rural life on the planet was a question of paramount importance in my thinking. The question is significant for the present inquiry in that it brings to focus the direction that has been set for the social and economic development of nations.

No one would claim that development objectives are set by consensus, through profound religious reflection on the nature and purpose of human existence, or through the scientific exploration of the options open to the human race. So simplistic a demand could not be made by anyone aware of the complexity of human affairs. Yet, it is not unreasonable to expect that, after these many decades, defining the aims of a significant global enterprise, which development has become, would no longer be approached haphazardly.

The present direction of development continues to be — in practice, if not in theory — modernization through an industrialization propelled by feverish activity to sustain technological progress. It was set by individuals whose experiences were shaped by World War II and by the breakdown of colonial empires. The theories that helped define it, Marxist or capitalist, viewed the city as the fairest fruit of civilization and the factory as the wellspring of wealth. They assumed that development would finally lead to a world in which rural dwellers would represent an extremely small percentage of the total population and that even these would have the characteristics of industrial workers.

Personally, I have never surrendered to romanticism about the beautiful past, the tranquil village life, or the spirituality of the rejection of means. The future I envision is highly technological, one in which scientific advances will have enabled humanity to live free from the struggle for mere survival. Nor do I see much value in speculating about the eventual form that cities and villages will take, although I find it difficult to believe that a mature humanity will live under the conditions we define today as either urban or rural. What seems to me indispensable is the creation of a viable future for the vast number of villages in the world so that their dwellers can participate meaningfully in building a world civilization. The poverty belts of Lima and Calcutta are not viable options.

A most disturbing fact about the current disintegration of rural life is that it is a direct result of policy. Beliefs that predict and applaud the rural–urban trend are self-fulfilling, for they are translated into strategies that impoverish the countryside and increase urban problems, thus absorbing more and more resources and accelerating the cycle. Colonialism transferred to the emerging cities of the South the abhorrent conditions that characterized so many European cities at the dawn of industrialization. Five decades of development have brought about the multiplication and growth of these cities whose problems seem insurmountable, despite the combined efforts of thousands of institutions toiling indefatigably to overcome them. But the victims of these erroneous policies are not only the broken families living partly in the village and partly in the slums of the city. The entire planet has suffered from its infatuation with a certain brand of industrialization and urbanization, as its leaders and policymakers, following their dreams and living in islands of prosperity, have lost touch both with the soul of the masses and with nature. Their relentless pursuit of what they have defined as progress is not sufficiently influenced either by the power of rigorous scientific inquiry or by the spiritual insights of religion.

THE DIRECTION OF DEVELOPMENT

Throughout the years, my colleagues and I in FUNDAEC participated in numerous deliberations on the nature and purpose of development and learned much from theories that focused attention on a growing set of interrelated themes, such as technological choice, the environment, basic needs, human development, and participatory research and action. Yet, it has always been difficult for me to see how the results of these deliberations can by themselves change the direction of development. Will a new direction ever be set if the masses of humanity continue to be considered mere beneficiaries of projects rather than the real protagonists of development? And can this change come about in the institutional vacuum that characterizes the life of such a vast number of human beings?

The majority of the interventions directed to "the poor" by government and nongovernmental organizations (NGOs) are of two kinds: the provision of services and the creation of groups that in one way or another cooperate to improve their own conditions. Usually, both kinds include a notable component of training. The objectives of training vary from preparing beneficiaries to receive services all the way to raising political consciousness and empowerment. No matter how extensive, however, these interventions and the accompanying training do not define the path of development for most nations. This is done largely through policies that crystallize in institutions charged with governing and administering the people's affairs, institutions that, alas, belong to and are chiefly accessible to a privileged minority, regardless of the fact that most people are constantly voting for this or the other candidate to run them.

Why the enhancement of institutional capacity among rural populations and the inhabitants of poor city neighbourhoods has been neglected by so many development plans is a question for which I have never had an adequate answer. The economists who set the tone for the entire enterprise at the beginning talked a great deal about the importance of institutions. But their focus on the traditional–modern dichotomy seems to have led them to concentrate on creating and strengthening institutions in the so-called modern sector. After all, the existence of the traditional sectors was coming to an end, and their members were to move gradually into a modern world that was being built for them. The dream, of course, did not come true. What has emerged, rather, is a world in which the majority not only lives in poverty but is increasingly marginalized from the institutional channels that would allow it a voice in shaping its future. The traditional institutions of most societies were not faultless or even viable in a world in rapid transition. The point is that they were mercilessly assailed by the forces of modernization without substitutes being offered to those who could only be passive witnesses to the disintegration of their systems and processes of life. The result is today's widening gulf that separates a technologically advanced society from the world in which the great majority of the human race lives.

161

The inability of development theory and practice to adequately address the creation, transformation, and strengthening of the structures of an emerging world civilization has been exacerbated by the long-standing conflict between two extreme views. At one extreme lies the conviction that change is basically effected at the level of the individual; at the other stands the conception of the human being as a mere product of society, and revolutionary structural change as the only way out of the predicament of most nations. The adherents of the first view include, of course, the followers of religious movements who see the solution to human problems in the salvation of souls, offered either to fixed numbers or to everyone on the planet. Although such a position would be frowned upon in development circles, it is surprising to note how many internationally supported development plans have sought to overcome poverty with minimum structural change by upgrading the skills of individuals through elaborate training programs designed to fit them to receive credit or employment. Insistence by those clinging to the second position, some of whom have gone so far as to label efforts to improve the human condition as mere attempts to postpone revolution, has done its share to divert attention from the challenges of institutional development. Perhaps today, when the debate between these extremes seems to have been exhausted, social theory can examine the transformation of human society in detached consideration of a complex set of interactions between profound changes within the individual and deliberate systematic re-creation of social structure.

The creation of the institutions of a global society, a web of interconnected structures that hold society together at all levels, from local to international — institutions that gradually become the patrimony of all the inhabitants of the planet — is for me one of the major challenges of development planning and strategy. Without it, I fear, globalization will be synonymous with the marginalization of the masses. I do not see how, in their present state, the social sciences can adequately address this challenge. The enormous scientific advance required by the task demands volition and a rigorous application of the methods of science. But method alone is not enough. A vision is needed, and the proper vision will never take shape if the entire spiritual heritage of the human race continues to be neglected.

TECHNIQUE, POWER, SPIRITUALITY, AND KNOWLEDGE

Finally, in my attempt to make explicit certain elements of personal belief and experience that influence my treatment of our theme of research, I should comment on the way I view a number of interrelated development concerns.

As mentioned before, my initial invitation to join the deliberations of a group on development was as a scientist expected to be concerned for scientific rigour. Soon I realized that what was required of me was to make technical contributions to the group. This I endeavoured to do with great pleasure. However, I gradually learned that to deal with development, and in fact with most social issues, at the level of technique is a growing and disturbing tendency of our times. I became increasingly aware of the limitations of a technocracy and grew weary of belonging to it. But the choice offered by the critics of technocratic rule was the veneration of politics and political power, which I found even less appealing.

That change and transformation entail the operation of power is an undeniable fact. That numerous issues in the field of development have a significant political dimension is also irrefutable. But the premise that political and economic power — interpreted as advantage enjoyed by persons or groups or as an attribute of individuals, factions, peoples, classes, and nations used to acquire, to surpass, to dominate, to resist, and to win — is the agent that will bring prosperity to the entire human race is untenable. Despite all claims to the contrary, there is no convincing historical evidence for this supposition. It appears to me that adherence to such a premise in the name of realism is in itself an indication of the confusion afflicting social thought.

The rapid expansion of Western civilization takes to every corner of the world both the blessings and the curses of the Enlightenment. The blessings include the systematic removal of the veils of superstition. But, unfortunately, this is accompanied by a coarseness of mind that tends to dismiss the ideal and to call real that which is ugly and base. The result, after a few centuries of insistence, is widespread forgetfulness of those many powers of the human spirit that are in fact responsible for some of the greatest accomplishments of humanity's past. Among these are the powers of unity, of humble service, of noble deeds, of love, and of truth. But even to mention the word *truth* in respectable discourse has become unacceptable; truth has been dethroned and reduced to something that is negotiable or a mere expression of dominance. The loudest message broadcast all over the world for an entire generation to hear is "he who is successful is right."

The only explanation I have found for how a process of intellectual enhancement, so intimately associated in its origins with the free investigation of reality, has led us to our present predicament is persistent neglect of the spiritual dimension of human existence. Modern scientific knowledge has shown its power to liberate us from the fetters of religion ruled by superstition and maintained by self-righteousness. But it has also demonstrated how it can lose its bearings when it falls victim to materialism. The knowledge system currently propelling the development of the world is fragmented. Its fragments by themselves cannot address the highly complex and interrelated problems of societies in dire need of profound transformation. Yet, the power that can ultimately raise humanity from its present condition is the power of knowledge. It is my perception of the role of knowledge in development that leads me to examine the theme of our research in the context of capacity-building, which is the subject of the fourth section of this paper.

163

FURTHER COMMENTS

In the remainder of this section, I address a number of points with direct bearing on the arguments of the preceding pages. These comments are intended to provide additional context for the ideas presented thus far and to lend them further clarity.

Definitions of science

In writing this document, I have tried to avoid explicit definitions of science. The literature of various fields is, of course, replete with such definitions. To none of them do I seriously adhere, convinced as I am that complex entities reveal their inner operations only if they are approached on a multitude of fronts. Statements of what science is and is not are useful so long as they are employed to offer insight and not to reduce. For the purposes of this paper, a phrase like "a system of knowledge and practice" seems sufficient, in that it allows me to discuss science in broad terms. I do hope, however, that what emerges is consistent with the notion of science as an expression of those faculties of the rational soul that, through both sensible and reasonable perception, shed light on the reality of inner and outer phenomena.

My own view of science has been shaped by theoretical physics, a modest amount of reading in the philosophy and history of science, and years of exposure to the social sciences as I worked in development-related fields. But the unshakeable faith I have in science, one that I trust comes through in the arguments presented in this paper, has its roots in religious belief as well as in scientific training. So insistent are the Bahá'í teachings about the critical role of science in the advancement of civilization that it would be difficult for a Bahá'í not to stand in awe of both the scientific heritage of humankind and its potential for future accomplishments. These teachings unambiguously declare as superstitious any religious belief that clearly disagrees with the confirmed results of scientific inquiry. Such statements as the following, from 'Abdu'l-Bahá, are representative of numerous passages on this subject:

> The virtues of humanity are many, but science is the most noble of them all. ... Science is an effulgence of the Sun of Reality, the power of investigating and discovering the verities of the universe, the means by which man finds a pathway to God.
> Science is the first emanation from God toward man. All created beings embody the potentiality of material perfection, but the power of intellectual investigation and scientific acquisition is a higher virtue specialized to man alone. ... The development and progress of a nation is according to the measure and degree of that nation's scientific attainments. Through this means its greatness is continually increased, and day by day the welfare and prosperity of its people are assured.
>
> BPT (1982, p. 49)

It would be misleading for me to give the impression, however, that science receives only praise in the Bahá'í writings. Also present are passages that warn of the harm science can do when it is divorced from spiritual perception. "The sciences of today are bridges to reality," stated 'Abdu'l-Bahá. "If then they lead not to reality, naught remains but fruitless illusion" (BPT 1997, 72:3).

Religion and development

The limitations of a discourse on development restricted by narrow definitions of the "scientific method," to which I have alluded, are not solely theoretical in nature; they affect the operation of development programs at every level. From its very beginnings, development thinking adopted the attitudes of a secular tradition, which, historically, has suffered from an inadequate conception of knowledge:

> This reductionist approach to knowledge leads most development specialists to become one-eyed giants: scientists lacking wisdom. They analyse, prescribe and act *as if* man could live by bread alone, *as if* human destiny could be stripped to its material dimensions alone.
>
> Goulet (1980, p. 481, emphasis in the original)

The attitudes toward religion fostered by the secular culture within which the field of development has flourished range from dismissiveness to outright hostility. Gunnar Myrdal's now classic *Asian*

Drama provides a candid — by no means exceptional — statement of this self-confident article of secular faith:

> Religion is, of course, crucial, but not the interpretation of old scriptures and the lofty philosophies and theologies developed over centuries of speculation. It is, indeed, amazing how much Western, as well as South Asian, writers think they are saying about the peoples of the region when they refer loosely to the impact of Hinduism, Buddhism, or Islam, which they think of as general concepts and often as intellectualized and abstruse. Religion should be studied for what it really is among the people: a ritualized and stratified complex of highly emotional beliefs and valuations that give the sanction of sacredness, taboo, and immutability to inherited institutional arrangements, modes of living, and attitudes. Understood in this realistic and comprehensive sense, religion usually acts as a tremendous force for social inertia. The writer knows of no instance in present-day South Asia where religion has induced social change. Least of all does it foster realization of the modernization ideals. From a planning point of view, this inertia related to religion, like other obstacles, must be overcome by policies for inducing changes, formulated in a plan for development. But the religiously sanctioned beliefs and valuations not only act as obstacles among the people to getting the plan accepted but also as inhibitions in the planners themselves insofar as they share them, or are afraid to counteract them.
>
> Myrdal (1972, pp. 48–49)

Magisterial statements of this kind long inhibited development workers from paying due attention to the force of religion, even when they themselves held firm religious beliefs. But now that five decades of intervention have revealed the strengths and weaknesses of dominant patterns of thought, development practitioners are becoming increasingly vocal in expressing their dissatisfaction with the consequences of this narrow approach to their field of expertise. This message comes through strongly in *Culture, Spirituality, and Economic Development: Opening a Dialogue*, William F. Ryan's (1995) account of his interviews with some 200 experienced individuals around the world, which served as the point of departure for our present endeavour.

To incorporate the subject of religion into development discourse is no easy matter. It is true that the field has been reasonably open to new ideas, but it has shown extraordinary reluctance to abandon its fundamentally materialistic mind-set. With painful slowness, people's participation, their culture, and their values have become accepted as legitimate matters to be addressed; even the mention of spirituality is now beginning to enjoy a certain acceptance. A thousand objections are raised, however, the moment the word *religion* is introduced. There is no opposition, of course, to what Goulet called an "instrumental" use of religious beliefs. These are "viewed *primarily* as mere means — aids or obstacles — to the achievement of goals derived from sources outside the value systems in question" (Goulet 1980, p. 484, emphasis in the original). Although development agents may be sensitive to local values, they

> usually derive their goals from outside these values: from develop-
> ment models or the common assumptions of their respective scien-
> tific disciplines. Thus, a demographer will strive to "harness" local
> values to his objective of promoting contraception or achieving zero
> population growth. Similarly, the agronomist will search for a
> traditional practice upon which to "graft" his recommendation to
> use chemical pesticides. Similarly, the community organizer will
> "mobilize" a population for political ends around traditionally
> cherished symbols.
>
> Goulet (1980, p. 484)

166

This instrumental treatment of religion is accompanied by a host of superficial remarks about the relationship between religion and progress that expose an unwillingness to study in any depth the way various religious traditions deal with the issue under discussion. A statement by W. Arthur Lewis illustrates the prevalent attitude:

> Does religion have an independent effect in shaping economic
> behaviour, or does religion merely reflect economic conditions? It is
> obvious that religious beliefs change as economic and social condi-
> tions change. Religious doctrines are continuously being reinter-
> preted, and adjusted to new situations. ...
>
> We cannot accept the conclusion that it is always economic
> change which causes religious change, and never religious change
> that causes economic or social change. It is not true that if economic
> interest and religious doctrines conflict, the economic interest will
> always win. The Hindu cow has remained sacred for centuries,
> although this is plainly contrary to economic interests. Or, to take
> another example, the failure of Spain to seize and exploit the
> economic opportunities presented by the discovery of the New
> World cannot be explained satisfactorily without taking into
> account religious beliefs and attitudes which hindered Spain in her
> competition with other countries. It is possible for a nation to stifle
> its economic growth by adopting passionately and intolerantly reli-
> gious doctrines of a kind which are incompatible with growth. Or
> it is possible, alternatively, for conversion to a new faith to be the
> spark which sets off economic growth.
>
> Lewis (1955, pp. 106–107)

The field of development

The word *development* — which spans an enormous range of meaning in the English language — is used in this paper chiefly to denote a partic-ular historical process. During the late 1940s and early 1950s, follow-ing the breakup of the colonial empires, a world poised for unprecedented social and economic transformation witnessed the emergence of a set of activities the purpose of which, apart from the reconstruction of Europe, was the "development" of the nations then considered backward. This field of activity, originally the concern of a band of development economists (see, for example, Meier and Seers 1984), rapidly grew into a gigantic global enterprise involving governments, a constellation of international agencies, the private sector, and an ever-increasing array of NGOs.

In its early years, development practice was intimately connected with foreign aid. In all but a few countries, however, the ratio of financial aid channeled through development programs to the funds expended by governments and private companies to effect social and economic change has gradually decreased until, today, in many cases it has become negligible. Yet, the field of development itself has steadily gained in importance, in terms of both the number of those who participate in its activities and the influence it exerts on public opinion and policy. Its successes and failures have become vital issues in the social and political lives of nations, challenging the intellectual resources of outstanding thinkers in a variety of scientific and professional fields. Its language has even entered the popular vocabulary, with terms like *the Third World*, *technology transfer*, *basic needs*, and *sustainability* now commonplace.

It is not unreasonable to claim, then, that today's multifaceted discourse on development is important for humanity's future and that the direction it should take in the coming years is a subject worthy of serious consideration. Given the magnitude of the forces at play, new ideas will become widespread only as their timeliness is proven, and this cannot be done without an adequate understanding of the evolution of development thought over the five decades or so since its inception. Although an extensive discussion of the subject is beyond the scope of the present examination, a few comments seem to be in order.

At a first glance, certain features of development discourse may suggest a linear evolution of thought through a series of well-defined and progressive stages. Indeed, the first three decades of activity have repeatedly been described in these terms. Dennis A. Rondinelli, for example, offered the following account in his 1983 work, *Development Projects as Policy Experiments*:

> The complex and uncertain changes that have come about in development policies and aid strategies can be seen in three major periods in the history of development theories. The industrial development policies of the 1950s and early 1960s sought maximum growth in the economies of developing nations and assumed that trickle down and spread effects would incorporate the majority of the poor into productive economic activities. The policies sought rapid and high rates of growth in national output with little

concern for distributive effects, and thus used largely untargeted aid strategies.

Development policies of the 1960s were designed to overcome obstacles and eliminate bottlenecks to economic growth by redistributing productive assets, developing human resources, controlling population growth, and increasing productive capacity in lagging sectors of developing economies. Sectoral development plans sought to change those social and economic conditions that were considered to be obstacles to development. These policies used semi-targeted aid: technical and financial assistance was more focused and concentrated on specific development problems and on groups of people with characteristics thought to be adverse to economic growth.

The policies of the 1970s sought economic growth with social equity; they were concerned as much with the distribution of benefits as with the rate and pace of economic output. They sought to channel aid to the poor majority and resources to subsistence populations in rural areas, provide for basic human needs in the poorest countries, and improve the living standards of "special publics" or groups of the poor. These objectives were largely pursued through targeted aid strategies.

Rondinelli (1983 pp. 23–24)

Accounts such as the above give a more or less accurate picture of what may be called "mainstream development effort" from the end of World War II to the early 1980s. To be complete, they would have also to describe the rise to prominence of the organizations of civil society, imperceptible at first, but already notable toward the end of the period. Thus expanded, they would be able to tell the story of how, through the interactions of two streams of endeavour, and in a little more than three decades, development discourse broadened its range of concern to include such essential issues as growth with equity, basic needs, appropriate technology, the status of women, planning and project implementation as instruments of learning, evaluation, participation, and community organization in people-centred development.

Despite this impressive accumulation of ideas, however, it would be difficult to argue that development policy and practice unfolded in systematic and successive stages. Already in the early 1980s, the signs of a breakdown could be detected. Rondinelli continued thus:

Turbulent changes in the world economy and in the economic, social and political conditions within developing nations in the early 1980s created an environment of greater uncertainty, in which the objectives and approaches to foreign assistance changed quickly. A new emphasis was placed on macro-economic adjustments to the rising cost of imports for developing nations and lower demand for their exports. Greater attention was given to private sector productivity. Less resources were available for international assistance, and the strong emphasis on meeting the needs and increasing the

productivity of the poor that had characterized development theories in the previous decade began to wane.

Rondinelli (1983, p. 24)

What had once seemed to be a forward movement, then, began to
look rather cyclical as development discourse resumed some of the attitudes that had characterized it at its beginning. The entire 1980s would
come to be regarded by some observers as a "lost decade." Others, however, would be less benevolent in their analysis of the spread of
poverty — especially in Africa — to which structural-adjustment policies had so decisively contributed. It is true that, during the same
period, concern with the sustainability of development began to take
centre stage, but, as the decade of the 1990s drew to a close, it was
becoming clear that the concept never did possess the power needed to
achieve its objectives. It proved unable to bring focus to the ever more
diversified set of activities striving to narrow the widening gap that separates the world's materially rich and materially poor, a condition that
strains the moral fibre of modern society.

169

It seems to me, then, that in our effort to explore the theme of
science, religion, and development, we would do well to remember
some of the opposing features of development discourse as it has evolved
over the past 50 years.

First, a great deal of knowledge has been generated that serves to
clarify the nature of the many interacting factors that contribute to the
highly complex development process. Development thinking, at least in
its literature, has become increasingly more profound as layer after layer
of interconnected issues have been discovered and analyzed, sometimes
with dazzling brilliance. Yet, policy and practice have tended to ignore
the lessons learned. The same mistakes have been repeated periodically,
and fads and fashions have been adopted with remarkable enthusiasm.
Strategies, dormant for a span of time, have been suddenly revived, and
substantial resources have been made available for favourite programs
and approaches as the leadership of influential agencies has changed.

Second, at every stage of this progress, development thinkers have
exerted their utmost to express their observations and theories in technical terms. Technocracy, with its familiar claim to freedom from value
judgments, has tended to dictate the prevailing mode of operation. Yet,
in ways apparent to everyone involved, important decisions have been
value driven and reached through political power play.

Third, the evolution of development thinking has led to an
increasing concern for people. Consequently, peoples' cultures, values,
traditions, and worldviews have come to be considered pivotal to development planning and implementation. Yet, despite the fact that spirituality is so central to the worldviews held by the vast majority of the
Earth's inhabitants, the premises of development theory and action have
remained almost entirely materialistic, oblivious of the spiritual dimension of human existence.

Development intervention

The ideas expressed earlier, under the heading "The inside–outside dichotomy," are elements of a broader category of consideration that may most accurately be termed "the ethics of development." As a field, development has to be constantly on its guard not to transgress those limits beyond which efforts to improve the lives of people degenerate into unethical interference. The question "Who gave me the right to intervene?" should always trouble the conscientious development practitioner. Majid Rahnema brings out, perhaps rather harshly, the disquieting aspects of the challenge:

> To prevent the development debacle from being followed by yet new forms of colonization and more pernicious systems of intervention, the very concept of intervention should be explored in depth. In particular, "activists," and the so-called agents of change, as well as intellectuals for whom the written or oral word tends to give life meaning, should try to examine the ethical dimensions of intervention.
>
> My personal, sometimes bitter, experience has taught me to be so cautious in this respect as to perceive intervention as an act bordering on the sacred. What right do I have to intervene in the life of another, whom I don't know, when I have only a personal, egocentric impression of his or her reality?
>
> There is, indeed, the spontaneous, compassionate gesture of the Good Samaritan who, without harboring any project of intervention, goes over to an apparently wounded and dying man on a desert road and comes to his aid. That act is not an intervention, in the sense used in the modern aid vocabulary. It is a gesture that has no other purpose but the act itself, and hence, it is an act of love and compassion, a "right action" in the Buddhist sense of the word. Here, the actor does not ask himself whether the person to receive help would some day be useful to him or not, whether he is a saint, a poor person, or even a would-be criminal. That is why the act of the Good Samaritan borders on sacred territory.
>
> The case is different with a project of intervention, which is prepared and developed somewhere, often in an institutional framework, with a view to changing the lives of other people, in a manner useful or beneficial for the intervener. That person must realize, at least, that he or she is launched on an adventure fraught with considerable danger. That awareness makes it necessary for interveners to start by questioning the whys and wherefores of their acts. Exceptional personal qualities are needed to avoid the possibility that well-intentioned interventions may end up producing the opposite of what is intended. Most of those qualities are actually qualities that are essential for any type of genuine relationship, in the true sense of the word.
>
> The most significant quality is to be open and always attentive to the world and to all other humans (*attentive*, meaning indeed to *attend*). *Attentive* implies the art of listening, in the broadest sense of

the word, being sensitive to what is, observing things as they are, free from any preconceived judgment, and not as one would like them to be, and believing that every person's experience or insight is a potential source of learning. Such an attitude is basically different from that of experts or highly paid consultants who generally act on the basis of a series of certainties coming from their "knowledge" or "professional experience." Such "authorities," particularly when they refuse to question their certainties, not only tend to mislead the people in whose lives they intervene, but also lose touch with the very objects of their knowledge. Because they are unable to listen, they find that their accumulated knowledge soon becomes obsolete and of little relevance to the changing realities they address. Militants and other votaries of various "isms," missionaries, charismatic politicians, and other professional "seducers," preachers, salespersons, and specialists of all kinds, including "scholars" in search of recognition and fame, are all examples of interveners whose incapacity to listen to and learn from their target audiences disqualifies them from any type of intervention. They seldom realize that they do to others what their all-powerful egos, with their seductive and manipulative tricks, do to them.

Intervention should therefore be envisaged only in the context of a constant exercise of self-awareness, of "meditative" state where one learns to see oneself as one is, not as one would like to be. Such intervention stands opposed to institutionalized aid and development, which represent the corruption and the complete opposite of the spontaneous, compassionate gesture of the Good Samaritan.

Rahnema (1997, pp. 8–9)

Human dignity

The following passage from Robert L. Heilbroner's *The Great Ascent: The Struggle for Economic Development in our Time* (1963) is quoted here, not for the relevance of its economic arguments, but to highlight the way development discourse has often treated the materially poor. By "the great ascent," Heilbroner meant the economic development of the entire world, a process by which more than 100 nations, most of which, according to him, previously "had no history," would become national entities living in "the chronicle of recorded events." This he considered "the first real act of world history." The book was published before political correctness had taught us to avoid sensitive phrases — alas, all too frequently without changing the attitudes underlying apparently technical arguments:

> From what we have learned about the strictly economic aspect of underdevelopment we know already what the core process of economic expansion must be. It must consist of raising the low level of productivity which in every underdeveloped area constitutes the immediate economic cause of poverty. This low level of productivity, as we have seen, is largely traceable to the pervasive lack of capital in a backward nation. ...

But how does a backward nation begin to accumulate the capital it so desperately needs? The answer is no different for a backward nation than for an advanced one. In every society, capital comes into being by saving. This does not necessarily mean putting money in a bank. It means saving in the "real" sense of the word, as the economist uses it. It means that a society must refrain from using all of its current energies and materials to satisfy its current wants, no matter how urgent these may be. ...

This release of productive effort directed to present consumption wants, in order to make room for effort directed at the future, does not present an overwhelming problem to a rich nation. But the problem is different in a poverty-stricken one. How can a country which is starving restrict its current life-sustaining activities? How can a nation, 80 percent of which is scrabbling on the land to feed itself, redirect its energies to building dams and roads, ditches and houses, railroad embankments and factories, which, however indispensable for the future, cannot be eaten today? The peasant painfully tilling his infinitesimal plot may be the living symbol of backwardness, but at least he brings forth the roots and rice to keep himself alive. If he were to build capital — to work on a dam or to dig a canal — who would feed him? Who could spare the surplus when there is no surplus?

In capsule this is the basic problem which most underdeveloped lands face, and on the surface it seems a hopeless one. Yet when we look more deeply into it, we find that the situation is not quite so self-defeating as it seems. For a large number of the peasants who till the soil are not just feeding themselves. Rather, in so doing, they are also robbing their neighbors. In the majority of the underdeveloped areas, as we have seen, the crowding of peasants on the land has resulted in a diminution of agricultural productivity far below that of the advanced countries. ...

Now we begin to see an answer to the dilemma of the underdeveloped societies. There does exist, in nearly all of these societies, a disguised and hidden surplus of labor which, if it were taken off the land, could be used to build capital. It is, to be sure, capital of a special and rather humble sort: capital characterized in the main by large projects which can be built by labor with very little equipment — roads, dams, railway embankments, simple types of buildings, irrigation ditches, sewers. However humble, these underpinnings of "social capital" are essential if a further structure of complex *industrial* capital — machines, materials-handling equipment, and the like — is to be securely anchored. Thus peasant labor released from uneconomic field work makes possible a crucially important first assault on the capital-shortage problem. ...

We have seen how an underdeveloped society can increase its agricultural output and simultaneously "find" the labor resources it needs for development tasks. But where is the saving — the release of consumption goods — we talked about? This brings us to a second necessary step in our process of capital creation. When agricultural productivity has been enhanced by the creation of larger farms (or by improved techniques on existing farms), *part of the ensuing crop must be saved.*

In other words, whereas the peasant who remains on the soil will now be more productive, he cannot enjoy his enhanced productivity by eating up all his larger crop. Instead, the gain in individual output must be siphoned off the farm. The extra crop raised by the fortunate peasant must be saved by him, and shared with his formerly unproductive cousins, nephews, sons, and daughters who are now at work on capital-building projects.

We do not expect a hungry peasant to do this voluntarily. Rather, by taxation of various sorts, or by forced transfer, the government of an underdeveloped land must arrange for this essential redistribution of food. *Thus in the early stages of a successful development program there is apt to be no visible rise in the peasant's food consumption, although there must be a rise in his food production.* Instead, what is apt to be visible is a more or less efficient, and sometimes harsh, mechanism for assuring that some portion of this newly added productivity is "saved" — that is, not consumed on the farm, but made available to support the capital-building worker. This is why we must be very careful in appraising a development program not to measure the success of the program by individual peasant living standards. For a long time, these may have to remain static — possibly until the new capital projects begin to pay off.

Heilbroner (1963, pp. 92–97, emphasis in the original)

It is encouraging to note that, over the years, numerous voices have been raised against such assaults on human dignity and are finally getting a hearing. *Ethical and Spiritual Dimensions of Social Progress*, a report prepared for the 1995 World Summit for Social Development, provides a helpful example:

A frightening trait of many cultures — ancient and modern — is that of associating different levels of dignity with a hierarchy of professions and activities. At the bottom of the totem-pole are, of course, adults who have never worked or have lost their jobs and cannot provide for their families. The "job" — not what he is or does — determines the individual's identity. One must have great courage and inner resources in order to resist the social and cultural pressure which strips the individual of his dignity when he is no longer "productive." At the international level, the dominant culture also tends to strip social groups and nations of their dignity when they do not contribute or no longer contribute to the growth and prosperity of the world economy. As with poverty eradication, the fight against unemployment and underemployment must begin with recognition of the dignity and value of all human labor, even if it is humble, insecure, "unprofitable" or unremunerated.

United Nations (1995, pp. 32–33)

Religion, of course, is a stronghold for the preservation of human dignity. It is unfortunate that, historically, its characteristic summons to freedom from the obsessive accumulation of material wealth has often

173

been grossly distorted. The result has been a tendency toward rejection of the world and the exaltation of a passivity that has invited oppression. Such distortions must be corrected for the force of religion to play its role in the struggle against today's cult of greed, and the signs are that this is indeed occurring in many religious movements.

One element of religious belief seems crucial in this respect, namely, the conviction that work done in the spirit of service to humanity is worship before God. It gives rise to attitudes that value economic progress but reject servitude to an erroneous notion of material productivity. In the words of 'Abdu'l-Bahá,

> In the Bahá'í Cause arts, sciences and all crafts are counted as worship. The man who makes a piece of notepaper to the best of his ability, conscientiously, concentrating all his forces on perfecting it, is giving praise to God. Briefly, all effort and exertion put forth by man from the fullness of his heart is worship, if it is prompted by the highest motives and the will to do service to humanity. This is worship: to serve mankind and to minister to the needs of the people. Service is prayer. A physician ministering to the sick, gently, tenderly, free from prejudice and believing in the solidarity of the human race, he is giving praise.
>
> BPT (1995a, 55:1)

The state and the market

The two ideologies that dominated the social and economic life of the planet after World War II held in opposition the state and the market, the former being regarded as the guardian of the collective good by the one side; and the latter being regarded as the protector of individual freedom by the other. The demise of the Soviet system has apparently brought to an abrupt end the deification of the state. But adoration of the workings attributed to the "invisible hand" has yet to exhaust itself. On the contrary, at least for the present, its exuberant voice can be heard more loudly than ever promising a prosperity that is clearly beyond attainment by the great majority of human beings. Meanwhile, the most readily observed phenomenon is marginalization. Is it too much to hope that the development field, concerned as it is with the conditions of the poor, could draw on its vast experience and lend wisdom to the pursuit of what seems to be an otherwise elusive dream of progress?

Although no clear commitment to this task is discernible, statements can be found in development literature that reflect a readiness on the part of some agencies to assume such a responsibility, provided the political will to do so is created. The World Bank's *World Development Report 1992: Development and the Environment* offers an example:

> The achievement of sustained and equitable development remains the greatest challenge facing the human race. Despite good progress over the past generation, more than 1 billion people still live in acute poverty and suffer grossly inadequate access to the

resources — education, health services, infrastructure, land, and credit — required to give them a chance for a better life. The essential task of development is to provide opportunities so that these people, and the hundreds of millions not much better off, can reach their potential.

But although the desirability of development is universally recognized, recent years have witnessed rising concern about whether environmental constraints will limit development and whether development will cause serious environmental damage — in turn impairing the quality of life of this and future generations. This concern is overdue. ...

There are strong "win–win" opportunities that remain unexploited. The most important of these relates to poverty reduction: not only is attacking poverty a moral imperative, but it is also essential for environmental stewardship. Moreover, policies that are justified on economic grounds alone can deliver substantial environmental benefits. Eliminating subsidies for the use of fossil fuels and water, giving poor farmers property rights on the land they farm, making heavily polluting state-owned companies more competitive, and eliminating rules that reward with property rights those who clear forests are examples of policies that improve both economic efficiency and the environment. Similarly, investing in better sanitation and water and in improved research and extension services can both improve the environment *and* raise incomes.

But these policies are not enough to ensure environmental quality; strong public institutions and policies for environmental protection are also essential. The world has learned over the past two decades to rely more on markets and less on governments to promote development. But environmental protection is one area in which government must maintain a central role. Private markets provide little or no incentive for curbing pollution. Whether it be air pollution in urban centers, the dumping of unsanitary wastes in public waters, or the overuse of land whose ownership is unclear, there is a compelling case for public action. Here there may be tradeoffs between income growth and environmental protection, requiring a careful assessment of the benefits and costs of alternative policies as they affect both today's population and future generations. The evidence indicates that the gains from protecting the environment are often high and that the costs in forgone income are modest if appropriate polices are adopted. Experience suggests that policies are most effective when they aim at underlying causes rather than symptoms, concentrate on addressing those problems for which the benefits of reform are greatest, use incentives rather than regulations where possible, and recognize administrative constraints.

World Bank (1992, p. 1, emphasis in the original)

Nobility

A striking aspect of Bahá'í belief is the extraordinary optimism it displays about humanity's future. Such hopefulness would be untenable were it not for a profound conviction, which arises from the Faith's

175

teachings, that the human being was created noble. The reader may find it useful to see a few examples of how the question is treated in Bahá'í scriptures.

The first adornment (*taráz*) of the human character, according to Bahá'u'lláh, is self-knowledge:

> The first Taráz and the first effulgence which hath dawned from the horizon of the Mother Book is that man should know his own self and recognize that which leadeth unto loftiness or lowliness, glory or abasement, wealth or poverty. Having attained the stage of ful-filment and reached his maturity, man standeth in need of wealth, and such wealth as he acquireth through crafts or professions is commendable and praiseworthy in the estimation of men of wis-dom, and especially in the eyes of servants who dedicate themselves to the education of the world and to the edification of its peoples. They are, in truth, cup-bearers of the life-giving water of knowl-edge and guides unto the ideal way. They direct the peoples of the world to the straight path and acquaint them with that which is conducive to human upliftment and exaltation. The straight path is the one which guideth man to the dayspring of perception and to the dawning-place of true understanding and leadeth him to that which will redound to glory, honour and greatness.
>
> BPT (1988, pp. 34–35)

Walking the straight path, with the perseverance it demands, would be impossible without faith in the nobility of one's own nature. Bahá'ís are to call to mind often the voice of an all-merciful Creator expressed in such exhortations as these:

> O Son of Being! Thou art My lamp and My light is in thee. Get thou from it thy radiance and seek none other than Me. For I have created thee rich and have bountifully shed My favor upon thee.
>
> BPT (1994, 2:11)

> O Son of Spirit! I created thee rich, why dost thou bring thyself down to poverty? Noble I made thee, wherewith dost thou abase thyself? Out of the essence of knowledge I gave thee being, why seekest thou enlightenment from anyone beside Me? Out of the clay of love I molded thee, how dost thou busy thyself with another? Turn thy sight unto thyself, that thou mayest find Me standing within thee, mighty, powerful and self-subsisting.
>
> BPT (1994, 2:13)

In no way does the Bahá'í belief in the inherent nobility of the human race, however, give credence to the romantic notion that, left to themselves, human beings will instinctively avoid evil actions. 'Abdu'l-Bahá emphatically rejected this position:

> There are some who imagine that an innate sense of human dignity will prevent man from committing evil actions and insure his spir-itual and material perfection. That is, that an individual who is

characterized with natural intelligence, high resolve, and a driving zeal, will, without any consideration for the severe punishments consequent on evil acts, or for the great rewards of righteousness, instinctively refrain from inflicting harm on his fellow men and will hunger and thirst to do good. And yet, if we ponder the lessons of history, it will become evident that this very sense of honor and dignity is itself one of the bounties deriving from the instructions of the prophets of God. We also observe in infants the signs of aggression and lawlessness, and that if a child is deprived of a teacher's instructions his undesirable qualities increase from one moment to the next. It is therefore clear that the emergence of this natural sense of human dignity and honor is the result of education.

BPT (1990, pp. 97-98)

In another passage, he stated the following:

The root cause of wrongdoing is ignorance, and we must therefore hold fast to the tools of perception and knowledge. Good character must be taught. Light must be spread afar, so that, in the school of humanity, all may acquire the heavenly characteristics of the spirit, and see for themselves beyond any doubt that there is no fiercer hell, no more fiery abyss, than to possess a character that is evil and unsound; no more darksome pit nor loathsome torment than to show forth qualities which deserve to be condemned.

BPT (1997, 111:1)

In the Bahá'í Faith, then, firm belief in the nobility of the human being is intimately connected with an equally strong faith in the power of education, but an education that sheds light on the path of true understanding, not one that perpetuates the tyranny of self.

FAITH AND REASON

Our eagerness to promote a discourse on the triple theme of science, religion, and development arises from the conviction that development theory and practice must give urgent attention to the spiritual dimension of human existence. That such a claim should find a sympathetic audience at all is, to some extent, a sign of the growing maturity of the development field. Yet, we have to admit that willingness to discuss spirituality is not the result of measurable theoretical advance; it is being forced on every area of human endeavour by a deepening crisis that is shaking the very foundations of social order. Materialistic philosophy has spent itself. Promises announced with immense self-assurance by its prophets have not been fulfilled. And everywhere the awakening victims of the systems and processes it has engendered raise their voices, calling it to account for its failures:

The time has come when those who preach the dogmas of materialism, whether of the east or the west, whether of capitalism or socialism, must give account of the moral stewardship they have presumed to exercise. Where is the "new world" promised by these ideologies? Where is the international peace to whose ideals they proclaim their devotion? Where are the breakthroughs into new realms of cultural achievement produced by the aggrandizement of this race, of that nation or of a particular class? Why is the vast majority of the world's peoples sinking ever deeper into hunger and wretchedness when wealth on a scale undreamed of by the Pharaohs, the Caesars, or even the imperialist powers of the nineteenth century is at the disposal of the present arbiters of human affairs?

BPT (1995b, p. 21)

It is tempting to argue, of course, that the need to incorporate spirituality into one's frame of action, no matter how incontestable, does not justify delving into religious matters. The prospect of becoming involved in what is widely perceived as an old debate between science and religion will be even less appealing, especially to those who see the urgency of applying immediate solutions to practical problems. But once aware of the need for spirituality, how does one avoid inquiry into religion — not sectarian disputation, but the exploration of a system of knowledge and practice that has played a determining role in the advancement of civilization? The issue is not a vague notion of spirituality — a spirituality that recent studies urge be made available as a product required to maximize satisfaction, a veneer of activities to sooth the nerves in a life that is materialistic at its very core. The questions before the development field, concerned as it must be with the prosperity of humankind, relate to the nature of the human being, the underlying purposes of individual and collective life, and the direction of society. Answers to these questions must shed light on the next stage of evolution in the relationships that are essential to existence and progress: between the species and nature, within the family, within the community, and between the individual and the institutions of society. Humanity must become increasingly engaged in a quest for meaning, and such a quest is inherently religious in nature.

In rejecting the materialistic approach to development, we do not claim that the issues at hand will somehow be resolved by religious considerations. The task before us is not the dethroning of science, as so many seem bent on doing. Given its extraordinary accomplishments, one could maintain that science deserves a higher station than humanity has so far been willing to bestow on it. To bring in the question of religion is not the same as return to superstition. Nor is the introduction of pseudoscience in its myriad forms the door to spiritual perception. Solutions to the pressing problems facing humankind must be sought through a rigorous application of science in the full meaning of that term. But to fulfill this expectation, science must engage in a serious dialogue with religion. At the 20th century ends, both systems, along with the rest of the social order, are in profound crisis. But crises in systems of knowledge are welcome occurrences, for they are invariably harbingers of progress. I hope to demonstrate in this paper that development theory and practice have, for the most part, been influenced by views of science and religion that are bound to disappear as both undergo rapid and radical transformation in the coming decades. I will argue that the field of development, by admitting a rigorous exploration of the issues related to faith and reason and acknowledging their relevance to its policies and programs, will achieve the great advance that all those committed to the work believe is possible, and doors to the discovery of effective strategies will open.

Scientific truth

We live in a time when science is blindly adored or rashly attacked by those who have an inadequate understanding of it. Many see science chiefly as the author of creations that verge on the magical. Unfortunately, this is often true even of individuals who, without having reflected in any depth on the nature of either science or technology, are engaged in narrow scientific activity. An assortment of courses on the scientific method offered to students on various career paths perpetuates deep-rooted misunderstandings.

Science starts with observation. Thus begins the commonly told story. The scientist uses his or her senses to observe things and occurrences. Scientific training ensures that such observation is carried out with an unprejudiced mind and the utmost objectivity. The immediate products of a purified and disciplined use of the senses are numerous "observation statements," from which laws and theories of science will finally emerge.

Observation statements are singular in the sense that they refer to a particular event at a particular time. But the trained mind is capable of arriving at more universal statements through the careful application of the principle of induction. For generalizations to be true, it is necessary to repeat observations in as wide a variety of conditions as feasible. The number of observation statements forming the basis of the generalization must be sufficiently large to justify the application of inductive reasoning. Once universal statements are discovered, the principles of deduction are used to explain other observed facts and to derive consequences that can then be checked through experimentation. The power of science to predict is one of its essential characteristics, one that gives validity to its claims to grandeur.

By presenting this simplistic view of science, I do not wish to suggest that even within what may be called the positivist camp, development theorists do not have considerable familiarity with far more sophisticated perspectives. In recent times, discussions of science have often referred to the complexities of the relationship between theory and observation and the strong influence the former exerts on the latter. By invoking the notion of probability and separating the way a generalization actually occurs from its subsequent justification, certain schools of thought have moved away from the simplistic explanation of "the scientific method" in terms of observation and induction followed by deduction and prediction. Elaborate and ingenious efforts to explain scientific reasoning in terms of falsification — scientific knowledge as a set of falsifiable hypotheses and theories in constant danger of being eliminated by fitter rivals — have led to valuable insights into the methods of science. The introduction into the discourse of science of the concepts of a scientific paradigm, on the one hand, and of competing research programs, on the other, has had a notable impact on most intellectual circles. Yet, strong convictions about the nature of scientific truth, which were arrived at on the basis of an essentially naive conception of science, not only survive but shape entire fields of human endeavour. The deplorable consequence is that an outmoded historical debate between science and religion is perpetuated, and meaningful dialogue between the two systems is blocked.

"Scientific knowledge is proven knowledge" is at the heart of such convictions. "Science in its uncorrupted form is objective and free from personal opinions." "Scientific knowledge is reliable knowledge because it is the result of the rigorous application of a method whose validity is beyond question." However, *objective*, *rigorous*, and *reliable* are not value-free words. Language plays tricks on the thought process. Science soon becomes the only source of indisputable truth, and every other source of knowledge comes to seem less valuable, less reliable, and ultimately valueless and unreliable. Under these conditions, how can religion receive a hearing so that the question of a harmonious interaction between the two may be explored? The contemporary crisis calls for a substantial change in humanity's perception of science, for the prevalent perception arose from early attempts to understand a new and powerful force and became popularized too quickly, before it was critically examined.

Whatever the precise nature of its processes and methods, science is clearly a dynamic system of knowledge and practice that defies attempts to reduce it to any simplistic formula. The fascinating and vital work of philosophers and historians of science leads to theories that explain some of its results and some of its processes. Like the other models that science makes of various portions of physical, intellectual, or social reality, each such explanation has a finite range of validity. Together, they bring to light many of its salient features, but none of them describes science in its totality.

Science clearly contains elements that are essentially articles of faith — to begin, faith in the existence of order in the universe and faith in the ability of the human mind to make sense of that order and express it in a precise language. In the words of Einstein (1954, p. 52), "those individuals to whom we owe the greatest achievements of science were all of them imbued with the truly religious conviction that this universe of ours is something perfect and susceptible to the rational striving for knowledge."

Scientific theories are all based on assumptions, some of which cannot be proven logically. They simply represent propositions acceptable to human reason, deriving their value from the success of the models and theories built on them. For centuries, accepted science assumed that the laws governing the behaviour of objects on Earth were different from those ruling heavenly bodies. Theories based on this assumption proved inadequate. Today, a basic premise of science is that the laws of physics are the same in the heavens as on Earth; the force of gravity, for example, is believed to determine much of the behaviour of space, time, and matter everywhere in the universe. For the time being, this assumption has led to models that seem to explain whatever we have observed, thus justifying its widespread acceptance.

181

The practice of science also draws on such specifically spiritual qualities of the human being as love of beauty and commitment to veracity. It is highly dependent on the use of the faculties of intuition, creativity, and imagination. These resources of the rational soul do not operate haphazardly in scientific activity. They are productive, as they are trained and disciplined and as the results of their operations pass the tests of a rationality acceptable to the community of scientists.

Science's main task is to make models of reality. Its models — called theories when sufficiently complex — seldom take the form of simple physical representations. Rather, they are structures in a language that uses both words and mathematical expressions. The language of science has characteristics unique to its aims. Among other things, it seeks to be rational in a highly defined way, unambiguous, and objective. Whether these qualities also distinguish all the processes through which science is generated is not easy to determine: scientific thinking itself is obviously too complex to be completely objective, faultlessly logical, or entirely devoid of ambiguity. By being bound to a strict language through which it must be expressed and communicated, however, science takes on many of the attributes for which it receives well-deserved praise.

Although the flaws intrinsic to positivism have been clearly exposed in recent years, the indispensable role of disciplined observation, albeit conditioned by theory, remains central to scientific practice. Generalization, formulation of hypotheses, deduction, testing of predictions, and falsification are vital components of any scientific method. But it should be borne in mind that they are not carried out mechanically by programed entities but by members of communities of scientists who are subject to the influence of social forces. These communities exhibit patterns of behaviour characteristic of groups made up of human beings. Specifically, they work within certain worldviews and theoretical frameworks that determine the kinds of questions they are willing to ask and the kinds of answers they are willing to explore. The concept of a paradigm, although not universally valid, is a highly useful tool for thinking about science. Scientific knowledge is accumulative only to a certain extent; some of the advances in science occur through pronounced shifts in paradigm, the dynamics of which evoke images of a revolution.

Scientific practice depends on a variety of coexisting research programs. Each program is essential to the very proposal of the theory to the building of which a community of scientists chooses to commit itself. One of the goals of such research is to extend the range of phenomena that a theory can successfully explain. But no community of scientists sets out to answer all the questions in the world. An indispensable element of any scientific model is a set of statements defining its range of validity. More advanced theories do not necessarily prove previous ones wrong but clarify the limits within which they operate and provide an understanding of why they work inside those limits. Thus, relativity and quantum mechanics, for example, do not "disprove" Newtonian physics; rather, they define the range of size and velocity for which the latter's predictions are totally reliable.

In making these remarks, I do not intend to be eclectic, somehow merging the work of Kuhn and Popper, Lakatos and Feyerabend. My intention is to argue that without entering into debate on the profound issues explored by philosophers and historians of science over the past decades, we can readily decide that the relation between science and truth is not the simplistic one propagated by naive descriptions of science. Certainly, the relationship between science and truth is enormously important. Scientific statements are about objective reality; they have an existence of their own and are not merely the products of the minds of a few scientists. Not satisfied with offering explanation only, science demands application and engenders technology — and policy, in the case of some of the social sciences — which in turn act on objective reality. In this sense, technology seems to be intrinsic to science; it is born of it and, together with other factors, defines the arena of its operations. Although driven by the powers of the rational soul, science is also an exigency of social existence, one of whose imperatives is technological advancement. Scientific knowledge is thus an expression of truth that sheds light on interconnected realities: the physical reality of the universe, social reality, and the inner reality of the human being.

RELIGIOUS TRUTH

With this perspective on science, let us now turn to religion. In doing so, we confront at the outset the question of whether scientific knowledge, with the degree of complexity intimated above, encompasses all of reality that is knowable to the human mind. What if the elements of faith underlying our worldview — not acquired by blind imitation, but through a process of observation, study, and reflection — include a belief in a spiritual reality beyond the world accessible to our senses? What if we cannot lend credit to the assumption — and it is only an assumption — that intelligence is a mere product of higher orders of organization, but regard it, instead, as a quality of being that transcends physical existence? What if that quality of being determines the structure and operation of the world, including the evolutionary appearance of a human mind capable of observing and thinking about the universe? What, indeed, if our inextinguishable sense of individual identity — which after all gives definition to the statement "I know" — finds the assumption that it will end with physical death quite meaningless and drives us on to explore the implications of timelessness and immortality?

The usual assertion that certain beliefs and premises are not needed and, therefore, according to some kind of minimalist principle should not be brought into the picture begs the question in at least two ways. First, it presupposes that the denial of an expanded reality is somehow objective and not, in itself, an assumption that has profound consequences for the direction of intellectual endeavour. Thus, it distorts the fact that the choice in each case is between two elements of faith, neither of which is provable, and not between "no assumption" and an "extraneous assumption." Second, it takes for granted the supremacy of science as the uniquely valid means for the investigation of reality and its claim to autonomy as somehow an irrefutable proof of this validity. Certainly, assumptions related to the spiritual dimension of existence are unnecessary in many scientific studies, but by what reason do we extend this to all investigation, denying the need for any other system of inquiry with which science must interact if it is not to become dogmatic and vulnerable?

Historically, religion has been the system concerned primarily with spiritual reality and its relation to individual and collective life. Like science, religion is a highly complex system of knowledge and practice, with a pattern of evolution particular to its nature and a history inextricably intertwined with the unfoldment of civilization. As a practice of human communities, it has inevitably had its share of folly, corruption, and abuse of trust. But it has also been the unfailing voice raising the call to transcendence, the ultimate source of every praiseworthy aspiration, and the light that has illumined human understanding and enabled it to distinguish between the base and the noble.

If we are to examine religion with an unprejudiced mind and discover how its interactions with science should occur, we need to set aside misgivings that, for whatever justifiable reasons, have gained widespread acceptance. The most notable of these is expressed in the opinion that there is no such thing as "religion," but merely numerous religions in fundamental disagreement with one another. Such a conclusion represents a highly restrictive view of religion. It is unarguable that religious strife, along with tribal, national, and racial conflict, has been a prominent feature of humanity's past and, like these other ills, continues to plague us during what may be seen as an age of transition. But if we accept that the path we must walk is one of both material and spiritual advancement, we must be willing to look more deeply into the spiritual heritage of the human race than so precipitate a judgment would encourage.

As science and its multiple structures exist and unfold, so do religion and its structures. Religious teachings and belief are expressed in myriad forms, and these expressions show significant differences. But this circumstance does not deny the existence of a dynamic knowledge system with its own field of inquiry and its own evolving methods and language. Once we free ourselves from a preoccupation with differences, we are astonished at the unity of themes explored by the major religions of the world and the continuity of the solutions they propose to the most perplexing problems. In this context, variety of expression becomes a source of richness of insight, rather than being a cause of contention. But such a perspective is possible only if each major religion is examined primarily through the eyes of those whose gaze has remained focused on the moral and spiritual teachings enshrined in its authentic scriptures. Separating these from the dogmas added by those who had an insatiable thirst for worldly power is, admittedly, a difficult task in some instances, but it is by no means impossible.

In the case of science, that which is understood and explained is a basically observable, objective reality — physical, psychological, or social. But what is the objective reality on which religion focuses in order to serve as a system of knowledge and practice within a community? To answer this question, it would seem essential to reflect on the body of teachings that lie at the core of each of the major religions of the world and have provided their primary impulse. Without entering into the familiar theological debate on transcendence versus immanence, one may simply observe that the encounter between human consciousness and the Divine has repeatedly resulted in a religious text, oral or written, at the heart of which are the pronouncements of the prophet–founder and a few historical figures intimately connected to this person. In the text is described life in both its material and its spiritual dimensions. It "reveals" aspects of spiritual reality, which, once uttered, can become the subject of exploration, not only by the individual soul, but also by entire populations. Without the revealed text, spirituality would be an expression of personal experience, never to be validated by the intellectual interactions that create social knowledge. For, by religious truth is not meant mere assertions about the esoteric, but statements that lead to experimentation, application, and the creation of systems and processes, whose results can be validated through observation and the use of reason. Humanity, by its very nature, is thus endowed with two Books, that of Creation and that of Revelation, the study of which, as "science" and "religion," propels the advancement of civilization.

HARMONY BETWEEN SCIENCE AND RELIGION

A note of caution is in order. Efforts to describe religion as a system of knowledge are always in danger of going too far by advancing arguments that would finally make religion a mere extension of science, a branch of scientific learning dedicated to the study of the unseen. That a system of knowledge is capable of penetrating every aspect of individual and social life does not imply that it has to be science. Clearly, as two major systems of knowledge and practice, religion and science will have many features in common. Articles of faith, assumptions, the use of various faculties of the soul, such as reason, intuition, and imagination, the ability to create models of reality — including the metaphysical and the inner life of individuals and communities — worldviews, and even something akin to a set of coexisting research programs are all elements readily observable in the operation and evolution of religion. Indeed, it can be persuasively argued that in many of its applications, the methods of religion are, and have to be, scientific. Yet, science and religion remain distinct knowledge systems, neither representing a subsystem of the other.

185

Of particular importance is the distinction that has to be made between the language of science and the language of religion. In many respects, the language in which religious truth is expressed, like scientific language, strives to be unambiguous and objective. But its primary challenge is to transcend the limitations of the language of science and to exploit poetic images, stories, parables, commands, admonitions, and exhortations so as to convey meaning and speak directly to the human heart in ways science does not pretend to do.

To emphasize the distinction between religious and scientific knowledge is not to deny interrelationship. The widespread belief in an intrinsic conflict between the two arose at a time of crisis in the history of Christianity, when the very conceptions of science and religion were inadequate to deal with rapid intellectual development. Today, several centuries later, the question before us is whether the type of understanding that has been achieved in recent times makes possible a new basis for interactions between the two systems. Is it not equally likely that harmony and not conflict should characterize these interactions? Indeed, is it not essential to demand such harmony to ensure that neither system degenerates into vain imagining and that both remain true to their nature?

Issues related to the harmony between science and religion can be addressed in a number of ways. It can be reasonably argued that the two systems are so distinct that there is no possibility of significant conflict between them. Science studies the material universe. The knowledge it generates becomes the basis for technological progress, and technology can be used either for the good of humanity or to its detriment, for building civilization or for its destruction. Science in itself does not have the ability to determine the uses to which its products should be put. Religion, in contrast, is concerned precisely with the spiritual dimension of human existence. Its task is to throw light on the inner life of the individual, to touch the roots of motivation, and to engender a code of ethics and morality to appropriately guide human behaviour. It can set the ethical framework within which technology can be developed and employed. The civilizing process depends on both these systems of knowledge; so long as each remains within the sphere of its own genius, there is no reason for them to come into conflict with each other.

This view of the harmony between science and religion is valid, but only at the level of application. Ultimately, in this approach, science and religion are separated and allowed to pursue their own ways, and what assumes importance is the interaction between technology and morality, the progenies of the two. But such an analysis of the relation between science and religion soon reaches its limits, for the two knowledge systems have too much in common and overlap in the range of phenomena within their realms of study. Commonalties include certain assumptions and elements of faith, qualities and attitudes, methods, and mental and social processes; other aspects of religion and science, while not contradictory, are needed in only one of the two. Overlap is intrinsic to the operation of the two systems and arises from the fact that a sharp division between matter and spirit is in itself impossible. Although for many practical purposes it is necessary to separate the two systems and allow their processes to run parallel to each other, attempts to deny their interconnectedness in the mind of the human being and in society can only rob them of the extraordinary powers they both possess.

In thinking about the relationship between religion and science, I have always found it helpful to draw upon some of the insights into the workings of the universe offered by the principle of complementarity. In its strict formulation, the principle asserts that the particle–wave duality clearly observable at the level of the smallest constituents of matter is inherent in the process of scientific observation and measurement itself. It is not that, for example, the electron is sometimes a wave and sometimes a particle; nor that it is both or neither. Complementarity takes us beyond the question of "either–or" and asks us to deal directly with the fact that under certain experimental "setups" the electron will always behave as a particle and under others it will always act as a wave. These two types of setup exhaust all the possibilities of measurement. It is impossible, that is, to establish an experiment in which one could ask, What is the electron really, a wave or a particle?

It is not my intention to claim that the complementarity of quantum mechanics is somehow directly applicable to the duality between science and religion. In fact, what is known as the Copenhagen interpretation, with which the above formulation is associated, has once again come into serious question in recent years. But whatever the resolution of the difficulties faced by the model, the fact remains that at the most fundamental level nature does not allow simultaneous measurements of certain quantities and lends itself to complementary descriptions. Given the intricacies of the process of measurement in science, such a statement cannot be only about the physical universe. Theoretical models elaborated by the human mind underlie the arrangement of instruments in the experimental setup, models that, as already noted, are structures in language. Therefore, complementarity, in any of its possible formulations, is telling us something fundamental about two coexisting realities and their interactions — human consciousness and objective reality. Particularly, it is offering insights into how the human mind can embrace aspects of the universe too complex to admit of a single description.

187

Accepting that this is the case, we cannot avoid asking ourselves related questions about levels of reality beyond the world of matter. Is it unreasonable to assume that when the object of exploration is the sum of both spiritual and physical reality, an object far more complex than the material universe, a single description would also prove to be inadequate? Is it not possible that to understand and explain this reality, humanity needs at least two languages, that of science and that of religion, which together enable it to penetrate its mysteries?

FURTHER COMMENTS

The following comments expand and elaborate on the arguments presented in the foregoing pages.

The purpose of religion

The passage quoted in the opening of this section on faith and reason comes from *The Promise of World Peace* (BPT 1995b), a statement written by the international governing body of the Bahá'í Faith. The document presents an analysis of the social and spiritual forces that contribute to the establishment of peace among the Earth's peoples, a condition that implies far more than the mere absence of armed conflict. It claims that world peace is inevitable but that its advent requires the collective will of the world's leaders and the application of a range of specific religious principles.

The arguments set out in *The Promise of World Peace* reflect the emphasis the Bahá'í teachings place on religion as an instrument to build civilization. But, although the role of religion as a positive social force is extolled, it is also acknowledged that it can be distorted through the manipulation of self-seeking leaders. Indeed, misunderstandings and confusion perpetrated in the name of religion are among the causes of the deplorable conditions of the world today. To attribute these conditions to the rise of secularism would be unfair. In many respects secularism is clearly a welcome development in the history of humanity, an inevitable and necessary reaction to religion fallen prey to fanaticism and superstition. Referring to religion as a means for human progress, Bahá'u'lláh stated the following:

> The purpose of religion as revealed from the heaven of God's holy Will is to establish unity and concord amongst the peoples of the world; make it not the cause of dissension and strife. The religion of God and His divine law are the most potent instruments and the surest of all means for the dawning of the light of unity amongst men. The progress of the world, the development of nations, the tranquility of peoples, and the peace of all who dwell on Earth are among the principles and ordinances of God.
>
> BPT (1988, pp. 129–130)

For Bahá'ís, as for millions of religious people from every tradition, the fact that religion, despite its originating impulse in the Divine, has been subject to the same distortion that affects all human constructs does not diminish the significance of its role in advancing civilization. What must be accepted is that religion stands in need of science if it is to avoid the pitfalls of fanaticism.

The crisis of science

Most readers of these pages will readily accept that, as is the case with much of civilization, religion is in crisis. But there are many who may hesitate to attribute a similar crisis to science as a system. The ethical problems faced by humanity as a result of accelerated scientific and technological advance are, of course, commonly acknowledged. It is possible, however, to regard these issues as challenges that emerge naturally in the course of progress and that will in time be addressed by science itself. The crisis to which I refer is a systemic one with many more dimensions than those that are purely ethical; it arises from inadequacies in the very process through which scientific knowledge is generated and applied. In his celebrated book of some years ago, *Scientific Knowledge and Its Social Problems*, Jerome R. Ravetz exposed the alarming consequences resulting from the lack of a "renewed understanding" of the nature of scientific inquiry:

> The activity of modern natural science has transformed our knowledge and control of the world about us; but in the process it has also transformed itself; and it has created problems which natural science alone cannot solve. Modern society depends increasingly on industrial production based on the application of scientific results; but the production of these results has itself become a large and

expensive industry; and the problems of managing that industry, and of controlling the effects of its products, are urgent and difficult. All this has happened so quickly within the past generation, that the new situation, and its implications, are only imperfectly understood. It opens up new possibilities for science and for human life, but it also presents new problems and dangers. For science itself, the analogies between the industrial production of material goods and that of scientific results have their uses, and also their hazards. As a product of a socially organized activity, scientific knowledge is very different from soap; and those who plan for science will neglect that difference at their peril. Also, the understanding and control of the effects of our science-based technology present problems for which neither the academic science of the past, nor the industrialized science of the present, possesses techniques or attitudes appropriate to their solution. The illusion that there is a natural science standing pure and separate from all involvement with society is disappearing rapidly; but it tends to be replaced by the vulgar reduction of science to a branch of commercial or military industry. Unless science itself is to be debased and corrupted, and its results used in a headlong rush to social and ecological catastrophe, there must be a renewed understanding of the very special sort of work, so delicate and so powerful, of scientific inquiry.

189

Ravetz (1973, p. 9)

Scientific facts

Reflections on the nature of scientific truth in the context of an emerging dialogue between religion and science can benefit from a careful reading of Ludwik Fleck's (1979 [1935]) monograph *Genesis and Development of a Scientific Fact*. In this insightful work, written originally in German, Fleck chose to examine in detail the emergence and final establishment of the fact that a serodiagnostic procedure developed in the 1920s, known as the Wassermann reaction, indicates, within acceptable statistical limits, the presence of syphilis in a patient. He described the complex set of factors that had to converge, over a long period of time, before syphilis would come to be considered a definite "disease entity" — beginning with an undifferentiated and confused mass of information about various chronic diseases that were characterized by skin symptoms and were frequently localized in the genitals, diseases that, in the 15th century, were all lumped together. Fleck showed how various beliefs and patterns of thought played crucial roles in the tortuous path leading to the unreserved recognition of this disease entity. For example, it was believed at the time that the "conjunction of Saturn and Jupiter under the sign of Scorpio and the House of Mars on 25.XI.1484" was the cause of carnal scourge, for "benign Jupiter was vanquished by the evil planets Saturn and Mars," and the sign of Scorpio "rules the genitals" (Fleck 1979 [1935], p. 2). Belief in carnal scourge laid the

ARBAB

"corner-stone of syphilology, ascribing to it a pronounced ethical character" (p. 3).

Next, we are told, "As a result of decades of practice, certainly spanning several generations, it became possible to distinguish and isolate from the host of chronic skin conditions a particular group which, when treated with mercury ointment, reacted favorably" (Fleck 1979 [1935], pp. 3–4). "Thus two points of view developed side by side, together, often at odds with each other: (1) an ethical–mystical disease entity of "carnal scourge," and (2) an empirical–therapeutic disease entity" (p. 5). This dual approach was then supplemented by a conviction that syphilis is associated with a change in the blood, which left its "natural state," becoming from the very outset of the disease "befouled by an infection attacking it without festering, and therefore relatively unnoticed" (p. 12). Later on, with the rise of the modern idea of pathogenic microorganisms, the agent causing syphilis was identified as *Spirochaeta pallida*. The discovery of the Wassermann reaction further refined and specified the association of the disease with the blood and "helped to classify tabes dorsalis and progressive paralysis definitely with syphilis. Since this spirochaeta was found in the lymphatic ducts very soon after infection, even the first stage of syphilis was no longer regarded as a localized disease" (p. 17).

In his analysis of the evolution of the concept of syphilis as a clearly defined disease entity and of the development of the Wassermann reaction and the emergence of serology as a scientific field, Fleck (1979 [1935]) introduced a number of ideas such as systems of opinion, thought styles, and thought collectives. The use of concepts of this nature is by no means free of problems. Yet, whatever one's disagreements with some aspects of the analysis, one can no longer be beguiled by simplistic definitions of scientific truth after reflecting on Fleck's brilliant arguments. One may seek to modify but cannot ignore his statement that

> Cognition is the most socially-conditioned activity of man, and knowledge is the paramount social creation. The very structure of language presents a compelling philosophy characteristic of that community, and even a single word can represent a complex theory. To whom do these philosophies and theories belong?
>
> Thoughts pass from one individual to another, each time a little transformed, for each individual can attach to them somewhat different associations. Strictly speaking, the receiver never understands the thought exactly in the way that the transmitter intended it to be understood. After a series of such encounters, practically nothing is left of the original content. Whose thought is it that continues to circulate? It is one that obviously belongs not to any single individual but to the collective. Whether an individual construes it as truth or error, understands it correctly or not, a set of findings meanders throughout the community, becoming polished, transformed, reinforced, or attenuated, while influencing other findings,

190

concept formation, opinions, and habits of thought. After making several rounds within the community, a finding often returns considerably changed to its originator, who reconsiders it himself in quite a different light. He either does not recognize it as his own or believes, and this happens quite often, to have originally seen it in its present form. The history of the Wassermann reaction will afford us the opportunity to describe such meanderings in the particular case of a completely "empirical" finding.

This social character inherent in the very nature of scientific activity is not without its substantive consequences. Words, which formerly were simple terms become slogans; sentences which once were simple statements become calls to battle. This completely alters their socio-cogitative value. They no longer influence the mind through their logical meaning — indeed, they often act against it — but rather they acquire a magical power and exert a mental influence simply by being used. As an example, one might consider the effect of terms such as "materialism" or "atheism," which in some countries at once discredit their proponents but in others function as essential passwords for acceptability. This magical power of slogans, with "vitalism" in biology, "specificity" in immunology, and "bacterial transformation" in bacteriology, clearly extends to the very depth of specialist research. Whenever such a term is found in a scientific text, it is not examined logically, but immediately makes either enemies or friends.

Fleck (1979 [1935], pp. 42–43)

191

Beauty

Examining the role played in his or her research by a scientific inquirer's attraction to beauty can open invaluable insights into the nature of science. Unfortunately, it is not possible in a brief exposition, and without the use of mathematics, to explore with any precision the concept of beauty, for example, in physics. In *The Mind of God: The Scientific Basis for a Rational World*, Paul Davies (1993) employed his admirable talent for making scientific ideas accessible to the nonspecialist to express the following:

It is widely believed among scientists that beauty is a reliable guide to truth, and many advances in theoretical physics have been made by the theorist demanding mathematical elegance of a new theory. Sometimes, where laboratory tests are difficult, these aesthetic criteria are considered even more important than experiment. Einstein, when discussing an experimental test of his general theory of relativity, was once asked what he would do if the experiment didn't agree with the theory. He was unperturbed at the prospect. "So much the worse for the experiment," he retorted. "The theory is right!" Paul Dirac, the theoretical physicist whose aesthetic deliberations led him to construct a mathematically more elegant equation for the electron, which then led to the successful prediction of the existence of antimatter, echoed these sentiments when he judged that "it is more important to have beauty in one's equations than to have them fit experiment."

Mathematical elegance is not an easy concept to convey to those unfamiliar with mathematics, but it is keenly appreciated by professional scientists. Like all aesthetic value-judgments, however, it is highly subjective. Nobody has yet invented a "beauty meter" that can measure the aesthetic value of things without referring to human criteria. Can one really say that certain mathematical forms are intrinsically more beautiful than others? Perhaps not. In which case it is very odd that beauty is such a good guide in science. Why should the laws of the universe seem beautiful to humans? No doubt there are all sorts of biological and psychological factors at work in framing our impressions of what is beautiful. It is no surprise that the female form is attractive to men, for example, and the curvaceous lines of many beautiful sculptures, paintings, and architectural structures doubtless have sexual referents. The structure and operation of the brain may also dictate what is pleasing to the eye or ear. Music may reflect cerebral rhythms in some fashion. Either way, though, there is something curious here. If beauty is entirely biologically programmed, selected for its survival value alone, it is all the more surprising to see it re-emerge in the esoteric world of fundamental physics, which has no direct connection with biology. On the other hand, if beauty is more than mere biology at work, if our aesthetic appreciation stems from contact with something firmer and more pervasive, then it is surely a fact of major significance that the fundamental laws of the universe seem to reflect this "something."

Davies (1993, pp. 175–176)

My own inclination is to suppose that qualities such as ingenuity, economy, beauty, and so on have a genuine transcendent reality — they are not merely the product of human experience — and that these qualities are reflected in the structure of the natural world. Whether such qualities can themselves bring the universe into existence I don't know. If they could, one could conceive of God as merely a mythical personification of such creative qualities, rather than as an independent agent. This would, of course, be unlikely to satisfy anyone who feels he or she has a personal relationship with God.

Davies (1993, pp. 214–215)

Davies is, of course, correct in assuming that a mere personification of creative qualities falls far short of the concept of God held by most religions. But the concept that the physical universe reflects in its structure the attributes of God is one that finds considerable resonance in religious discourse. Bahá'u'lláh, for example, whose teachings uphold the existence of a God forever unknowable in essence, stated that

Whatever is in the heavens and whatever is on the earth is a direct evidence of the revelation within it of the attributes and names of God, inasmuch as within every atom are enshrined the signs that

192

bear eloquent testimony to the revelation of that most great Light. Methinks, but for the potency of that revelation, no being could ever exist. How resplendent the luminaries of knowledge that shine in an atom, and how vast the oceans of wisdom that surge within a drop!

BPT (1983b, pp. 100–101)

Rationality

All too often, rationality is identified with one or another specific way of thinking. The rational soul is a unique characteristic of the human being; its powers include scientific investigation, comprehension of meaning, and contemplation of beauty. These powers can express themselves in the creation of more than one mode of rational thought and action. Only if we are willing to abandon narrow definitions of rationality will we appreciate the underlying harmony between science and religion. The definitions at which we arrive should allow for the scepticism that characterizes any scientific method, but we should also acknowledge the need for repeated leaps of faith, for it is an undeniable fact of life that one without the other leads nowhere. The following passage from David Bohm's *Wholeness and the Implicate Order* illustrates what I mean by a "way of thinking":

193

> Nevertheless, this sort of ability of man to separate himself from his environment and to divide and apportion things ultimately led to a wide range of negative and destructive results, because man lost awareness of what he was doing and thus extended the process of division beyond the limits within which it works properly. In essence, the process of division is a way of *thinking about things* that is convenient and useful mainly in the domain of practical, technical and functional activities (e.g., to divide up an area of land into different fields where various crops are to be grown). However, when this mode of thought is applied more broadly to man's notion of himself and the whole world in which he lives (i.e. to his self–world view), then man ceases to regard the resulting divisions as merely useful or convenient and begins to see and experience himself and his world as actually constituted of separately existent fragments. Being guided by a fragmentary self–world view, man then acts in such a way as to try to break himself and the world up, so that all seems to correspond to his way of thinking. Man thus obtains an apparent proof of the correctness of his fragmentary self–world view though, of course, he overlooks the fact that it is he himself, acting according to his mode of thought, who has brought about the fragmentation that now seems to have an autonomous existence, independent of his will and of his desire.
>
> Bohm (1981, pp. 2–3, emphasis in the original)

Complementarity

Attempts to apply the principle of complementarity to areas other than physics do not enjoy every scientist's blessing. For one thing, physicists do not agree on the precise meaning of complementarity, nor do they share all the philosophical views expressed by the architects of the Copenhagen interpretation, primarily Niels Bohr. One issue on which profound differences exist, for example, is whether human ideas can grasp the essence of things. Bohr was clearly doubtful of such a possibility; for him, as Henry P. Stapp (1993) put it, "progress in human understanding would more likely consist of the growth of a web of interwoven complementary understandings of various aspects of the fullness of nature." "Such a view," Stapp continued,

> though withholding the promise for eventual complete illumination regarding the ultimate essence of nature, does offer the prospect that human inquiry can continue indefinitely to yield important new truths. And these can be final in the sense that they grasp or illuminate some aspect of nature as it is revealed to human experience. And the hope can persist that man will perceive ever more clearly, through his growing patchwork of complementary views, the general form of a pervading presence. But this pervading presence cannot be expected or required to be a resident of the three-dimensional space of naïve intuition, or to be described fundamentally in terms of quantities associated with points of a four-dimensional spacetime continuum.
>
> Stapp (1993 p. 70)

Personally, I am not at ease with every aspect of the Copenhagen interpretation of quantum mechanics, least of all its extreme pragmatism. But in relation to human knowledge, the ideas I have expressed in this paper resonate far more with the above statement than, say, the belief that all explanation will be finally reduced to the ramifications of a single overall scientific theory.

Duality

There is a vast difference between the duality of quantum mechanics and the dichotomies on which the mechanistic worldview seems to have thrived. One of the most significant contributions of "new physics" to a pattern of thought that is emerging in the world today is its rejection of this worldview. In *The Quantum Self: A Revolutionary View of Human Nature and Consciousness Rooted in the New Physics*, Danah Zohar (1991) gave an insightful analysis of the alienation resulting from the mechanical interpretation of the universe:

> The three "pernicious dichotomies" left us wondering how we conscious human beings related to ourselves (our own bodies, our own past and future, our own sub-selves), to each other or to the world of nature and facts. In trying to resolve these questions, our psychology, our philosophy and our religion fragmented into opposite extremes. As Yeats said of this era, "Things fall apart, the centre cannot hold."
>
> The split between mind and body, or between inner and outer, gave rise to the dichotomy between extreme subjectivism (a world

without objects) and extreme objectivism (a world without subjects). Thus Idealism denied the reality or importance of matter and reduced everything to mind, while materialism denied the reality or importance of mind and reduced everything to matter. Freud assumed that the inner was real and accessible, while the outer was all projection, and many strains of mysticism mirrored this view — for example the world is the veil of Maya, a veil of illusion. At the other extreme, Behaviourism assumed the outer was real but denied the relevance of the inner. It became psychology without the psyche.

The split between the individual and his relationships led on the one hand to an exaggerated individualism, to a selfish will to power and possession, and on the other to an enforced communitarianism like that of Marxism, which denied the meaning or importance of individuals at all while stressing the absolute primacy of relationship.

The split between culture and nature led both to relativism of all sorts — factual, moral, aesthetic and spiritual (value judgments) — and to dogma and extreme fundamentalism. There seemed no middle ground between the two extremes of saying that a given way of looking at things was only one of many contingent and relative ways of looking at them, or between saying there was only one, true and absolute way of looking at them. There seemed no way to say that we were not either wholly creatures of culture, and therefore unrooted in any established facts, or wholly creatures of nature (of the given), with no flexibility or room for creative development.

In the West, these dichotomies robbed our individuality of its context and landed us in the deepest isolation, leading to narcissism. We were cut off from an outer confirmation of our inner life, leading to nihilism, and denied the confirmation of our ideas, leaving us with relativism and subjectivism. Each nourished a form of alienation, and the sum total of this alienation is the curse of modernism.

Zohar (1991, pp. 217–218)

As we try to promote a discourse on science, religion, and development, the greatest challenge before us is to overcome the habits of mind described by Zohar in the above passage. What is daunting is that our discourse has to focus primarily on development, the very process that took it upon itself to propagate these habits throughout the planet.

SPIRITUAL PRINCIPLES AND THE ROLE OF KNOWLEDGE

Development programs will continue to be relevant to the life of society only to the extent that they are formulated and carried out in the context of an emerging world civilization. This is not to argue that the field of development must broaden its scope to touch on every aspect of human existence. On the contrary, as a global enterprise its value lies in its consecration to the task of fostering prosperity among the diverse inhabitants of the planet. Yet, to achieve the required vitality, systematic effort to bring about the social and economic development of nations must be conceived in the context of a greater process that will carry humanity into the next stage of evolution.

No matter how cursory, a survey of the historical forces that are shaping the structure of society — along with the devastating upheavals that these forces have already precipitated and the prodigious changes they have engendered — should convince even the staunch defenders of today's global policies that unchecked material progress is not what is needed. A dual cry can everywhere be heard rising from the heart of the great masses of humanity. It demands the extension of the fruits of material progress to all peoples, and, at the same time, it calls out for the values of spiritual civilization. For material civilization "is like a lamp-glass. Divine civilization is the lamp itself and the glass without the light is dark. Material civilization is like the body. No matter how infinitely graceful, elegant and beautiful it may be, it is dead. Divine civilization is like the spirit, and the body gets its life from the spirit" (BPT 1997, 227:22). True prosperity has both a material and a spiritual dimension.

That humanity is being impelled irresistibly toward some kind of coherent global form of existence can no longer be disputed. The choice lies in that which is to be globalized: the basest of human desires or noble ideals and aspirations. The ideas set forth in these pages originate in the conviction that the apparent dominance currently enjoyed by the former is an illusion; it is the latter that will have the final say in the destiny of the human race. The vision projected here, therefore, is optimistic, not in relation to the immediate but a more distant, yet entirely foreseeable, future.

It is a characteristic of numerous forms of existence that they undergo successive stages of transformation before reaching the level of maturity destined for them. Even the human being must pass through the stages of infancy, childhood, and adolescence before the full powers of the human spirit begin to manifest themselves. The attributes of the adult are not defined by the imperfections of childhood; nor do the vicissitudes of adolescence last beyond the age of transition. Does history not suggest a similar pattern in the collective life of humanity?

If humanity is indeed approaching adulthood, the revolutionary changes occurring with bewildering swiftness in every department of its collective life assume the character of two parallel processes, one integrative and the other of ruinous disintegration. The operation of both is necessary during such a tumultuous period when the barriers raised by the thoughts, attitudes, and habits of the childhood of the race must be uprooted and the structures of a new civilization that can reflect the powers of maturity must be shaped. If this assessment is a reasonably accurate view of the contemporary crisis in civilization, then it is imperative that those of us who work in the global enterprise we call development, which is to contribute to the emergence of the institutions and practices of adulthood, understand the nature of the dual process affecting our endeavours. For, inevitable as the final outcome may be, disintegration can be painfully prolonged by the decisions of world leaders who refuse to respond to the exigencies of a new age.

This interpretation of the nature of our times can help us free ourselves from excessive attachment to the standards of the past and move on to find new and viable paths of development. If old conventions are allowed to persist, the fate of humankind will be a global society ruled by the interests of a relative few and held in the grip of political and economic forces. Such a society will be unacceptable to a human race that has successfully shed the habits of adolescence. In this context the view of development as something that is handed over by the "developed" to the "underdeveloped" or as the imitation by every nation of the pattern of industrialization that historically led certain countries to material prosperity cannot survive as a realistic option. Equally inadequate is a vision of development as a haphazard process whose aims emerge from within its own dynamics. The transition to maturity referred to here anticipates the attainment by humanity as a whole of a new level of collective consciousness. As this increasingly occurs, the only acceptable development strategies will be those that centre on people and their institutions as the real protagonists of change — all of humanity and the institutions that legitimately serve its interests. If development is to be defined at all, then it will have to be in terms of the building of capacity in individuals, communities, and institutions to participate effectively in weaving the fabric of a materially and spiritually prosperous world civilization.

SPIRITUAL PRINCIPLES

Clearly, the relationship between spiritual and material civilization, introduced above, is not a simple one. Matter and spirit interact in intricate patterns and at various levels. In the field of development, an essential interaction should occur at the level of principle. Recognizing the need to modify the statement at a later stage, I would like to propose that progress in material civilization receives its impetus fundamentally from the force of science. It results from diverse applications of the rational faculty of the human soul, for example, to understand the laws of nature and society, to promote agriculture and industry, to learn the lessons of history, to gain insights into viable social organization, and to devise just methods of human governance. Yet these applications must respond to, and be governed by, the principles of spiritual civilization, without which material progress leads as much to misery as to happiness.

In today's world, it will not be easy to argue that development practice should be guided by spiritual principle. The prescription that the "end justifies the means" has been so long and so widely accepted by so many that it is now a feature of culture, and the accompanying idea that success is the final arbiter of truth compounds the problem. Consider, for example, the question of justice. If justice is to be a binding principle of development practice, then the purposeful creation of injustice even as a temporary measure to achieve prosperity at a future date is not permissible. Yet, not only did development thinking endorse such policies to that effect in its early years, but three decades later, after painfully acquired experience, similar policies, albeit expressed in vocabulary designed to make them more palatable, emerged and continue to survive up to the present day.

The effort to incorporate the discussion of spiritual principles into deliberations on social and economic development entails other difficulties, most of them rooted in a long history of misbehaviour on the part of religious movements. Even the suggestion brings to mind experience of the arrogance of self-righteousness and inevitably generates resistance. Yet, as argued elsewhere in this paper, extreme reactions by enlightened minds to corrupt forms of religious belief have taken a heavy toll on humanity, and it is time to show discipline in this respect. To believe in principles and to uphold them does not imply a sense of spiritual superiority. There is a difference between believing in high ideals and claiming to be their embodiment. To translate principles into action, one must engage in a process of learning, a process whose methods must be scientific. Furthermore, effective learning depends on a posture of humility, and our fear of hypocrisy should not prevent us from giving humility its due merit. The discussion of principles that follows, then, is not a treatise on religiosity; it is presented in the context of learning as the ideal mode of operation in the development field.

The oneness of humankind

The hallmark of the age of maturity will be the unification of the human race. The principle of the oneness of humankind is not a mere expression of a romantic notion of brotherly love or the praise of some vague ideal of tolerance and respect. It is not a summons to uniformity. It has nothing in common with the aggressive advance of a superficial culture that idolizes the unfettered gratification of desire and devours every culture it encounters in the name of universality.

To believe in the oneness of humanity, as advocated here, implies the rejection of theories that explain the collective life of human beings in families, groups, tribes, cities, and nations solely in terms of the imperatives of survival. Rather, the evolution of such collective life and its institutions is viewed as a gradual unfoldment of the potentialities of the human spirit. This evolutionary process will attain a stage of fulfillment when humanity is at last able to undertake the task of laying foundations for a unified and advanced civilization. Progress toward such a goal demands rapid and organic change in the very structure of society, accompanied by an equally profound change in human consciousness.

Efforts to understand the operation of this principle should bear in mind that oneness must necessarily express itself in infinite variety. Diversity and oneness are complementary and inseparable. Diversity does not invariably give rise to enmity and opposition. The differences of ethnicity, nationality, and race that exist today can be appreciated in the context of a historical process that has entailed progressive stages of unity. Differences that are perceived as causes of division and conflict should in fact be treated as sources of stability. Diversity brings enormous strength to the composition of the whole as unification occurs.

Gradual awareness of the significance of interconnectedness in the workings of the universe is arising from not only religious and philosophical but also scientific observation. Several advances in the past decades — for example, in understanding the evolution of biological and learning systems, in ecology, in the study of the cosmos and its tiniest particles — have made obsolete a worldview that was founded on the mechanics of a clock and the interactions of billiard balls. Development thinking must similarly be challenged to leave behind visions of society that have originated in minds given to fragmentation and seek in emerging scientific paradigms the ideas and tools it needs to perform its tasks.

199

The analogy that seems to demonstrate the operation of the principle of oneness in society is the human body. Within that system, millions of cells, with an extraordinary diversity of forms and functions, collaborate to make the existence of a human being possible. They give and receive whatever is needed for their individual function, as well as for the growth and welfare of the whole. No one would try to explain the life of a healthy body in terms of some of the principles we use so freely in our social theories, such as competition among the parts for scarce resources. The principle that governs the functioning of the body is cooperation. But this is not cooperation without a purpose — existence for the sake of existence. The outcome of this complex set of interactions is a system that serves as the temple of the soul. The rational faculty appears, and intelligence, a quality that seems to be present deep in the structure of the universe, manifests itself. Could not society also become the arena for harmonious interactions among human beings, interactions whose purpose is not the mere enjoyment of a few fleeting moments on this Earth, but the appearance of a higher form — human civilization?

Viewed in this way, the principle of the oneness of humankind would enter development discourse at three levels. The first would be at the level of policy and direction. That which furthers separateness, consolidates isolation, and strengthens the ascendancy of one group of people over others — even in the guise of unity and globalization — can hardly be considered development. The second would be at the level of approach and methodology. Development understood as extending prosperity to all cannot be advanced through the glorification of conflict, whether of class or of ideology. Nor can the pursuit of selfish aims and competition be considered the organizing principle of society and the only path to excellence, although one may accept that ideas and products should be allowed to compete with one another. Excellence will be achieved if the noble qualities of the human soul are allowed to flourish in the environment of freedom created by cooperation. The third level at which the principle of oneness would be felt is that of program activity. The cementing together of human hearts and the progressive achievement of unity of purpose, unity of thought, and unity of action must be incorporated in both the goals and the methods of development projects; so, too, have to be measures that promote the integration of peoples everywhere into a growing network of global relations. It is in this sense, I believe, that the well-known phrase "Think globally, act locally" takes on its true significance.

Justice

To say that justice must be a fundamental concern of development strategy is to express a truism. There is, however, little agreement on the means by which justice can be worked into actual plans and promoted in action. Recognizing that justice is primarily a spiritual principle, an exigency of the human spirit, helps overcome the difficulty and opens doors to possibilities that are not available when discussion is limited to the distribution of income or the rule of democracy. As a concept inapplicable to the web of connections defining the animal kingdom, justice is irrefutably a requirement of a life that transcends animal existence. Beyond mere concern with social issues, justice as a spiritual principle touches the individual at the deepest level of consciousness. Its influence motivates participation, raises awareness to new levels, and empowers individuals, communities, and institutions.

The spiritual roots of the principle are to be found in that faculty of the human soul that enables us to see with our own eyes and not with the eyes of others. The cultivation of this faculty creates in the individual the responsibility to investigate reality free from the chains of tradition perpetuated through imitation. When sufficiently developed, it protects the individual, for example, from being a naive victim of market propaganda, constantly induced to buy things, services, and ideologies. The elimination of such credulity is, clearly, a requirement of a development process that calls for the participation of the people in tracing their own path of collective advancement.

Understood as a spiritual principle, justice helps policymakers avoid the pitfalls of uniformity while still respecting the exigencies of equity. The analogy of the human body discussed in relation to the ideal of oneness takes on new meaning when examined in the light of this principle. Rather than defining relationships among the members of society in terms of a sameness foreign to the very structure of creation, one is moved to see individual and collective well-being as the result of the intricate operations of a system that measures needs, aspirations, talents, motivations, and performances and rewards all equitably. When appropriately brought to bear on social issues, justice is the single most important instrument for the establishment of unity.

Without justice, the goals of development become distorted. They either are dictated by the interests of dominant ideologies and powerful groups or represent simply no more than the beliefs, admittedly often rooted in altruism, of those who work professionally in the development field. Consider how loudly the praise of defective approaches to globalization is sung and how much effort is expended on covering up the resulting marginalization of the masses. Review the thousands of projects that have set out to alleviate poverty but have merely succeeded in offering a small group of beneficiaries a few advantages while the gap between the rich and the poor in the area under their influence has continued to widen. Surely, at every stage of activity — from the formulation of policies, to the design of programs, to the implementation of specific projects — the principle of justice has to be made the final arbiter.

201

Equality of men and women

There can be no doubt that the equality of men and women will be a distinguishing characteristic of the civilization destined to emerge from the present passage through an age of transition. The challenge is to ensure that, on the one hand, the principle is permitted to give direction to development strategy and, on the other, its translation into proper structures and attitudes is accepted as an integral goal of specific projects.

Acknowledging that the equality of men and women is an elementary spiritual principle closes all those arguments that, overtly or in subtle ways, sustain the notion of the superiority of men. To promote, as an element of religious belief, the conviction that the soul of the human being has no sex — as is the case with race or colour — is to attack the very foundations of the age-old prejudice against women. Science, of course, does much to shatter erroneous belief. But history is replete with examples of entire peoples who readily accepted error as scientific truth because their inherited preferences inclined them to do so.

Unfortunately, so far as the treatment of women is concerned, the record of most major religions has been anything but impressive. To denounce religion as the perpetrator of inequality between women and men, however, is not justified. Religious teaching has been progressive, certain elements of it addressing only the historical reality of the people among which it was promulgated. These have to be understood in the context of an ongoing process through which spiritual truth has been brought progressively to bear on the challenges of civilization.

Contemporary society is ill-served by a prevailing tendency to relegate certain principles, even after their value has been acknowledged, largely to the realm of rhetoric and academic discussion. If the principle of the equality of women and men is not to meet this fate, it must be given sustained expression through the adoption of one goal: ensuring that men and women work shoulder to shoulder in all fields of human endeavour — scientific, political, economic, social, and cultural — with the same rewards and in equal conditions. For the vast majority of women in the world, the most immediate implication of such a goal must be to make education available to them, an education that is of the same scientific quality as that being offered to men, and it is therefore of great significance that the education of the girl child is finally being recognized internationally as an indispensable theme of policy. The seriousness of this commitment can be appreciated in the care being taken to complement the emphasis on the education of women with measures to change the attitudes of men.

However welcome, attitudinal change is nevertheless only part of the answer in a society organized according to past prejudices. The principle of the equality of men and women has profound implications for the changes of structure that will characterize humanity's coming of age. It is no exaggeration to claim that the rigorous application of this principle will revolutionize every institution of society, from the family to government, from the smallest productive unit to large financial organizations, from structures that support individual creativity to the most complex channels for the collective expression of culture. For the objective is not the mere opening of opportunities to women to do everything that men do today, so much of which is shameful and cruel. The principle of the equality of men and women sheds light on how the true qualities of the human soul are to govern social existence. It is a statement about human reality, and its application constitutes a requisite for the establishment of peace, a definite move away from violence, an exigency of the long-awaited spiritual civilization. Without it, development simply will not occur.

Stewardship of nature

The modern scientific era has witnessed a well-justified rebellion against religious views that preach the abandonment of this world in exchange for rewards in the next. For people everywhere, it became increasingly apparent that placing the spiritual and the material in forced opposition engenders passivity, itself a major influence in the perpetuation of poverty through oppression. The creed of materialism that accompanied rebellion against the tradition, however, did not mend humanity's relationship with the material world in which it lives. As God was set aside, the answer to every question was to be sought in the workings of nature, vaguely defined as all that was accessible to the senses. But with this shift, there vanished also the reverence for nature that had been a vital feature of earlier stages of social evolution. The Earth became basically a reservoir of material resources to be exploited within an approach that could only be characterized as hostile and irresponsible. The resulting ecological disaster now forces world leaders to reexamine the meaning of progress and the appropriate relationship between humanity and nature.

Much of the blame for the great imbalance created in the ecosphere is placed on the anthropocentrism of today's civilization. The alternative often suggested, however, is a biocentrism that seems equally untenable. In its extreme formulation, this philosophy is but another brand of materialism, a worship of nature that ignores the exigencies of a consciousness unique to the human species and absent from the material universe. Once again, the focus is exclusively on the survival of the race. Can human beings now be induced to believe that their only purpose is to pass a few scores of years on this planet in harmony with nature, as do the fish and the bird?

The principle of stewardship advocated in this paper takes as a given the human aspiration to transcend the limitations of the material world, but does so while maintaining an attitude of respect and cooperation with nature that is in harmony with the oneness of existence. It upholds a vision of wholeness and interconnectedness throughout creation, which includes both nature and human consciousness, the former being an expression of God's will in the contingent world and the latter an imperative of a higher order of existence. Stewardship of nature, then, constitutes an inescapable role that humanity, from among countless species in the biosphere, must play — the role of being a conscious, compassionate, and creative participant in the evolution of the life of the planet. Far from considering the present ecological crisis a cause for despair, development thinkers should recognize it as a providential turning point in the evolution of human consciousness, a turning point in which fragmentation gives way to wholeness.

Work and wealth

As has been the case with nature, wealth has received contradictory treatment in every period of social evolution. Repeatedly, the pendulum has swung from one extreme to another, from contempt for wealth as the corrupter of the human soul to its adoration as the ultimate dispenser of happiness. The concept, clearly, needs to be reexamined in the context of a development process that can contribute to the spiritual and material advancement of the human race.

The spiritual principle that can help define a proper attitude toward wealth is one that is consistent with the real nature and purpose of work. Work is both an exigency of life on this planet and an urge inherent to human character. Through it, essential requirements of the human soul find fulfillment, and many of its potentials are realized. To accomplish its purpose, however, work cannot be reduced to a mere struggle for survival. Nor can its aim be solely the satisfaction of the demands of the self. Work's highest station is service to humanity, and when performed in that spirit, it becomes an act of worship.

The noblest fruit of work is spiritual and intellectual attainment. But work must also produce the material means to sustain the individual and society and make progress possible. The prosperous world civilization now within humanity's grasp will call for the production of wealth on a scale hitherto unimagined. The success of such an effort will depend on a rigorous definition of the parameters of the ownership of wealth so as to avoid the pitfalls of both excessive state control and the unbounded accumulation of riches by the relatively few. Extremes of wealth and poverty are closely interconnected; the latter cannot be abolished while the other is allowed to exist.

Seen in such a light, personal wealth is acceptable so long as it fulfils certain conditions. It must be earned through honest work, physical or intellectual, and its acquisition by the individual must not be the cause, no matter how indirectly, of the impoverishment of others. Moreover, the legitimacy of material possessions depends equally on how they are earned and how they are used. One should enjoy the fruits of one's labours and expend one's wealth not only for the good of one's family, but also for the welfare of society.

Freedom and empowerment

At the heart of spirituality is the yearning of the human soul for freedom from the chains and struggles of material existence. Paradoxically, the impulse is opposed by another: licence to follow the dictate of one's desires. Throughout history, these two urges have coexisted and have become intertwined, spinning dozens of ideologies, each appealing to noble aspirations and each carrying within it the seeds of its own destruction. Revolution has followed revolution — driven initially by legitimate longing to be free, only to be co-opted later by the cruelest manifestations of a lower nature. The despair that characterizes today's society owes much of its force to the confusion of those who cannot distinguish between true freedom and surrender to animal desire.

Science provides tools and methods that can be used to achieve freedom. But it is the light of religion that separates nobility from baseness. From a religious point of view, true liberty is compliance with divine teachings. For only to the extent that human beings awaken to the capacity for love, generosity, justice, compassion, trustworthiness, and humility can they manifest the extraordinary powers with which they have been endowed.

Certainly, freedom from oppression is a cause to be upheld throughout the age of transition from childhood to maturity. Those working toward this goal will have little trouble detecting the oppressive behaviour of tyrannical regimes and the political and economic measures instituted by one group to suppress another. What is somewhat more difficult to appreciate is that the reigning version of democracy, so closely tied to the operations of the market, breeds other forms of oppression, subtle but equally damaging, for the greatest crime of oppression is that it robs people of their true identity. Its weapon is the prolongation of ignorance through the manipulation of information and the denial of access to knowledge. Ironically, the perpetrator and the victim both find themselves deprived of opportunities to develop the potentialities on which fulfillment ultimately depends. A central task of development, then, is the systematic propagation of spiritual and material knowledge for the clear purpose of empowering people.

THE ROLE OF KNOWLEDGE

If development practice is to be governed by spiritual principles, the role it assigns to the generation and application of knowledge must be reevaluated. Materialism, whether cogently defined or hidden in implicit assumptions, has little choice but to place economic activity at the centre of human existence. In one way or another, all other processes of social life end up subordinate to this activity, deriving the greater part of their significance from the contributions they make to the generation of material comfort and wealth. Specifically, knowledge, too often confused with information, acquires much of its value from its enormous potential to drive economic progress.

205

An alternative claim, one advanced in this paper, is that a worldview that is cognizant of the spiritual dimensions of consciousness would regard the generation and application of knowledge as the very central process of social existence. Clearly, the creation of wealth and its just distribution would continue to be indispensable. But economic activity would not be seen as an end in itself. Beyond attention to the needs of survival, it would concern itself with the multiplication of means through which humanity would pursue goals of a higher purpose.

In the final analysis, whether the necessity to make such a fundamental shift in our perception of social life is acknowledged or dismissed depends on one's convictions about life's meaning and purpose. But whatever these convictions, it is becoming increasingly difficult to ignore the evidence that points overwhelmingly to the inability of development practice rooted in dogmatic materialism to ensure even the material well-being of the great masses of humanity. Indeed, how can one escape the conclusion that economic and political oppression is inherent in the materialistic view of existence? No matter how heroic the struggle against misery may be, oppression, the main cause of misery, will prevail in one or another of its myriad forms until society becomes the expression of the higher imperatives of human nature.

The building of a world civilization — the content within which, I have argued here, the field of development needs to organize its operations — calls for a level of capacity far greater than anything humanity could have imagined during its long childhood. Reaching such a level will require an enormous expansion of knowledge. But if all that is accomplished is growth in magnitude, the practical results will be sad indeed. If the current arrangements that assign the ownership of modern science to small sectors of society are maintained, the consequence will be no more than the widening of the gap between the poor and the rich. Development, that is, cannot be viewed as the mere preparation of the majority of humankind to become efficient users of the products of science and technology. A fundamental concern of any program of social and economic development has to be the right of the masses of humanity not only to have access to information, but to participate fully in the generation and application of knowledge; the extent of each human being's participation should be determined only by the measure of his or her capacities.

The availability of good-quality education to every member of the human race will clearly play a crucial role in bringing about the level of participation being proposed here, as will the extension of the work of sophisticated research centres to every region. But beyond these, the flow of knowledge in the world will have to be rearranged.

For the most part, what may be referred to as modern scientific knowledge is currently generated in universities and specialized research centres of the industrialized countries. Replicas of these institutions in the South participate in this process to only a limited degree. The majority of the people in the world receive from this elaborate research and development system an inadequate formal education, instructions by agents of governments and NGOs on the proper use of technological packages, and a variety of short courses on the many aspects of a modern life into which the masses of humanity are to be incorporated. They are simultaneously subjected to the commercial, political, and cultural propaganda of innumerable groups and organizations constantly competing for their attention.

That highly sophisticated centres in the world dedicated to research and development in the frontiers of modern science are essential is undeniable. The need for efficient channels through which individuals and communities receive beneficial services in areas such as health, education, and production is equally evident. What is widely ignored is that, in addition to training and the delivery of services, the application of knowledge for the purpose of transforming complex social realities requires the generation of new knowledge through dynamic and effective research and the participation of an ever greater diversity of minds.

Further, it is surely self-evident that research on development cannot have as its sole purpose the enlightenment of academic circles or be carried out by scientists from outside the population whose progress is being promoted. Valuable as the fruits of such research may be, it fails to promote the development of the institutional capacity within the population to deal with the generation and application of knowledge, not necessarily in the forefront of modern science and technology, but in areas where the natural and social sciences must together tackle specific problems of specific people. It is addressing this latter need that constitutes one of the primary challenges facing the field of development. If successfully met, the result will be to break the present pattern of flow of knowledge in the world, dissociate development from an ill-conceived and destructive process of modernization, and focus attention on true cultural advancement.

FURTHER COMMENTS

The following two comments seem necessary to clarify the nature of the principles I have attempted to describe here.

Relation to Bahá'í text

As mentioned earlier in the paper, the methodology adopted for this research project invites each participant to make explicit the religious beliefs underlying the arguments he or she is advancing. This sub-section is primarily an exposition of some of the Bahá'í teachings relevant to capacity-building, the topic to be treated in the next section. Although the ideas expressed represent my own understanding of these teachings, I have tried to follow Bahá'í texts as closely as possible. Let me give an example to illustrate how I have gone about doing this. My brief description of the concept of humanity's coming of age is based on a number of passages from the Bahá'í writings. Bahá'u'lláh made repeated reference to the opening of a new stage in the life of humanity:

> This is the Day in which God's most excellent favors have been poured out upon men, the Day in which His most mighty grace hath been infused into all created things. It is incumbent upon all the peoples of the world to reconcile their differences, and, with perfect unity and peace, abide beneath the shadow of the Tree of His care and loving-kindness. It behoveth them to cleave to whatsoever will, in this Day, be conducive to the exaltation of their stations, and to the promotion of their best interests.
>
> BPT (1983a, IV)

'Abdu'l-Bahá, interpreting his father's teachings, further elaborated on this idea:

> From the beginning to the end of his life man passes through certain periods, or stages, each of which is marked by certain conditions peculiar to itself. For instance, during the period of childhood his conditions and requirements are characteristic of that degree of intelligence and capacity. After a time he enters the period of youth, in which his former conditions and needs are superseded by new

requirements applicable to the advance in his degree. His faculties
of observation are broadened and deepened; his intelligent capacities are trained and awakened; the limitations and environment of
childhood no longer restrict his energies and accomplishments. At
last he passes out of the period of youth and enters the stage, or station, of maturity, which necessitates another transformation and
corresponding advance in his sphere of life activity. New powers and
perceptions clothe him, teaching and training commensurate with
his progression occupy his mind, special bounties and bestowals
descend in proportion to his increased capacities, and his former
period of youth and its conditions will no longer satisfy his matured
view and vision. Similarly, there are periods and stages in the life of
the aggregate world of humanity. ...

From every standpoint the world of humanity is undergoing a
reformation. The laws of former governments and civilizations are
in process of revision; scientific ideas and theories are developing
and advancing to meet a new range of phenomena; invention and
discovery are penetrating hitherto unknown fields, revealing new
wonders and hidden secrets of the material universe; industries have
vastly wider scope and production; everywhere the world of
mankind is in the throes of evolutionary activity indicating the
passing of the old conditions and advent of the new age of
reformation. ...

This is the cycle of maturity and reformation in religion as well.
Dogmatic imitations of ancestral beliefs are passing. ... Bigotry and
dogmatic adherence to ancient beliefs have become the central and
fundamental source of animosity among men, the obstacle to
human progress, the cause of warfare and strife, the destroyer of
peace, composure and welfare in the world. ...

This reformation and renewal of the fundamental reality of religion constitute the true and outworking spirit of modernism, the
unmistakable light of the world, the manifest effulgence of the
Word of God, the divine remedy for all human ailment and the
bounty of eternal life to all mankind.

BPT (1982, pp. 438–439)

The operations of two processes, one of integration and the other
of disintegration, through which the "coming together" of the peoples
of the world is to be realized, are also the subject of detailed exposition
in Bahá'í texts. Bahá'ís are called on, then, to do all they can to promote
the forces of integration in society but to understand well the inevitable
effects of the destructive forces that are at work in their own lives and
in the lives of others. As they do so, they are to keep before their eyes a
vision of a future that is depicted in terms such as the following:

National rivalries, hatreds, and intrigues will cease, and racial animosity and prejudice will be replaced by racial amity, understanding and cooperation. The causes of religious strife will be
permanently removed, economic barriers and restrictions will be
completely abolished, and the inordinate distinction between
classes will be obliterated. Destitution on the one hand, and gross

accumulation of ownership on the other, will disappear. The enormous energy dissipated and wasted on war, whether economic or political, will be consecrated to such ends as will extend the range of human inventions and technical development, to the increase of the productivity of mankind, to the extermination of disease, to the extension of scientific research, to the raising of the standard of physical health, to the sharpening and refinement of the human brain, to the exploitation of the unused and unsuspected resources of the planet, to the prolongation of human life, and to the furtherance of any other agency that can stimulate the intellectual, the moral, and spiritual life of the entire human race.

BPT (1991, p. 204)

The reader unfamiliar with the Bahá'í Faith may find these ideas utopian and deterministic. For Bahá'ís, they do not carry such connotations. When examined in the context of the totality of the belief system, which places great emphasis on individual and collective choice, these statements are understood as descriptions of a process of organic growth, the unfolding of the potentialities with which human existence has been endowed.

Knowledge, love, faith

The principles briefly analyzed in this section of the paper represent the convictions of a growing number of people from many religious and secular backgrounds today. For Bahá'ís, they are considered essential elements of their belief system and receive extensive treatment in their scriptures. Given the theme of this research project, the beliefs I have tried to make explicit are related primarily to the transformation of society. This, I fear, could convey a narrow view of the Bahá'í Faith as a religion. In fact, a high percentage of the Faith's literature pertains to the mystical aspects of life, to matters of worship and religious practice, and, of course, to theological concepts. Although these do not bear directly on the issues under discussion, I should express my conviction that without them the principles I have discussed lack the force needed to bring about transformation. Knowledge must be accompanied by the will to act if ideals are to be translated into reality. For a religious person, the will to act receives its impulse from two main forces: that of love and that of faith. According to 'Abdu'l-Bahá, "Love is heaven's kindly light, the holy spirit's eternal breath that vivifieth the human soul. ... [it] revealeth with unfailing and limitless power the mysteries latent in the universe" (BPT 1997, 12:1). And faith, according to him, is "the magnet which draws the confirmation of the Merciful One," whereas service is "the magnet which attracts the heavenly strength" (BPC 1930, 1:62). "By faith is meant, first, conscious knowledge and second, the practice of good deeds" (BPT 1930, 3:549).

"In the garden of thy heart plant naught but the rose of love" is Bahá'u'lláh's admonition (BPT 1994, 2:3). "Only by love," says the

Bhagavad Gita, "can men see me, and know me, and come unto me" (11:54). "Many waters cannot quench love," we are assured by the Song of Solomon, "neither can floods drown it. If a man offered for love all the wealth of his house, it would be utterly scorned" (8:7). From Buddhist teachings, we learn that "the man of faith is revered wherever he goes: he has virtue and fame, he prospers" (Dhammapada, 21:303). "If ye have faith as a grain of mustard seed," Jesus promised, "ye shall say unto this mountain, Remove hence to yonder place; and it shall remove; and nothing shall be impossible unto you" (Mt 17:20). And the testimony of the Qur'an is equally emphatic: "God is the protector of those who have faith: from the depths of darkness He will lead them forth into light" (Q 2:257).

CAPACITY-BUILDING

In an attempt to explore the characteristics of a development theory that takes into account the spiritual dimension of human existence, I have outlined certain principles that I propose should govern both strategy and project operation. The view of development set forth has been one of a global enterprise whose purpose is to bring prosperity to all peoples, an enterprise that, I have claimed, must pursue its aim in the context of the emergence of a world civilization. I have argued that humanity is experiencing an age of transition, best appreciated as a passage from collective childhood to collective maturity, and that, to be effective, development efforts must transcend the behavioural patterns of adolescence. I have singled out the force of knowledge as the propeller of civilization and asserted that participating in the generation and application of knowledge is an inalienable right of every human being on the planet. Within this context, I have proposed that development focus on the building of capacity in individuals, communities, and institutions — the three protagonists who must participate in the construction of material and spiritual civilization.

If we accept that development is to be shaped by the exigencies of humanity's transition from its collective childhood to collective maturity, we need to acknowledge that in the process the conceptual building blocks of cultures and ideologies must undergo profound changes of meaning. The list of terms to be redefined is long — *man, woman, youth, work, leisure, wealth, honour, loyalty, freedom, nation, state, governance,* and so on. Particularly urgent is the task of rethinking conceptions of the individual and the community and the relationship of each to the institutions that make organized life on the planet possible.

Those who founded development as a distinct field of endeavour in the middle years of this century convinced themselves that the world was essentially populated by two types of individuals. On the one side were placed the vast majority of humankind, who, depending on the propriety of the occasion, would be labeled as backward, lethargic, tradition bound, constrained by the demands of the extended family and the community, ruled by taboos, content with too little, and lacking in initiative. On the other side stood "modern men" — and they were men — energetic, hardworking, disciplined, self-motivated, and rational. Development aimed at gradually changing the former into the latter. Fifty years later, thinking about the inhabitants of the planet is far more sophisticated, and the greater part of modern man's behaviour has been subjected to severe questioning. Unbridled individualism has taken an appalling toll on society and nature, and an overly self-confident liberalism has proven a fertile breeding ground for despair and confusion. The need for a clear understanding of the rights and responsibilities of the individual has become a pressing concern.

While maintaining such decided views on the individual, early development thinkers showed remarkable ambivalence toward the notion of community — but then the concept had been in crisis for decades in the West, and its nature and role in the modern world were not well defined. Thus, despite the heroic efforts of a variety of programs, community life disintegrated and the traditional social structures crumbled, without being replaced by institutions able to hold the community together. For a while it seemed that small communities, especially those in rural areas, were doomed to disappear and that the only option open to human beings was to live in overcrowded, soulless cities. Then suddenly, extraordinary advances in communications technology in recent years began to introduce unexpected elements into the picture. The need to centralize, characteristic of industrialization in the past, rapidly diminished to the point that it has become possible to claim that a relatively small local community, at once conducive to participatory collective endeavour and connected globally to a vast reservoir of information, may be an attractive and viable alternative for growing numbers of people. It is evident that the concept of community is also in need of redefinition.

The idea I would like to put forward is that new definitions of the individual and the community will emerge only as we are willing to reexamine the concepts of authority and power in depth. Further, as development is to be intimately connected to knowledge, fresh insight into the nature of authority and power will have to come from a dialogue between science and religion.

POWER AND AUTHORITY

In the opening section of this paper, I expressed certain misgivings about the way power has been perceived and used throughout humanity's childhood and subsequently during its adolescence. I will argue here that, as maturity approaches, power should be viewed primarily as an attribute of the individual and the local community — power to carry out, at the prompting of the human spirit, the tasks required by the common purpose of creating civilization.

For this conception of power to become widely accepted, we need a new understanding of what it means to exercise individual initiative and participate in collective enterprise. Individual initiative is not the same as the pursuit of whatever the heart desires or random motion according to some romantic definition of creativity. To be fruitful and to avoid the alienation that results from unrestricted individualism, creativity must accept discipline, and initiative must move in the direction of oneness.

Discipline needs to be maintained by the force of inner conviction. When discipline is imposed, it succeeds only in quenching the fire of creativity. Yet, it would also be misleading to view inner discipline simply as a product of the individual's will. The human soul manifests its latent powers as it learns submission to a higher authority, fundamentally the authority of the spiritual and material laws governing existence. These laws are explored in the texts of science and religion. Understanding them not only influences individual conscience but also gives meaning to the authority society bestows on its institutions. The latter is, in its essence, the authority to channel the powers of the individual and the group to achieve a common good, an authority all too often abused, degenerating into the power to control and to manipulate.

Conflict between the individual and the institutions of society — the one clamouring for ever greater freedom and the other demanding ever more complete submission — has been a feature of political life throughout the ages. The model of democracy vigorously propagated in the world today takes this state of conflict for granted but tries to fix the parameters so that the individual's rights are not transgressed in the process. Beyond any question, the version of democracy so far achieved is preferable to the despotic systems of governance to which humanity has been subjected time and again. But the historical process of democratization does not have to end here, at its current immature stage; the interaction between institutional authority to decide and individual power to accomplish has only begun to realize its possibilities. Better arrangements will emerge, however, only when institutions cease to be seen as instruments for imposing on society the views of a particular faction, whether democratically elected or not. To the extent that institutions become channels through which the talents and energies of the members of society can be expressed in service to humanity, a sense of reciprocity will grow in which the individual supports and nurtures institutions and these, in turn, pay sincere attention to the voice of the people whose needs they serve.

Social existence, of course, cannot be reduced to the interplay between individuals and institutions. These can only exist and interact in an environment from which they must derive sustenance and to the enrichment of which they must dedicate themselves. Thus, a new understanding of power and authority has profound implications for the nature of community life and hence for culture. On the community rests the challenge of providing that environment where individual wills blend, where powers are multiplied and manifest themselves in collective action, where higher expressions of the human spirit can appear.

With these brief remarks on the character of the three protagonists of development, I now turn to the subject of capacity-building, first to discuss it in general terms and then to analyze a few specific capabilities I consider indispensable to the progress of a people.

DECISION-MAKING AND IMPLEMENTATION

Capacity-building, as proposed here, entails the enabling of the individual to manifest innate powers in a creative and disciplined way, the shaping of institutions to exercise authority so that these powers are channeled toward the upliftment of humanity, and the development of the community so that it acts as an environment conducive to the enrichment of culture. The challenge to all three is to learn to use the material resources of the planet and the intellectual and spiritual resources of the race to advance civilization. Meeting this challenge implies a fundamental change in the process of decision-making, both individual and collective. Today, unbridled competition, obsession with power, and the abuse of authority vitiate the way decisions are made. The process suffers from extremes: apathy or overenthusiasm, attachment to technique or haphazardness, devotion to minutia or the propensity to deal only with abstractions. What is vitally needed is a mode of operation into which systematic learning has been woven.

To facilitate the discussion here and in the rest of this paper, I will present my arguments in the context of one region of a country, a region that embraces several towns, many villages, and possibly one or more cities. Such regions, usually with well-defined ecological, cultural, and political identities, are often the focus of development programs in which international agencies, the government, and some of the organizations of civil society all have distinct parts to play.

We can safely assume that the majority of the inhabitants of our typical region have seldom had a voice in substantial decisions affecting their collective life — for example, those related to physical infrastructure, the nature and size of agricultural and industrial production, technology, education, or communications. These decisions are made either outside the region or by a regional elite who, depending on the extent of decentralization achieved in the country as a whole, play a more or less important part in the overall structure of power through which the nation is governed. The elite itself is divided in numerous factions, this whether or not the political arrangements are democratic in character.

The region being described here is not one from which political processes are absent. Democratization, with its recurring cycles of triumph and setback, has encouraged the rise of institutions that touch the life of the individual in the towns and villages. As acceptance of the values of decentralization has advanced, a measure of authority may have even been devolved on these local institutions. But what is in place is a far cry from a political system conducive to the participation of people in the administration of their own affairs. In reality, even elected councils in the smallest of villages function as instruments in the hands of the appointees of various political bosses. These use their connections to bring resources to their people and in turn deliver allegiance, increasingly in the form of votes as more and more nations join the ranks of those who hold democratic elections.

Despite all these inadequacies, it would be a mistake to regard the situation of the region as hopeless. The elite is not impervious to reform, and individuals of uncompromising integrity do rise to influential positions. Corruption is widespread, but there is frequently also a genuine desire to bring prosperity to the masses. Altruism and greed exist side by side in constant opposition to each other.

A great source of hope for the region is the gradual ascent of nongovernmental development organizations. These have now been labouring in every corner of the world for a few decades. Much of their work is effected through grass-roots organizations — cooperatives, associations, clubs, and so on — endowing civil society with indispensable social, political, and economic structures. Important as their work may be, however, even these institutional arrangements are no substitute for a proper system of governance. In the absence of such a system, nongovernmental bodies, too, tend to reinforce the power of local interest groups that are ready to absorb the resources of whatever development projects appear on the horizon.

Effecting a fundamental change in this condition clearly involves creating and strengthening authentic structures of governance, especially at the local level. But where, the question must be asked, are development thinkers to look for those concepts that would help fledgling institutions engage in a sound process of decision-making and implementation? It would be naive to expect that politics as practiced in the region would be a source of helpful inspiration. After all, the purpose is not to learn to manipulate, to amass personal wealth and consolidated group power to the detriment of others, and to be skilful players in an endless game that has already led to the impoverishment of the masses.

What, then, of the processes characteristic of materially advanced countries? Are they the models that should be emulated by the rest of the world? Do they embody the values needed to enable the inhabitants of our region, until now marginalized from decisions governing their collective life, to forge a path of progress for themselves? Are the past contributions of these political processes to the affluence of some nations sufficient proof of their ability to bring about the transformations that will engender material and spiritual prosperity of the human race as a whole?

If we were to follow the mood of our times, we would be enthusiastic about the latter alternative as long as measures were instituted to avoid corruption. To attribute the obvious inadequacies of current modes of political behaviour solely to corruption, however, is to ignore deeply rooted flaws in certain fundamental conceptions. For example, it is true that the use of physical force, a cherished instrument of authority throughout history, has lost credibility and appeal in recent years. But democracy, defined as the dividing of people according to interest, talent, and ideology, who then "negotiate" decisions, continues to embrace violence. The purpose of each component group is to win. The means to this end are economic advantage and the mobilization of support to overwhelm the opponent. So strong is this legacy of "he who wins is right" that it essentially determines the way justice is administered. Are we to accept this as the crowning achievement of the evolution of collective decision-making on the planet?

215

Rather than defining collective decision-making as the mastery of the art of political manipulation, development strategy would do well to view it as the collective investigation of reality and the rational analysis of options. Such a process is open to the use of methods that, although not necessarily sophisticated or complex, are fundamentally scientific. Indeed, over the years, programs concerned with community action have devised highly imaginative methods to detect needs, analyze causal chains, weigh alternative courses of action, plan, and monitor. It is true that some of these efforts involve an almost mindless application of technique. But there are also programs that have clearly assisted groups of people to acquire the intellectual tools to deal with collective decision-making, understood as the systematic investigation of reality. The particular features of these methods are not at issue here. What is significant is that valuable knowledge already exists within the social sciences and could be incorporated into mainstream activity if policy looks favourably upon this dimension of development.

That the power of science can be brought to bear on the design of effective mechanisms for collective decision-making is half the story. The success of a consultative process that takes on the characteristics of the investigation of reality and does not easily degenerate into conflict and power play depends also on the spiritual qualities of the participants. Honesty, fairness, tolerance, patience, and courtesy are a few that readily come to mind. To make a list of such attributes is not difficult. The question is how to develop them. What force can enable people to oppose their passions, to cling to truth even when it does not gratify some of their own perceived interests, and to accept a discipline that invokes both the courage to express frank opinion and the wisdom to become an active participant in a consensus? Clearly, this inner force is religious in nature.

To insist on the acquisition of qualities that a dispassionate investigation of reality demands is not to ignore self-interest. Nor can one deny the difficulties in reaching consensus on matters that affect the well-being of the participants in a consultative process. All that is being asked is that people draw upon the resources of science and religion to develop in decision-making bodies certain abilities required of them by their functions in society. These include the abilities to maintain a clear perception of social reality and of the forces operating in it; to detect some of the opportunities offered by each historical moment; to properly assess the resources of the community; to consult freely and harmoniously as a body and with one's constituency; to realize that every decision has both a material and a spiritual dimension; to arrive at decisions; to win the confidence, respect, and genuine support of those affected by these decisions; to effectively use the energies and diverse talents of the available human resources; to integrate the diversity of aspirations and of activities of individuals and groups into one forward movement; to build and maintain unity; to uphold standards of justice; and to implement decisions with an openness and flexibility that avoid all trace of dictatorial behaviour.

Even a cursory review of these abilities suggests the need to re-create the decision-making bodies of our region as learning organizations. What is at stake is the transformation of the present mode of governance, based on traditional concepts of power and authority, into one shaped by a genuine posture of learning. There is no denying that the task will demand a commitment to principle that development projects have seldom managed to muster. Yet, is not the shift from governing by force to administering by learning one of the distinguishing features of humanity's passage from childhood to maturity?

THE UNIVERSITY

For development efforts to operate entirely in a learning mode, something more than the experiential learning of communities and organizations is required. Every developing region is in need of an institution devoted to the formal generation, application, and propagation of knowledge. I will refer here to this institution as the university. The extent to which this university undertakes the traditional tasks assigned to it — those of offering higher education and carrying out research in the frontiers of modern scientific endeavour — will depend on the specific conditions of the region under consideration. In the context of development as capacity-building, its essential functions are research, action, and training related to the entire spectrum of processes of social, economic, and cultural life of the population it serves. What is being suggested is not mere academic activity, but research carried out with the participation of the population in the very spaces where they are engaged in such undertakings as agricultural and industrial production, marketing, education, socialization of values, and cultural enrichment.

In its relation to regional development, then, the university is an institution present in almost every instance of social action, accompanying the population, systematizing existing knowledge, generating new knowledge, incorporating the results of systematic learning into programs of formal and nonformal education, and providing decision-making bodies with insights and enlightened perspective. Establishing such an institution and defining its mode of operation are crucial components of capacity-building in any region — a challenge that calls for creativity and the ability to innovate. Traditional models of an already stagnant higher education have little to offer. New parameters have to be set for both research and action. The goal is to create a social space, every one of whose structures — the farm, the factory, the school — serves as a dynamic centre of learning.

DEVELOPMENT, TRANSFER, AND ADOPTION OF TECHNOLOGY

One of the most demanding tasks before the people of our region, a task that will claim the constant attention of the university and decision-making bodies at various levels, is that of making proper technological choices. The subject of technology has been integral to development discourse since its inception, and by now has been examined from almost every angle possible. An array of adjectives — *large* or *small*, *capital* or *labour intensive*, *modern*, *advanced*, *intermediate*, *indigenous*, *energy efficient*, *environmentally sound* — has been used to describe the appropriateness of technology in one or another of its various forms. Its associated processes of transfer, innovation, research and development, adaptation, and diffusion as applied to most fields of human endeavour have been scrupulously analyzed and the findings fully debated. The interplay between technology and the economic, cultural, political, and social determinants of a nation's life has also been studied in detail. It is puzzling, then, that discussions of technology in the development field have remained so inconclusive. In most developing countries, formulating effective science and technology policies continues to be a formidable challenge. Every time the topic of technology takes centre stage, a host of other factors, largely economic and political, are introduced, with the result that focus is shattered.

Apart from the complexity of the issues involved, technological advance is itself an elusive theme, for it is both a goal of development and a means of effecting it. Much of modernity is defined in terms of the use of modern technology. This does not reflect a misconception, as technological change is inherent in material progress. Thus, when running water is brought to a village, the inhabitants can rightfully claim that access to this new technology constitutes a step forward in development. By the same token, the introduction of computers into a society can be considered a contribution to its advancement. The problem arises when the essential link between material and spiritual progress is ignored and material civilization is allowed to race forward with little or no attention paid to spiritual reality. The role of technology as a means of fulfilling higher aspirations slips from view. Instead, technology becomes a mysterious and autonomous force that defines the shape of the future. People recede into the background, as if they had no choice but to follow whatever trend the invention of a new technology establishes.

The solution to the dilemma is obviously not to deny the intrinsic value of technological progress, much less to perpetuate defective notions of spirituality and harmony with nature. What is needed, rather, is to foster in the inhabitants of each region the capacity to make increasingly more valid choices, both individually and collectively, regarding the development, transfer, and adoption of technology.

In a world all too given to twisting words to suit economic interests, the capacity to make proper technological choices could easily become synonymous with the possession of the skills of a good consumer. This is clearly not what is intended here. The type of capacity under discussion represents a complex set of attitudes, convictions, understandings, skills, and habits, all of which characterize the behaviour of individuals and organizations in their daily interaction with technology.

A major determinant of such behaviour is what may be called a scientific and technological culture of the people. The inability of development strategy to address this aspect of culture and to seek to achieve change through it — preferring to focus on fragments of modern science and technology — is responsible for many of its past failures. The university, I believe, is the institution that can remedy the situation by introducing in the region a dynamic process of learning about technology at various levels.

As defined earlier, the university is to operate in a variety of social spaces, from the most sophisticated intellectual circles to the farms and factories of the region it serves. It can use these learning centres to promote a discourse on science and technology that is balanced in its approach to change. Militant defence of traditions is almost always an expression of fear on the part the masses and those who control them. Disdain for and neglect of knowledge systems already present among the people of a developing region similarly stem from insecurity, in this case the insecurity of those who wish to impose change; among the undesirable outcomes of this special form of arrogance are alienation and resistance. The university must strive to cultivate a healthy relationship between the cultural heritage of the population whose education it fosters and the fruits of modern science, thus enabling the people to take possession of the new knowledge generated by the interaction of the two.

For such a sense of ownership to be meaningful, it must be accompanied by the understanding that technology is not neutral. The notion that technology can be good or bad depending on how it is used has validity, but only within a very limited context: clearly, a knife can be used to kill or to cut bread. But at a more fundamental level, technology carries with it an ideology and pronounces on the way individual and social life should be organized. Technological choice bears on every other choice made about the quality and direction of life in a region. It is itself an expression of values — political, social, cultural and, ultimately, moral and spiritual. The task of the university would be to so infuse this understanding into the general thinking of the people that it becomes an undisputed element of the culture.

Creating an adequate understanding of the nature of technology in the population of a region is only an initial step in building its capacity to face technological choice, not as a helpless victim of the market, but as a conscious entity in charge of its own destiny. The university must pursue ceaselessly the goal of promoting a dynamic discourse on science and technology in the region, cognizant that at any moment the forces of political and commercial propaganda can disrupt the process of learning set in motion. The point is not to turn development programs into courses of philosophy and become lost in endless academic debate; selected technologies have to be disseminated widely and applied properly for material progress to become a reality. The challenge is to ensure that such dissemination does not occur as a series of isolated events whose implications for social transformation are never taken into consideration.

At least two types of effort should move forward in a region if technological change is to be a deliberate process open to the scrutiny of an informed population. First, steps have to be taken to make explicit the values underlying the operation of each set of interrelated products, instruments, processes, and procedures introduced in the region. Unfortunately, in recent years, the word *values*, like a number of other important terms brought into fashionable social discourse, has been tossed about so carelessly that it has nearly been rendered useless. The kind of exploration into the subject being proposed here implies courageous opposition to an aggressive culture that cannot deal properly with the question of values and seeks, therefore, to reduce it to a matter of personal taste. How could it be otherwise in a moral and spiritual vacuum in which purpose and identity represent no more than derivatives of activity itself? In a culture still connected to its religious roots, in contrast, values arise from spiritual teachings that shed light on individual and collective identity and define the purpose of constructive endeavour.

219

Second, measures should be adopted to develop in the region the ability to comprehend the science behind the technology being propagated. Specifically, at least part of the scientific text responsible for each step forward in technological progress should be introduced into the knowledge system of the region. The level of sophistication at which this is done depends on the nature of the technology, the complexity of the particular scientific text, and the previous achievements of the population. To accomplish this goal, the university has various means at its disposal, from publications and films that popularize particular scientific themes to formal curricula for every educational level. It also has in its armoury research, if not at the cutting edge, then substantive enough to move the population from the position of mere receiver and user of technology to being its owner.

In addition to concern for culture, the technological dimension of building capacity in a region has clear implications for the autochthonous agencies charged with the development, adoption, and propagation of technology. These agencies need to be strengthened in taking up their many crucial responsibilities, which include assessing the technological requirements of the development process; surveying the natural resources of the region as well as the by-products of ongoing activities and determining how they should be put to use; planning and monitoring the transfer of specific technologies and measuring their effects; carrying out high-quality research and finding technological solutions to concrete problems; and attending to the needs of technical education. All these tasks must be performed with intimate and detailed knowledge of the ecology of the region and a profound understanding of the evolving social reality of the population; to ensure that learning does indeed occur, the university needs to accompany the agencies and institutions involved in these processes.

From the immensity of the tasks described above, it is clear that no single development program with a focus on a specific region can endow its population with the capacity to make sound technological choices. Technology is a global issue, and its role in the advancement of civilization has to be explored and clarified in that context. The discourse on science and technology — several elements of which have been mentioned here — has to extend beyond regional boundaries. The university referred to in these pages is to be but a component of a larger network of learning institutions operating in every society independent of its degree of material attainment. What is really needed is an open, worldwide exploration of issues related to technological choice, one not easily co-opted by privileged groups bent on setting the direction of material progress and receiving a giant share of the power it generates. This vigorous endeavour must be scientific in its approach to problems but should also be allowed to draw freely on the religious heritage of humanity to clarify questions of value and purpose. The present revolution in communication makes such a global effort eminently practicable.

The revolution itself now opens possibilities for rapid technological change in every corner of the world in ways unthinkable when, several decades ago, the field of development was born.

THE EDUCATION OF CHILDREN AND YOUTH

From the beginning, enhancing the ability of the world's governments to impart education to their citizens has been a major component of development strategy. Initially, the emphasis was largely on infrastructure, but, over the years, other matters related to curriculum, administration, educational technology, teacher training, and even the relationship between the school and the community were also addressed. It must be acknowledged that enormous progress has been made in these interrelated areas of endeavour, particularly in the context of the universalization of primary education. Yet, there is a widespread feeling that despite these impressive accomplishments, education is not living up to its promises, indeed that educational systems everywhere are in crisis.

A thorough analysis of the ills afflicting modern education lies beyond the scope of this paper. But one point needs to be briefly discussed so that the line of reasoning being followed here can be made clear. Apart from a relatively small number of fortunate students attending exceptional schools, the majority of the world's children and youth today receive an increasingly superficial education that systematizes the fragmentation of the students' minds, advancing thereby the fragmentation of society. The solution to the problem cannot be sought in simply better management of the parameters and relationships that define the school, improvement of teaching–learning dynamics in and outside the classroom, application of the latest technology, or elaboration of a stream of documents that define an impressive set of objectives for every course and every area of study. These measures are important in themselves and certainly create the image of a progressive movement ever engaged in educational reform in country after country. The roots of the crisis gripping education, however, are to be found in the way knowledge is perceived and treated in many educational systems.

In most schools, curricula are organized by subject matter. Although more advanced approaches allow for educational activities that try to integrate two or three subjects, the choice of the content of every course is made within a framework that divides knowledge into distinct and disconnected components. Division into disciplines is seen as virtually inherent to knowledge itself, which is defined in terms of its fragments — as the sum of all the disciplines in natural and social sciences, arts and humanities, and professional fields such as engineering and medicine. Year after year, the students accumulate knowledge in separate categories without becoming aware of the essential relationships uniting the parts, without perhaps even getting a glimpse of the underlying interconnectedness of social existence, much less of the material universe.

The problem is exacerbated by the emphasis that is placed on the assimilation of facts rather than on the understanding of profound concepts. Rote learning is categorically condemned but is blandly replaced by the mastery of techniques to manipulate information. Even the attractive pedagogy of learning by doing becomes distorted by an exaggerated attitude of play. Nowhere is this more apparent than in so-called modern approaches to science education where, in the name of individual discovery, tinkering is presented as the essence of scientific inquiry, and appreciation of the complex structure of science as an evolving body of knowledge receives little attention. Morality, if addressed at all, is treated as another fragment, another discrete subject matter. The notion of service to humanity is minimally present, and the fostering of a spiritual consciousness is almost entirely ignored. A dichotomy between theory and action results in a tendency to teach practical and manual skills to some and book-learning to others, the ability to participate in planning and decision-making to the few and to carry out orders to the majority. And in those infrequent circumstances when learning to think is given priority, the analytical method is essentially assumed to fill the requirements. The result is a population of sharp-minded individuals who can focus increasingly on more and more minute parts of reality, to the point of being incapable of seeing larger, particularly historical, contexts. Not surprisingly, as such individuals rise to positions of leadership, they are prone to making judgments without awareness of the moral and ethical implications involved. They are capable of denying to themselves the noblest of human sentiments in the name of the "bottom line" or expediency. Only now does the havoc wrought in our physical and social environment by such polished and ostensibly educated minds, with alarmingly narrow ranges of understanding, begin to be recognized.

Today, the task of expanding the coverage of education fortunately enjoys general and enthusiastic support. If the foregoing assessment of education's plight is at all plausible, however, the reformation of the educational system must have the highest priority in the development plans of our typical region. Here again, in an approach that places learning at the heart of all efforts to transform society, the university must play a preponderant role in fostering a proper educational process among the population it serves. By its very nature, the university is concerned with education at higher levels. What is required of it in the context of so specific a dimension of capacity-building is a concerted effort to systematically develop the contents and methods of three programs of education: preschool, basic education for children from 6 to 14 years of age, and high school focusing on the intellectual and moral development of 15- to 18-year-old youth.

The university's greatest challenge in this respect is harnessing relevant knowledge to the creation of pedagogically sound programs that respond to the exigencies of each stage of the intellectual and emotional development of the students. In an era of accelerated progress in science and technology, no one will deny the need for specialization and high expertise in narrow fields of human endeavour. But before specialized training takes place — whether in a trade or profession or in research and development — the basic structure of the mind of the student has surely to be addressed. Most of today's textbooks seem to assume that every student is being prepared to specialize in the specific subjects with which these texts are dealing. The result is neither sound intellectual development nor a reasonable knowledge of any one discipline. An indication of the seriousness of the problem is the concern commonly expressed by universities everywhere about the quality of education received by the majority of their entering students.

223

The situation calls for a fresh look at the universe of knowledge and for a new way to bring together its diverse elements in curricula that respect the wholeness of knowledge yet anticipate specialization at a later stage. The focus of each set of interrelated educational activities should be the development of one or more capabilities — scientific, artistic, technical, social, moral, and spiritual — endowing the individual with the understanding of concepts, knowledge of facts, and mastery of methods, as well as the skills, attitudes, and qualities he or she needs to lead a fruitful life. Specifically, in this age of transition, it is imperative to endow youth with a twofold moral purpose: to take charge of their own intellectual and spiritual growth and to make significant contributions to the transformation of society.

The claim being advanced here, one for which I have ample evidence, is that an educational process organized around the development of a set of carefully selected capabilities can impart far more knowledge to children and youth than programs concerned with covering the usual array of skills and subject matter. Cultivating such capabilities makes special demands at each of the three stages of the pedagogical enterprise. Preschool needs to emphasize the building of character. It should pay attention to the emotional makeup of each child and help with the acquisition of the spiritual qualities that will finally shape the attitudes and outlooks of the future youth. It must teach joy and freedom by instilling self-discipline and laying the foundations of a lasting moral structure. It needs to foster habits of investigation and reflection and encourage the early manifestations of clear thinking and eloquent speech. Such objectives are entirely harmonious with the development of the various types of dexterity and powers of perception that have tended to preoccupy so many preschool programs earnestly being propagated internationally.

Whatever one's definition of basic education, an appropriate level of proficiency in such areas of knowledge as mathematics, the natural sciences, history, geography, language, and literature is clearly an important element. But the approach advocated here would allow educational systems to go far beyond today's rather modest goals. We must ask what attributes some 8 years of schooling should have cultivated in a 14-year-old adolescent so as to enable him or her to make a clear-cut transition from childhood to youth. We can readily identify a few that are especially helpful in exposing the nature of the education being called for: the realization that it is chiefly service to humanity and dedication to the unification of humankind that release creative powers latent in one's nature; the understanding that not only knowledge of principles but the exercise and application of will is essential to both personal growth and social change; a conviction that honour and happiness lie not in the pursuit of wealth and power for their own sake, but in self-respect and noble purposes, in integrity and moral quality; and a disposition to analyze and a desire to understand the features of different forms of government, law, and public administration. To these must be added other attributes that enhance social effectiveness: an adequate understanding, at least in the local context, of the concerns of programs of social progress in such areas as health and sanitation, agriculture, crafts, and industry; some development of the power of intellectual investigation as an instrument of successful individual and collective action; certain ability to analyze social conditions and discover the forces that have caused them; the corresponding ability to express ideas and to contribute to consultation on community problems; the capacity to take part in community action as a determined yet humble participant who helps overcome conflict and division and contributes to the establishment of a spirit of unity and collaboration; and a reasonable degree of excellence in at least one productive skill through which to experience the truth that work is worship when performed in a spirit of service.

These are admittedly demanding objectives for the 8 years of basic education. But a good beginning can be made in every one of these directions. High school, then, must assume the responsibility of ensuring that such capabilities — concerned with both the acquisition of knowledge and the qualities of the mind and spirit — develop to the point that each man and woman can go on to play a fulfilling role in the life of the human race. This is not to imply, however, that the high-school program should be a mere continuation of basic education. On the contrary, the transition calls for a qualitative change, particularly in terms of scientific rigour, use of language, and social content, for it is in this stage of education that vague hopes and ideals regarding one's future and service to humanity must crystallize into the twofold moral purpose mentioned above. The student must now become a purposeful agent in charge of his or her own education. Every effort needs to be made to raise the student's consciousness to a higher level — a consciousness of the ramifications of personal choices being made, of the social forces to which one's community is subjected, and of the nature of the historical processes in which one is immersed.

There is no doubt that the design and implementation of these three programs present a daunting challenge both to the university and to the school system in any region. It can only be met if a global development enterprise is willing to come to the aid of every population and ensure the availability of creative imagination and financial and human resources. For this to happen, it is imperative that we learn from the experience of the nearly five decades of development. New generations have to be empowered — as opposed to being simply instructed — if development is to offer more than superficial solutions to ever-occurring social and economic crises.

225

MATERIAL MEANS

To illustrate the challenge of building the capacity of a population to set the direction of its own development, I have presented a brief analysis of two processes — one related to technological choice and the other to education. A more thorough treatment of the subject would have also to cover such diverse capacities as those of dealing efficiently and accurately with information, rather than responding unwittingly to political and commercial propaganda; interacting with other cultures in a way that leads to the advancement of one's own culture and not to its degradation; manifesting rectitude in private and public administration; and imbuing social interaction with an acute sense of justice. In focusing on the technological and educational dimensions of capacity-building as examples, it has not been my intention to belittle the importance of economic development. As mentioned earlier in the paper, to place the generation and application of knowledge at the heart of the development process is not to deny the indispensable nature of material means. Development as envisioned here requires the multiplication of material means at the disposal of the diverse populations of the world at a scale never achieved by the human race.

Enhancing the capacity of a typical region to achieve the material and spiritual prosperity of its people involves the strengthening of its economy, a process that includes but is not identical to economic growth. Such an effort must, of course, take place in the context of some kind of economic thinking. The search for an appropriate theoretical framework, however, is far from easy at a time when the fundamental concepts of today's "economic thinking" — considered the embodiment of rationality for many decades — are being vigorously questioned. The resulting loss of faith is steadily exacerbated by the deepening environmental crisis and by the rise and fall of economic systems whose performance receives extravagant praise until they begin to disintegrate and expose the real conditions under which their victims live.

Criticisms of mainstream economics come from both within and without; they call for a revision of both methodology and the conceptual framework of analysis. According to the critics, economists, unlike scientists in many other fields, have shown little willingness to examine in a detached spirit the nature of their methodology or to understand its origins. Admiration for classical physics has inspired them to abduct metaphors and methods without taking into account the disparity between the objects of study. The mechanistic structure of their mindset has prevented them from giving proper attention to such crucial factors as knowledge, purpose, and qualitative change. The concept most central to their analyses has been an imaginary "man," the sole judge of his own whims and desires, making decisions to optimize his utility. The mechanism through which these "rational" choices are supposed to be realized has been an abstraction of the market, an abstraction well beyond what is allowed in reasonable scientific practice. And, in a curious way, both the physical world, the origin of all material resources, and culture, the milieu within which human resources are shaped, are relegated to secondary consideration.

I do not feel competent to analyze in depth the arguments of the critics and the defenders of present-day economic theory. At this point, however, it does seem clear that the gates of a mighty fortress, until recent times presumed unassailable, are now being successfully stormed. What this rapidly expanding intellectual activity will bring and how it will affect development strategy are not easy questions to answer. But the few indications about the nature of the "new economic thinking" are most encouraging. One can safely assume, for example, that new economics will not ignore the question of values or be allowed to hide them behind the convenient veil of externalities. It will uphold the principle of the equality of women and men, acknowledge the role and needs of the community, and cease to promote unrestrained individualism. And, one may confidently state, it will pay considerable attention to the question of natural resources and the environment.

Promising as the new directions being explored may be, a breakthrough in economic theory cannot be anticipated in the near future. For one thing — and this is to be expected of a science that has entered a period of crisis — the range of exploration is too broad and there is a tendency to look for a theory that touches on too many aspects of individual and social existence. Admittedly, humanity needs a renewal of moral philosophy. But it is also true, at least from the point of view of development strategy and planning, that we require a science of economics, one that is directly concerned with the generation, distribution, and utilization of material means. This science must be rigorous without being reductionist. It will need to choose methods appropriate to the object of study and not blindly follow some inadequate impression of physics. It will have to be concerned with purpose and make explicit its assumptions and the values underlying them. Above all, it must be a science capable of progressively modifying its premises — especially those related to human conduct — as the process of civilization-building advances. Recognizing that the policies it engenders have the capacity to change value systems, it will have to take into account its own inter-actions with a changing object of study and allow for a constant reexamination of the facts about human beings and social structures out of which it builds its models of economic development and behaviour. Whether such a science is possible is a question that I hope we will address in our discourse on science, religion, and development in the future.

It is not the purpose of this paper to comment substantively on economic theory. What is being emphasized is that a development strat-egy based on capacity-building needs to pay enormous attention to those dimensions of regional capacity that have to do with the creation and utilization of material means — from specific instances of economic activity such as commercial agricultural production and small family farms, industrial production in units of various sizes including micro-enterprises, and a vast variety of services both private and governmen-tal, all the way to the formulation and implementation of economic policies that enable the region to participate in a global economy, not as a helpless victim but as a strong and self-reliant contributor. The work required to achieve such strengthening of regional economy is complex under any circumstances, but evermore so today when economic theory must undergo a thorough and fundamental revision. Once again, the institution whose participation in the process is indispensable — if we accept the approach being proposed in this paper — is the university. As defined here, it is the only institution that can shoulder the twin responsibilities of keeping abreast of progress in the worldwide search for new theories and of coordinating learning in various spaces where economic activity takes place in the region.

A word of warning, however, is needed. It would be a mistake to assign responsibility for economic development to programs that focus only on the poor. Indispensable to the creation of prosperity for humankind is the elimination of the extremes of wealth and poverty. Development strategists, then, would do well to heed the statement attributed to 'Abdu'l-Bahá that wherever you find great poverty, look close and you will find extreme wealth. This is true for a region, an entire country, or globally for the community of nations and peoples.

FURTHER COMMENTS

Capacity-building is a vast subject that I have only touched upon in these pages. The following comments offer further insights.

The concept of the university

In my references to the university, I have drawn upon my own experience at FUNDAEC, where the conceptual framework and mode of operation of the rural university mentioned in the first section of this paper were developed. Throughout those years of intense research and action, I was often asked why I insisted on using the title of "university" for what appeared to be another, albeit innovative, development organization. I hope that the ideas presented in this paper somehow justify this use of the term. Basically, what is being said is that at the heart of the development of any people must be a learning process. It is always highly desirable that learning occur in international decision-making circles and influential academic institutions. But this, by itself, is insufficient. In each region, too, development programs must operate in a learning mode, with the population of the region assuming an active role in the process. Such systematic learning cannot occur in an institutional vacuum. There is a need for an institution to take charge of collective learning, and the university is the one candidate with the intellectual discipline required by the function.

Unfortunately, in most developing regions, the university has become irrelevant to the life of the people; it is focused almost entirely on the routine process of producing graduates for various careers. The desire to re-create the university, then, arises from two considerations. One is the need for coordination of learning in the context of development; the other is the urgent necessity to save this pivotal institution of society from its current state of stagnation.

Autonomous technology

As I was reflecting on the theme of the present project — science, religion, and development — I revisited a book that had significantly influenced my thinking about the field. The work is the brilliant *Autonomous Technology: Technics-out-of-Control as a Theme in Political Thought*, by Langdon Winner (1978). More than 20 years ago, at a time when our research in the area of technology at FUNDAEC had advanced considerably and we were eager to share our results and insights with other institutions, Winner's rigorous and thorough analysis proved invaluable to me. It was clear to me at the time that despite the great popularity of the appropriate-technology movement there was a general tendency to treat technology hastily and not in sufficient depth. Winner's arguments convinced me that we owed much of this unfortunate situation to the widespread idea that technology is an autonomous force inducing change in society in ways beyond the control of human beings. Some celebrated the operation of this force, and others lamented it. But both groups were victims of the subtle paralysis of thought that such a belief produces in everyone who submits to it. The realization underlined for me the enormity of the task of persuading development programs to engage in the building of capacity to make technological choices in the populations they served — a notion with which we were already working at FUNDAEC — and abandon the habit of seeking solutions to the problems caused by haphazard technological change in newer and better technological fixes.

In expressing his conclusions — as true today as when they were written — Winner seized on the imagery of Mary Shelley's *Frankenstein*:

> The best single statement of her view comes on the title page of the book, a quotation from Milton's *Paradise Lost*:
>
> > Did I request thee, Maker, from my clay
> > To mould me man? Did I solicit thee
> > From darkness to promote me? —
>
> Suggested in these words is, it seems to me, the issue truly at stake in the whole of *Frankenstein*: the plight of things that have been created but not in a context of sufficient care. The problem captures the essence of the themes my inquiry has addressed.
>
> Victor Frankenstein is a person who discovers, but refuses to ponder, the implications of his discovery. He is a man who creates something new in the world and then pours all of his energy into an effort to forget. His invention is incredibly powerful and represents a quantum jump in the performance capability of a certain kind of technology. Yet he sends it out into the world with no real concern for how best to include it in the human community. Victor embodies an artifact with a kind of life previously manifest only in human beings. He then looks on in surprise as it returns to him as an autonomous force, with a structure of its own, with demands upon which it insists absolutely. Provided with no plan for its existence, the technological creation enforces a plan upon its creator. Victor is baffled, fearful, and totally unable to discover a way to repair the disruptions caused by his half-completed, imperfect work. He never moves beyond a dream of progress, the thirst for power, or the unquestioned belief that the products of science and technology are an unqualified blessing for humankind. Although he is aware of the fact that there is something extraordinary at large in the world, it takes a disaster to convince him that the responsibility is his. Unfortunately, by the time he overcomes his passivity, the consequences of his deeds have become irreversible, and he finds himself totally helpless before an unchosen fate.
>
> Winner (1978, pp. 312–313)

229

Having argued that the entire world now faces this same problem, Winner continued:

> Beyond these dominant beliefs and attitudes, however, lies something even more fundamental, for there is a sense in which all technical activity contains an inherent tendency toward forgetfulness. Is not the point of all invention, technique, apparatus, and organization to have something and *have it over with?* One does not want to bother anymore with building, developing, or learning it again.

One does not want to bother with its structure or the principles of its internal workings. One simply wants the technical thing to be present in its utility. The goods are to be oriented without having to understand the factory or the distribution network. Energy is to be utilized without understanding the myriad of connections that made its generation and delivery possible. Technology, then, allows us to ignore our own works. It is *license to forget*. In its sphere the truths of all important processes are encased, shut away, and removed from our concern. This more than anything else, I am convinced, is the true source of the colossal passivity in man's dealings with technical means.

Winner (1978, pp. 314–315, emphasis in the original)

The purpose of education

Some of the comments made earlier may seem overly critical of the world's educational systems. But it is difficult to assume a detached position in this matter knowing how thirsty are children and youth in every society for knowledge and having experienced the enthusiasm with which they engage in educational activity when their spirit is touched. A highly successful program developed by FUNDAEC as part of its efforts to define the parameters within which a rural university would operate is known as Sistema de Aprendizaje Tutorial. It covers the final stages of what in this paper I have called basic education, as well as the program of high school in its entirety. It now reaches some 40 000 students in the rural areas of Colombia and is gradually entering other Latin American countries. Each time I have visited a group of youth participating in the program and observed their activities, I have been filled with a mixture of joy and sadness. The level of intellectual performance of the participants is astounding. But I have never been able to feel satisfied with FUNDAEC's accomplishment knowing that it is only a small step toward an educational process commensurate with the enormous potentialities latent in every human being.

A characteristic of the curriculum developed by FUNDAEC is the effort it makes to progressively raise the students' level of consciousness. This applies to the process of education as well as all the other transformational processes in which they are engaged. For example, in a unit whose main purpose is to strengthen capabilities in the area of language during the last year of high school, students are presented with a series of readings, with the corresponding exercises, which make explicit the fundamental concepts underlying their own education. To illustrate some of the ideas I have briefly discussed, I would like to quote from a number of these readings:

[From Reading 1]

For an educational process to be truly successful, it must encourage students to reflect on the conceptual foundation of their own education. The units entitled "Basic Concepts" are to provide you with the opportunity to engage in such reflection. As with other units in the area of language, their purpose is to assist you in developing your skills of expression. Their content, however, will explore fundamental concepts that you have encountered in various courses without having had a chance to examine them in depth.

Let us begin by looking at the purpose of your education. You have been told time and again that your education is purposeful. What is this purpose and how does it manifest itself in the educational program you have been following now for a number of years?

To say that your education has a purpose does not, by itself, have a great deal of significance. Every educational system sets out to accomplish laudable aims. To become a useful citizen, to contribute to the progress of one's country, to become a productive member of society, to achieve happiness, to find work and improve one's standard of living, such expressions abound in books and documents on education. Why is it, then, that today, in spite of these explicit aims, the majority of students in the world are confused about the purpose of their education? Why are there so few who are truly motivated to learn? What has motivated you to show zeal and enthusiasm during the course of your studies? Does your understanding of the purpose of your education have anything to do with your high level of motivation?

If we were to summarize everything we have discussed on the subject of education throughout the years, we would say that the purpose of your education is your growth as an individual and the development of your capacity to contribute to the transformation of society. This is a simple statement with numerous ramifications. The readings that follow shed light, each in its own way, on the meaning and implications of this statement.

FUNDAEC (1998, p. 1)

[From Reading 3]

The enhancement of understanding is one of the most fundamental aims of the educational process in which you are participating. The next two readings are taken from a series of lectures on curriculum development given by one of the founders of FUNDAEC. *They contain a number of ideas — some of which are more or less self-evident — that will be useful to you in reflecting on your own education, even if the secondary education you received was not through* FUNDAEC.

The verb "to understand" obviously has to have a subject and an object. The subject of the verb is the human mind and heart, which need to fulfill certain conditions in order to reach the shores of true understanding. "Objects of understanding" are those things that the human mind and heart are supposed to understand; they are extremely varied and fall into many seemingly unrelated categories.

A cursory examination of a few statements made in conversation points to some of these categories:

"I don't understand why you act this way."
"I don't understand why suffering exists in the world."
"He doesn't understand our friendship."
"I wish I could understand chemistry."
"Do you understand how this gadget works?"
"I understand what you are saying."
"I don't understand what you are driving at."
"You should try harder to understand his feelings."
"I fully understand his views."
"We need to gain a greater understanding of the dynamics of crisis and victory."
"We need to understand the true nature of man."

From these few examples it is easy to see that objects of understanding fall into categories such as subject matter, relationships, feelings, views, interactions, the causes of things, the reason for things, the meaning of things, the purpose of things, the workings of things, and the reality or essence of things. To this you may add visions, contexts, approaches, attitudes, results, conventions — and undoubtedly a myriad other things — and you will have a rather formidable list of categories of things to be understood. What is important for you to realize is that in the course of your education, we were careful to address a sufficient number of objects of understanding from various categories so as to sharpen your faculties and to equip you with those mental tools needed to achieve an understanding of yourself and the world that surrounds you.

Two of these mental tools, both extremely powerful in the process of investigation of reality, are worthy of mention. One is analysis, that is, breaking things into smaller parts and then examining the relations and interactions of these parts. The other is placing things in larger and larger contexts in order to gain insights into causes and reasons for their existence and behavior. ...

FUNDAEC (1998, pp. 15–16)

[From Reading 5]

The educational process in which you are participating is characterized by its emphasis on moral and ethical considerations. Concern with morality, however, is not expressed in the form of sermons on good behavior; the discussion of moral and ethical issues is incorporated into every element of the curriculum. The next two readings consist of a few paragraphs from a document exploring a framework for moral education appropriate for this period of human history, a period to which the document refers as the age of transition from humanity's childhood to maturity. Slight modifications have been made in order to render the readings suitable for this unit.

In order to act effectively during the present period of transition in human society, individuals must, above all, be imbued with a strong sense of purpose that impels them both to transform their own selves and to contribute to the transformation of society. On a personal level, this purpose is directed towards the development of one's vast potentialities, comprising both those virtues and qualities that should adorn every human being and those talents and characteristics that are the individual's unique endowment. On a social level, it is expressed through dedication to the promotion of the welfare of the human race. These aspects of the sense of twofold purpose are fundamentally inseparable, for the standards and behavior of individuals shape their environment, and in turn are molded by social structures and processes. Unless the transformation of both individual character and environment are addressed simultaneously, the full potential of humanity's age of maturity cannot be realized.

A profound awareness of the reciprocal relationship between personal growth and organic change in social structures is, then, essential to moral education. One cannot develop virtues and talents in isolation, but only through effort and activity for the benefit of others. Idle worship and prolonged withdrawal from society, advocated by some philosophies of the past, can neither promote individual development nor aid humanity's progress. To focus one's sense of purpose only on the development of one's own potential is to lose objectivity and perspective. With no outside interactions and social goals, one has no standard by which to judge personal progress and no concrete results by which to measure one's development. A person forgetful of the social dimension of moral purpose is prone to subtle forms of ego — combinations of guilt, self-righteousness and self-satisfaction.

Conversely, a sense of purpose driven only by the desire to transform society, with no attention to the need for personal growth and transformation, is easily misdirected. The person who blames society for every wrong and ignores the importance of individual responsibility loses respect and compassion for others and is prone to acts of cruelty and oppression. Social transformation, if divorced from the desire to transform one's own character, is an extremely fragile enterprise. ...

FUNDAEC (1998, p. 35)

[From Reading 7]

By the term "capability" we mean *developed capacity to think and to act in a well-defined sphere of activity and according to a well-defined purpose.* We use the word to refer not to individual skills but rather to complex spheres of thought and action each requiring a number of related skills and abilities. Moreover, we place great importance on the notion that the gradual acquisition of a given capability, in addition to the mastering of skills, is dependent on the assimilation of relevant information, the understanding of a set of concepts, the development of certain attitudes, and advancement in a number of spiritual qualities.

Classification, for example, is a capability, in this case a mathematical one, which an individual can acquire at different levels of competence. At the most elementary level, say, at the beginning of secondary school, it involves acquiring an understanding of the concepts of sets, of an element of a set, and of belonging to a set. It also requires an understanding of the concept that things can be divided into sets according to common properties. But, even at this level, such an understanding is not sufficient. The ability to recognize the properties according to which the elements in question are to be classified, as well as some relevant information about those elements, is also necessary. For example, if someone is to classify objects according to size, the skill of estimating or measuring the size of the objects in question becomes essential. As to attitudes, carefulness and appreciation for order are clearly desirable. At a more fundamental level, truthfulness is a spiritual quality that helps generate positive attitudes towards precision and care.

In language, to cite another example, the mechanics of reading and writing are skills, but to read at a certain level of comprehension is a rather complex capability. Another language capability is that of describing what we observe in the world around us in ever greater contexts. To describe the world around us quantitatively is a mathematical capability. Examples of highly desirable scientific capabilities are those of making organized observations of phenomena and designing experiments to test a hypothesis. Participating effectively in consultation is a capability needed in the social realm, as is the capability of participating in collective enterprises. To manage one's affairs and responsibilities with rectitude of conduct is a moral capability. Another essential moral capability is that of building environments of unity based on an appreciation of diversity.

FUNDAEC (1998, pp. 60–61)

[From Reading 8]

The approach we adopted to curriculum design, organized around capabilities rather than subject matters, helped our students learn with extraordinary rapidity. That the capabilities we were trying to develop all had the same explicit social purpose enabled us to address one of the basic challenges of curricular integration: how to overcome the dichotomy between theoretical and practical knowledge. Most current educational systems tend to teach practical and manual skills to some and book-learning to others. The capacity to participate in planning and decision-making is developed in a few, while the majority are trained to carry out orders. What we tried to achieve is to maintain the interest of the students simultaneously in concrete and abstract activities. For example, the skills of animal husbandry were taught in conjunction with the study of animal physiology, and the steps to establish a village store with the analysis of abstract social and economic theories. To the degree that we succeeded in integrating theoretical and practical knowledge, we saw prejudices and false scales of prestige gradually disappear and be replaced by a purposeful attitude towards learning and change.

But the most difficult challenge of our educational innovation proved not to be the fusion of elements of knowledge of the physical universe and society. A far greater task was the integration of material and spiritual concepts into a knowledge system that would enable individuals and entire populations to contribute to the creation of a world civilization, towards which, we felt, humanity is inexorably moving. To meet this challenge, we did not develop specific courses on religion; nor did we engage in humanistic studies of ethics and social behavior. Spirituality was treated as a state, an inner condition, that should manifest itself in action, in everyday choices, in profound understanding of human nature and in meaningful contributions to community life and society. Following this interpretation, we tried to integrate spirituality into every educational activity: every act had to be a means for the clarification and application of spiritual principles.

In doing so, we found that a number of issues needed to be tackled. Spirituality has to be built into curricula without denying material well-being or relegating prosperity to another life. What has to be done is to elevate everyday activities to a more sublime station by imbuing them with the spirit of service. However, identifying spirituality exclusively with service poses the danger of conveying the notion that spirituality arises from actions that lead to well-being. To counterbalance this effect, the manifestations of the most profound yearnings of the human soul, such as the search for nearness to God through prayer and meditation, also have to be given due consideration. "Being" and "doing" are intimately connected and should not be artificially separated.

Furthermore, this integration of the spiritual and the material calls for increasing understanding of the delicate balance that must exist between the many forces at work in the human mind and heart: balance between personal liberty and social obligation, between being the master of nature and living in harmony with it, between humanism and science, the rational and the emotional. To achieve such a balance, one has to go beyond the attributes of the mind and touch those qualities of the soul that are the foundation of human character. An essential requisite for achieving a balance between the forces at work in the human mind and heart is, then, the development of spiritual qualities, such as justice, love, generosity, compassion, humility, and truthfulness. Moreover, if these qualities are to give rise to attitudes and behavior which are a true reflection of spirituality, they must be developed in such a way that they moderate one another. Otherwise, all that is achieved in the name of spirituality is self-righteousness and fanaticism. Further, it is only through understanding the interaction of spiritual qualities that we learn to distinguish moderation from mediocrity — justice moderated by compassion, not half-justice; lavish generosity together with humility, not cautious giving; absolute truthfulness acting in the medium of love, not the mixing of truth with lies whenever it is convenient.

FUNDAEC (1998, pp. 71–72)

235

REFERENCES

Bohm, D. 1981. Wholeness and the implicate order. Routledge and Kegan Paul, London, UK. 224 pp.

BPC (Bahá'í Publishing Committee). 1930. Tablets of Abdul-Baha Abbas. 3 vols. BPC, Chicago, IL, USA. 730 pp.

BPT (Bahá'í Publishing Trust). 1982. The promulgation of universal peace: talks delivered by 'Abdu'l-Bahá during his visit to the United States and Canada in 1912. BPT, Wilmette, IL, USA. 513 pp.

———— 1983a. Gleanings from the writings of Bahá'u'lláh. BPT, Wilmette, IL, USA. 346 pp.

———— 1983b. The Kitáb-i-Íqán: the book of certitude. BPT, Wilmette, IL, USA. 274 pp.

———— 1988. Tablets of Bahá'u'lláh revealed after the Kitáb-i-Aqdas. BPT, Wilmette, IL, USA. 299 pp.

———— 1990. The secret of divine civilization. BPT, Wilmette, IL, USA. 126 pp.

———— 1991. The world order of Bahá'u'lláh: selected letters. BPT, Wilmette, IL, USA. 234 pp.

———— 1994. The hidden words. BPT, Wilmette, IL, USA. 52 pp.

———— 1995a. Paris talks: addresses given by 'Abdu'l-Bahá in Paris in 1911. BPT, London, UK. 208 pp.

———— 1995b. The promise of world peace. BPT, Wilmette, IL, USA. 40 pp.

———— 1997. Selections from the writings of 'Abdu'l-Bahá. BPT, Wilmette, IL, USA. 359 pp.

Davies, P. 1993. The mind of God: the scientific basis for a rational world. Simon and Schuster, New York, NY, USA. 254 pp.

Einstein, A. 1954. Ideas and opinions (based on *Mein Weltbild*, edited by Carl Seelig, and other sources, with new translations and revisions by Sonja Bargmann). Crown Publishers, Inc., New York, NY, USA. 377 pp.

Fleck, L. 1979 [1935]. Genesis and development of a scientific fact (edited by T.J. Trenn and R.K. Merton and translated by F. Bradley and T.J. Trenn). University of Chicago Press, Chicago, IL, USA. 203 pp.

FUNDAEC (Fundación para la Aplicación y Enseñanza de las Ciencias). 1998. Basic concepts: education. Palabra Publications, Riviera Beach, FL, USA. 79 pp.

Goulet, D. 1980. Development experts: the one-eyed giants. World Development, 8 (7/8), 481–489.

Heilbroner, R.L. 1963. The great ascent: the struggle for economic development in our time. Harper and Row, New York, NY, USA. 189 pp.

Lewis, W.A. 1955. The theory of economic growth. Richard D. Irwin, Inc., Homewood, IL, USA. 453 pp.

Meier, G.M.; Seers, D., ed. 1984. Pioneers in development. Oxford University Press, New York, NY, USA. 372 pp.

Myrdal, G. 1972. Asian drama: an inquiry into the poverty of nations. Random House; Vintage Books, New York, NY, USA. 464 pp.

Rahnema, M. 1997. Signposts for post-development. Revision: A Journal of Consciousness and Transformation, 19 (Spring), 4–12.

Ravetz, J.R. 1973. Scientific knowledge and its social problems. Oxford University Press, New York, NY, USA. 449 pp.

Rondinelli, D.A. 1983. Development projects as policy experiments. Methuen and Co., London, UK. 167 pp.

Ryan, W.F., S.J. 1995. Culture, spirituality, and economic development: opening a dialogue. International Development Research Centre, Ottawa, ON, Canada. 67 pp.

Stapp, H.P. 1993. Mind, matter and quantum mechanics. Springer-Verlag, New York, NY, USA. 248 pp.

United Nations. 1995. Ethical and spiritual dimensions of social progress. United Nations, New York, NY, USA. 115 pp.

Winner, L. 1978. Autonomous technology: technics-out-of-control as a theme in political thought. MIT Press, Cambridge, MA, USA. 386 pp.

World Bank. 1992. World development report 1992: development and the environment. Oxford University Press, New York, NY, USA. 308 pp.

Zohar, D. 1991. The quantum self: a revolutionary view of human nature and consciousness rooted in the new physics. HarperCollins Publishers; Flamingo, London, UK. 245 pp.

237

Our Way of Proceeding

William F. Ryan, S.J.

This publication, on the International Development Research Centre's (IDRC's) Science, Religion, and Development project, features personal essays on the human-level interaction of science, religion, and development (SRD). The appearance of this publication at this juncture of human history is both timely and insightful. Calls for more "people-centred" development and for a higher quality of life beyond the culture of consumption are increasing. This implies what some are calling a qualitative step in human consciousness. Significant changes have occurred in the world agenda and in scholarly reflections on these changes since my earlier research on behalf of IDRC. The results of my work, carried out in 1994, were published under the title *Culture, Spirituality, and Economic Development: Opening a Dialogue* (Ryan 1995). This unconventional research was intended to respond to a concern voiced in a conversation with a Muslim leader that development research did not seriously take into account the influence of local cultural and religious values, systems, and institutions. A series of interviews conducted in a number of developing countries uncovered a strong consensus among nearly 200 theoreticians and practitioners in the international development field that local cultural and religious values must be better integrated into research on sustainable and equitable development.

That early study has generally been welcomed. The major objections to it have come from Western researchers who fear that if cultural and religious values form part of the development paradigm, it will jeopardize some human advances stemming from the Enlightenment. With justification, they resist the spectre of reintroducing paralyzing and self-defeating concepts and practices, such as fatalism and the subordination of women, which are still prevalent in some traditional

239

cultures and religions. Of course, those who are still convinced that the global free market's invisible magic is adequate to the job of increasing human well-being see no need to introduce culture or religion into the development paradigm.

The field of research on religion and development is much more crowded in 2000 than it was in 1994. IDRC can no longer claim to be a pioneer in it, although its attempt to articulate the relationship among the fields of SRD still sets it apart. But now other organizations are taking up related questions. Space limitations require that I mention but a few of these endeavours. I offer as an indication of the sheer volume of these new inquiries a bibliography issued by the Centre for Development Research in Copenhagen, Denmark, in February 1998, *Religion and Development: A Bibliography* (CDRLS 1998). It lists 435 new entries between 1 January 1993 and 17 April 1997. This is a spectacular increase in work on this ambiguous topic for so short a period, especially considering that the Danish listing is still far from complete. Most of the works listed in this bibliography seem to have been written in response to recent world developments in the dynamic process of globalization. Many people, assuming that the current global free-market paradigm, with its Western accompaniments, is inevitably universal believe that globalization is threatening to homogenize local cultural and religious values and institutions.

The various faiths have themselves long been involved in development efforts, but recognition of the relationship between religion, development, and world affairs has also come from other, more unexpected quarters. James Wolfensohn, the president of the World Bank, himself a practicing Jew, recently initiated a dialogue with the leaders of nine of the world's faiths to find a way to cooperate in their efforts to rid the world of poverty and misery. Likewise, the US State Department, confronted with the reality of Islamic fundamentalism, recently abandoned its long-accepted taboo against reporting religion in official diplomatic dispatches as an influence or causal factor in world affairs. Another recent and unexpected champion for the powerful, if ambiguous, influence of religion and culture in shaping civilizations is Samuel Huntington, a well-known political scientist from Harvard University. In his controversial book, *The Clash of Civilizations and the Remaking of World Order* (Huntington 1996), he argued that cultures and religions are key factors in shaping world affairs. This perspective clearly flies in the face of *The Economist*'s persevering declaration that "Asian values" have had no significant influence on Asia's recent rapid economic development.

Ecologists, too, are turning to religion for sympathetic support and motivation. For example, the Center for the Study of World Religions (CSWR) at Harvard University has, over the last few years, involved more than 1 000 scholars — religionists, scientists, and ecologists — in its ongoing forum on the religions of the world and ecology. The forum aims to recover vision and meaning from religious teachings to enlighten and motivate people to act decisively on the current global ecological agenda.

Among economists, however, Herman Daly still seems to be uncommon: in his recent book, *Beyond Growth: The Economics of Sustainable Development* (Daly 1996), he specifically invoked religious insight from the Hebrew scriptures to ground the ethical principles he considers necessary for managing, through public policy, limits to both natural capital and personal income to achieve sustainable development.

It is also evident, I believe, that the conversation between science and religion has intensified at the opening of the new millennium. In the last 2 years, articles have appeared in publications such as *Science* ("Science and God: A Warming Trend?" [Easterbrook 1997]), *The New York Times on the Web* ("Science and Religion: Bridging the Great Divide" [Johnson 1998]), and *Newsweek* (as a front-cover feature) ("Science Finds God" [Begley 1998]). But popular articles discussing questions like these represent only the front edge of a long-standing research problematic. J.M. Templeton and the John Templeton Foundation have long been investing significant resources in numerous efforts to bring rapprochement and increased understanding between science and religion. John Paul II's remarks on the occasion of the 300th anniversary of Newton's *Philosophiae Naturalis Principia Mathematica* (mathematical principles of natural science) are also highly relevant: "'The unprecedented opportunity we have today is for a common interactive relationship' in which science and religion retain their own integrity and yet are 'open to the discoveries and insights of the other'" (John Paul II 1988, p. 375). And at the September 1998 CSWR conference on ecology and religion, scientists brought the following question to the table: Can religions of the world adjust their own world visions, stories, and myths of creation to enhance and put soul, meaning, and motivation into scientists' current theory of how the universe is unfolding since the initial "big bang"?

Increased desire for citizen participation and accompanying cynicism about public institutions, especially government, have led to a worldwide explosion of nonprofit nongovernmental organizations (NGOs) and coalitions of such NGOs. This offers us another good example of the new awareness and incorporation of religion into discourses until recently considered secular; increasingly, groupings of NGOs in every sector of society include faith-community membership. Recent NGO successes include lobbying for the International Land Mine Agreement, stalemating the proposed Multilateral Agreement on Investment, and blocking the construction of the Narmada Dam in India. These are just a few of the more significant and current international issues in which NGOs have played a large role. Some people have become optimistic — probably too quickly — that these new balances of power, much aided by the Internet's ability to connect millions of like-minded

241

people worldwide, signify the ultimate death knell for monopoly power in all its multiple forms.

For my present purpose of reflecting on our authors' essays, perhaps the most significant development is the widespread deprivatization of religion and churches to give them a more active role in the public forum. This process was well-documented in the work of sociologist José Casanova of the New School for Social Research. The central thesis of his book, *Public Religions in the Modern World* (Casanova 1994), is that we are witnessing everywhere the deprivatization of religion. Casanova supported his thesis through sociohistorical case studies in Brazil, Poland, Spain, and the United States and corroborating references to similar happenings on other continents, such as the Islamic revolution in Iran. He documented the fact that "religious traditions throughout the world are refusing to accept the marginal and privileged role which theories of modernity as well as theories of secularization had reserved for them" (Casanova 1994, p. 234). In other words, for Casanova, the narrow secular point of view that holds that religion is dying or withering away is itself now dead. And more and more sociologists are recognizing this trend. But this is not the place to develop Casanova's unexpected thesis; it is enough to take seriously the cocky challenge he threw at reductionist social scientists in the final paragraph of his book:

> Western modernity is at a crossroads. If it does not enter into a creative dialogue with the other, with those traditions which are challenging its identity, modernity will most likely triumph. But it may end up being devoured by the inflexible, inhuman logic of its own creations. It would be profoundly ironic if, after all the beatings it has received from modernity, religion could somehow unintentionally help modernity to save itself.
>
> Casanova (1994, p. 234)

The issue, then, is no longer whether there should be a dialogue between the fields of SRD. It is already happening, piecemeal, in various sectors. Rather, the key question is how to find a productive methodology for this type of conversation. How can these very different kinds of knowledge, diverse kinds of rationality, be brought together so that they can benefit from the insights of the others without encroaching on the integrity of the other realms of knowledge? We are not without historical precedents for such interactions. Religious belief has long accepted the unity and interconnectedness of all creation, which science is just now coming to understand and endorse. And modern science painfully brought Christians to the realization that the sun did not, in fact, circle the Earth, as they had always assumed. But these historical shifts offer little in terms of models for the mediation of constructive interaction.

For some, the answer lies in a new and more compelling global rational ethic. Experience shows us, however, that for the great majority of people, reasonableness alone simply does not lead to decisive action as effectively as belief. Belief, whether religious or secular, engages the human will and emotions, as well as the human intellect; indeed, it engages the whole human being. So what is to be our way of proceeding? Obviously, it has to be interdisciplinary in the sense that each side has to recognize humbly both the strengths and the weaknesses of the other's approach. A jousting of infallibilities will prove futile. The goal cannot be religious conversion, although a degree of intellectual conversion is probably necessary for the participants to become open and empathetic to each other's beliefs and convictions. Even the politely tolerant approach of certain scientists, such as distinguished biologist E.O. Wilson, would likely prove counterproductive. As he reiterated at the CSWR meeting, he accepts the usefulness of, even the need for, dialogue between science and religion but steadfastly holds that a time will come when biology will no longer need any help from religion, because it will itself have decoded the whole human story.

243

This IDRC team of researchers chose the essay approach to present evidence of how individual scientists–believers can harmonize their personal understandings of the various epistemologies, rationalities, and assumptions involved in the discourses of SRD. If we, as individual believers–scientists, can experience a unity of consciousness and understanding in our daily work, why should it not be possible for other groups of scientists and believers to achieve, or at least appreciate, the benefits of an analogous experience of shared consciousness and understanding?

Some believers, such as the renowned Islamic scholar Seyyed Hossein Nasr, have long been advocating the development of a new (or rediscovered) cosmology as an overarching framework to provide, as in earlier times, a common point of reference to facilitate dialogue between religion and science. I believe that Dr Baharuddin is sympathetic to this approach in her own efforts to establish that her Islamic faith is not in contradiction with her science of biology. A key insight in this approach is, I believe, that many statements in science and religion are not contradictories as they at first appear. Rather, they are contraries — different ways of understanding the same reality that can often be harmonized at a different level of knowledge or integrated within ancillary fields (such as development) that have human well-being as their primary goal. For example, Dr Baum is at peace with his understanding that scientific and religious approaches produce different kinds of knowledge that can be mutually beneficial to each other, provided that scientists and believers are at least empathetic to each other's beliefs and convictions, whether secular or sacred. Like an increasing number of social scientists, he has little difficulty acknowledging the personal influence of religion on his scholarship or adding religion as an endogenous variable in his sociological analysis.

Today, most believers want evidence that their faith is not conceptually in contradiction to the findings of science. They also want to know that their faith is an evident force for good in shaping human history. For example, Dr Kapur seeks to understand and articulate how the Hindu faith has, over the centuries, been a fertile environment for human material development grounded in spiritual principles, even if the Hindu tradition has not always been actively supportive of such development. Dr Arbab's personal experience of seeing flawed development models foisted on marginalized people in Colombia led him to discover a more holistic and participatory model of human development in the vision and tenets of the Bahá'í Faith. His commitment to the tasks of development is realized through concrete methods and programs, based in religious and spiritual principles, that promote the personal human capacity of poor people.

Following the preparation of this volume, a still larger group of 10–15 people, with diverse experiences of SRD, was invited to bring further personal experiences, insights, and approaches to this discussion. They were believers from different faiths or scientists empathetic to the role of belief systems in the process of development. They came from countries in the South and countries in the North. This group met with the original essayists at an international conference in November 1999. The purpose of this meeting was to agree on a way of proceeding with the SRD discourse and to legitimize the discourse for wider dissemination. The participants at this meeting were clearly invigorated and excited by the possibilities of seeing worldviews that integrated both faith traditions and science to help guide development research. Participants created bonds spanning disciplines, religions, and nationalities, demonstrated in their desire to maintain contact and collaborate with the other researchers, scientists, and NGO participants at the meeting, and talked of ways to bring this discourse into their respective fields. Finally, they agreed on a third and final publication, in which the proceedings of the meeting would be disseminated and for which they would transform the documents they had prepared for the meeting into messages for youth — messages of hope and invitation for the young to explore new ways of looking at the world.

Through the three volumes generated by this project, the fruits of the SRD research process may prove helpful to both theoreticians and practitioners in the field of development, concerned religious leaders, and a future generation of researchers, scholars, practitioners, and policymakers. Our ultimate hope is that this dialogue will engender a creative, new consciousness — both personal and public — of how science and religion can work together effectively to their mutual benefit and create a more humane and just world. Should this happen, IDRC will be abundantly rewarded for undertaking what seemed at first a daunting experiment in unconventional research.

REFERENCES

Begley, S. 1998. Science finds God. Newsweek, 20 Jul, 46–52.

Casanova, J. 1994. Public religions in the modern world. University of Chicago Press, Chicago, IL, USA. 320 pp.

CDRLS (Centre for Development Research Library Staff). 1998. Religion and development: a bibliography. Centre for Development Research, Copenhagen, Denmark. CDR Library Paper 98.1. 54 pp.

Daly, H. 1996. Beyond growth: the economics of sustainable development. Beacon Press, Boston, MA, USA. 253 pp.

Easterbrook, G. 1997. Science and God: a warming trend? Science, Aug, 890–893.

Huntington, S. 1996. The clash of civilizations and the remaking of world order. Simon and Schuster, New York, NY, USA. 367 pp.

John Paul II. 1998. A dynamic relationship of theology and science. Letter from John Paul II to Jesuit Father George Coyne, Director of the Vatican Observatory. Origins, Nov, 375.

Johnson, G. 1998. Science and religion: bridging the great divide. The New York Times on the Web. Internet: http://www.nytimes.com/library/national/science/063098sci-essay.html

Ryan, W.F., S.J. 1995. Culture, spirituality, and economic development: opening a dialogue. International Development Research Centre, Ottawa, ON, Canada. 67 pp.

Contributing Authors

Farzam Arbab

Farzam Arbab's doctorate in theoretical particle physics led him to Colombia to work with the University Development Program of the Rockefeller Foundation to strengthen the Department of Physics at the Universidad del Valle. While there he began to study the relationship between science, technology, and educational policy and their effects on development, which led him and a group of colleagues to form the Fundación para la Aplicación y Enseñanza de las Ciencias (Foundation for the Application and Teaching of Science). This organization still functions as a successful development program in Colombia and has earned an international reputation for its application of spiritual principles in education and development. In 1993, Dr Arbab was elected to the international governing body of the Bahá'í Faith, on which he currently serves.

Azizan Baharuddin

Dr Baharuddin's degrees in biology and the history and philosophy of science allowed her to pursue her interest in the relationship between Islam and science. Her research interests and teaching areas include the history and philosophy of science; science and religion; ethics, environmental ethics, and bioethics; gender studies and human development; and futures studies. She has written various publications on the issues of science and faith and ethics and the environment. Dr Baharuddin is an associate professor in the Department of Science and Technology Studies at the University of Malaya.

Gregory Baum

With degrees in mathematics, sociology, and Catholic theology, Dr Baum has for 40 years been a professor of theology and religious studies. He currently teaches religious studies at McGill University in Montréal, Quebec. He has written more than 20 books on ethics and economics, solidarity, and various approaches to social justice within the Christian churches. He is a member of the Karl Polanyi Institute at Concordia University and was a member of a research team on environmental ethics at Université du Québec à Montréal. He is also an officer of the Order of Canada.

Pierre Beemans

Pierre Beemans has degrees in education and philosophy and has worked in the field of international development for more than 30 years, including living and working for extensive periods in Latin America and Africa. He has held both field and management positions with CUSO and the Canadian International Development Agency and was for 3 years a policy adviser in the Privy Council Office of the Government of Canada. Since 1992, he has been Vice-President, Corporate Services Branch, of the International Development Research Centre.

Sharon Harper

Her degrees in journalism, law, and theology led Sharon Harper to seek a position that would allow her to explore the scriptures and practice of the world's religions and their manifestations, roles, and effects in the public sphere. After graduating from Harvard Divinity School, she became the project officer for the International Development Research Centre's Science, Religion, and Development project. She is a lawyer and legal researcher with experience in human-rights and discrimination issues, both domestic and international; an experienced writer and editor; and a program manager who is knowledgeable about mediation and arbitration techniques, issues of gender and research for development, and feminist ethics and epistemologies.

Promilla Kapur

With degrees in psychology and sociology, Dr Kapur has worked as a researcher, teacher of sociology, and counselor–therapist for more than 30 years. She specializes in the sociology of women, family, and marriage and has done extensive empirical research on women, adolescents and girl children, working women, family violence, and sex workers. She has published extensively in these areas, with books in English, Hindi, and Japanese. She has been a student of Indian culture, Hinduism, interfaith dialogue, and integrated human development. Since 1984 she has been the director of the Integrated Human Development Services Foundation, a charitable organization providing counseling and crisis intervention based on the principle of whole health, which includes human and spiritual values. She has been honoured by the British

International Biographical Centre, the American Biographical Institute, and the All India Conference of Intellectuals.

William Ryan, S.J.

Dr Ryan entered the Jesuit Order in 1944 and was ordained into the priesthood in 1957. He has an MA in labour relations and a PhD in economics from Harvard University and has been very active in Canada and the United States thinking, writing, and organizing around social-justice, ethics, and economic issues. He was the founding director of the Center of Concern (Washington, DC) and has been a senior research fellow at the Canadian Institute for International Peace and Security and held the chair in Social Faith and Justice at St Paul University in Ottawa. He is the director of the Jesuit Project on Ethics in Politics in Ottawa and was recently appointed coordinator of the Jesuit Centre for Social Faith and Justice. Dr Ryan is the author of many articles and lectures on multinational corporations and the new international economic order, the poor, the relationships between faith and social justice and between faith and culture, and the role of religious people in socioeconomic change. He has been working with the Science, Religion, and Development project since its inception in 1993.

249

Acronyms and Abbreviations

CSWR	Center for the Study of World Religions
DAV	Dayanand Anglo Vedic
FUNDAEC	Fundación para la Aplicación y Enseñanza de las Ciencias (Foundation for the Application and Teaching of the Sciences) [Colombia]
IDRC	International Development Research Centre
IIIT	International Institute of Islamic Thought
IMF	International Monetary Fund
MAIS	Malaysian Academy of Islamic Science
MINDS	Malaysian Institute for Development Studies
NGO	nongovernmental organization
S&T	science and technology
SAP	structural-adjustment policy
SRD	science, religion, and development
TNC	transnational corporation
UNDP	United Nations Development Programme